Gender and Culture in Psychology

Gender and Culture in Psychology introduces new approaches to the psychological study of gender that bring together feminist psychology, sociocultural psychology, discursive psychology, and critical psychology. It presents research and theory that embed human action in social, cultural, and interpersonal contexts. The book provides conceptual tools for thinking about gender, social categorization, human meaning-making, and culture. It also describes a family of interpretative research methods that focus on rich talk and everyday life. It provides a close-in view of how interpretative research proceeds. The latter part of the book showcases innovative projects that investigate topics of concern to feminist scholars and activists: young teens' encounters with heterosexual norms, women and men negotiating household duties and child-care, coercion and violence in heterosexual encounters, the cultural politics of women's weight and eating concerns, psychiatric labeling of psychological suffering, and feminism in psychotherapy.

EVA MAGNUSSON is Professor of Psychology and Gender Studies at the University of Umeå, Sweden. She is also affiliated with the Centre for Gender Studies at the University of Umeå and has been a director of the Centre.

JEANNE MARECEK is William R. Kenan Professor Emerita of Psychology at Swarthmore College, Pennsylvania, USA, where she also has been a member of the Program on Gender and Sexuality Studies and the Asian Studies Program.

Gender and Culture in Psychology

Theories and Practices

Eva Magnusson and Jeanne Marecek

CAMBRIDGE
UNIVERSITY PRESS

CAMBRIDGE UNIVERSITY PRESS
Cambridge, New York, Melbourne, Madrid, Cape Town,
Singapore, São Paulo, Delhi, Tokyo, Mexico City

Cambridge University Press
The Edinburgh Building, Cambridge CB2 8RU, UK

Published in the United States of America by
Cambridge University Press, New York

www.cambridge.org
Information on this title: www.cambridge.org/9781107649514

First published in Swedish in 2010 under the title
Genus och kultur i psykologi: teorier och tillämpningar by
Natur & Kultur, Stockholm

ISBN: 978-91-27-11818-8

First published in English 2012

Printed in the United Kingdom at the University Press, Cambridge

A catalogue record for this publication is available from the British Library

Library of Congress Cataloging-in-Publication Data
Magnusson, Eva, 1947–
  Gender and culture in psychology : theories and practices / Eva Magnusson,
Jeanne Marecek.
     p.   cm.
  ISBN 978-1-107-01803-7 (Hardback) – ISBN 978-1-107-64951-4
(Paperback) 1. Feminism–Psychological aspects. 2. Gender identity–
Psychological aspects. 3. Culture–Psychological aspects. I. Marecek,
Jeanne, 1946– II. Title.
  HQ1206.M224 2012
  305.3–dc23
                                                                    2011037985

ISBN 978-1-107-01803-7 Hardback
ISBN 978-1-107-64951-4 Paperback

Contents

Contents

Preface

We wrote this book to place the psychology of gender in conversation with the knowledge about gender and sexuality produced in other disciplines. In our view, gender is best understood as a social practice that is embedded in culture. This book illustrates how psychologists can make use of this way of understanding gender in theoretical work, in research projects, and in applied work and clinical practice.

We are teachers and researchers in psychology. We also count ourselves as members of local and international communities of gender studies scholars. Over the past forty years, these multidisciplinary communities have offered trenchant analyses of social life and have pioneered innovative methods of inquiry. One of our goals is to bring this work into the purview of psychology. We also have worked as professional psychologists, engaging issues of gender, sexuality, and social justice in our work. This has brought us face to face with the vicissitudes of mundane and institutional power. Another of our goals is to argue that a psychology of gender must attend to power in its many forms.

Our collaboration crosses national boundaries: One of us works in Sweden and the other in the USA. Both of us also have spent a good deal of our professional lives working in countries other than our own. Our collaboration and our experiences in societies outside our own have persuaded us that psychology – whether as discipline, profession, or body of knowledge – is indelibly marked by its cultural surround.

Our ideas have been developed in conversation with colleagues and students in psychology, gender studies, and other disciplines. We thank feminist scholars in psychology and in other fields for work that is both inspired and inspiring, as well as for stimulating conversations. We thank the many critical psychologists, theoretical psychologists, and historians of psychology whose close scrutiny of the discipline has spurred our own scrutiny. Over the years, many psychologists who were not specialists in the psychology of gender have called on us to explain it to them. We thank them for their questions, which have compelled us to clarify our thinking. We are especially grateful to our students. Many of the ideas in this book had their origins in conversations about their research projects or in the classroom.

We thank Umeå University and Swarthmore College for providing intellectual environments that enabled us to grow as scholars. We thank the Centre for Advanced Study at the Norwegian Academy of Science and Letters, where we were appointed as Fellows in 2011. Lena Albihn at Natur & Kultur Press provided valuable advice and support on the earlier Swedish version of this book. Finally, we thank Hetty Marx and her staff at Cambridge University Press for their support.

Eva Magnusson
Umeå, Sweden
Jeanne Marecek
Colombo, Sri Lanka

1   Gender and culture in psychology: a prologue

Gender, the equality of the sexes, and societal inequalities more generally have been intensely debated and studied by social scientists in the last several decades. In the wake of the debates, new fields of study and new ways of thinking about old issues have emerged. This is as true of psychology as of other social sciences. When psychologists take contemporary scholarship on gender, ethnic groups, sexuality, and other social categorizations into account, foundational assumptions and practices in psychology begin to shift.

To begin with, new and different psychological questions emerge and new topics are brought forward. To answer such new questions and address new topics, new research methods have been devised. This, in turn, has caused gender researchers to become attentive to epistemological questions. In this book, we discuss these three innovations associated with gender scholarship: (1) in content, that is, new knowledge about gender and culture; (2) in method, that is, alternate ways of doing research and practice; and (3) in epistemology, that is, new ways of thinking about psychological knowledge. We approach these innovations from several different angles.

We present theoretical tools for thinking about gender, culture, and psychology, as well as methodological tools for doing research about these issues. We present research projects that illustrate innovative method and theory. We also present overviews of issues that have been central to psychological theorizing about gender and culture. And we present debates among gender researchers about such issues. In our presentations we draw upon fields outside psychology, including anthropology, history, sociology, political science, feminist studies, and science studies. We also draw upon several fields within psychology, including critical psychology, feminist psychology, sociocultural psychology, discursive psychology, rhetorical psychology, post-structural psychology, and critical history of psychology. Psychologists in these fields have analyzed the influence of political processes, cultural patterns and forces, and national contexts, as well as social subordination and exclusion, on the knowledge that psychology has produced. Many have questioned the idea of universal, ahistorical, "generic" human beings, and many have also advanced epistemological and methodological critiques of psychology.

We are psychologists with long experience of teaching, doing research, and engaging in practical work in psychology, in gender studies, and at the intersection of psychology and gender studies. We work in two very different regions of the world: Eva in Sweden; Jeanne in the USA. We study regions that are even more different: Eva, the Nordic countries; Jeanne, Sri Lanka, an island off the south coast of India. We have seen increasing interest among students and psychologists in incorporating knowledge about gender and other social categorizations into the corpus of psychological knowledge and in bringing a critical cultural perspective to bear on psychological knowledge. Our efforts to integrate such knowledge into courses and study programs have led us to see the need for the book we are offering here: a book that explores the challenges that scholarship about gender and culture brings to psychology. Integrating such knowledge demands more than adding new bits of information to the existing body of psychological knowledge. It also goes beyond devising new techniques to measure gender or measure culture. It is much more. This is what our book is about.

The roots of the new psychological scholarship on gender and culture

Psychological scholarship about gender and culture constitutes a rich and varied field of knowledge that has flowered over the last forty years. It began with psychological researchers and psychotherapists who were active in the women's liberation movement in the 1960s and 1970s. They established a field of knowledge, then called the psychology of women, which challenged many taken-for-granted ideas in psychology. They argued, for instance, that psychology was *androcentric*; that is, that the discipline and many of its practices had been shaped by the interests and experiences of men, primarily white, middle-class men in western, high-income parts of the world.

Outside psychology, the multidisciplinary field now often called gender studies emerged around 1970 in the midst of the women's movement, with its broad political goal of improving conditions and opportunities for women. The earliest gender studies programs (then called women's studies) developed as a part of this social movement and drew intellectual inspiration, energy, and political support from it. The programs often envisioned themselves as a heady combination of an academic department, a site of political activism and mobilization, and a space of solidarity for women students, faculty members, and staff in the university and, sometimes, for feminists in the community at large. Researchers in these academic programs came from several different disciplines, among them psychology. They took seriously the project of forging connections between their scholarly pursuits and their political commitments. For many, this was a matter of ethical principle. Yet they were mindful that they walked a tightrope between academic strictures regarding the objectivity of research and their feminist commitments to bettering the lives of women and girls.

In psychology, researchers who studied women also had to contend with the discipline's disregard for "applied" research, which was viewed as less valuable than "pure" or "basic" research. In the eyes of the discipline, research about women (in contrast to research about men) was not seen as "general" research about humans, but as research about a special group, often with solely utilitarian value. Feminists in psychology took up research aimed at challenging discriminatory and oppressive cultural views and fostering societal changes that would expand options for women and girls. The topics mirrored the social issues being addressed by the feminist movement. Researchers in the 1970s, for example, studied the effects of mothers' paid work outside the home on their children; the consequences of unintended childbearing and abortion; the effects of discrimination, sexual harassment, or sexual violence on victims; and the well-being and adjustment of children raised by lesbian women. Feminist psychologists also focused attention on ways that psychological theories reproduced (sometimes deliberately, sometimes unwittingly) the culture's template of good femininity, which included motherhood, domesticity, and a conventional division of family labor.

As a consequence of connecting their research to their political commitments, some researchers turned their backs on the psychology laboratory, as well as the reliance on college students as research "subjects." Conventional research methods were not suited to the questions they wanted to answer. Moreover, in situating research in the "real world," studying "real" problems framed in everyday language, and taking into account the multiple social identities and investments of those they studied, researchers came to see that societal and cultural forces had to be reckoned with.

In this period, feminists inside and outside psychology began to challenge established psychological wisdom about men and women – both the claims made by clinical theories and the knowledge produced by psychological research. Feminists in psychology claimed that psychology's teachings about women were laced with invidious stereotypes and dubious assertions (Sherif, 1979; Sherman, 1978; Weisstein, 1971/1993).

They pointed out that a good deal of the accepted scientific knowledge in psychology unwittingly incorporated cultural assumptions regarding male and female nature. As in the culture, so too in the discipline, these assumptions served to legitimate the subordination of women in the family and in society. Feminists in psychology challenged flawed theories and concepts and they criticized bias in personality tests, intelligence measures, and indices of psychopathology. They also showed that no research method could insulate the research process from the standpoint of the researchers.

Soon feminist scholars argued that the social location of researchers was of crucial importance in constituting the researchers' worldview and forming their view of which topics were worthy of study and which ways of studying them were legitimate (Haraway, 1988; Harding, 1986, 1987). In other words, feminist critics did not accept the idea of neutral researchers who "study nature," but argued that all researchers, whether openly expressing a political commitment or not, inevitably have an *interested* position. They argued that one's experiences as a human being who inhabits certain categories and social positions indelibly stamp one's perspective and choices of topics, methods, and theories. They went on to argue that the discipline needed to rethink more or less all the knowledge it proffered about women. Very soon thereafter, their voices were joined (and their message intensified) by the voices of psychologists who were not white and psychologists who did not identify as heterosexual.

We have used the words *feminist* and *feminism* several times in the text, and we need to clarify what we mean by them. Put succinctly, someone who calls herself or himself a feminist holds that women and men are equally valuable. He or she also thinks that, in order for all women to be able to live safe and satisfying lives, societal changes are necessary.

Gender and culture in psychology: three kinds of issues

In this book, we keep our sights on the three concerns about gender, culture, and psychology that we pointed to earlier. First is the set of *content-oriented* concerns, which have their origin in the particular topics that gender scholars studied. Second are the *methodological* concerns: How can we best conceptualize and study particular psychological topics? This has been a major subject of discussion among gender scholars in psychology. If we take seriously the challenges that these scholars have brought to the discipline, a third set of concerns – *conceptual* and *epistemological* ones – emerges: How does psychology construe its objects of study? And how does it make its theories?

Psychologists who work on questions of gender, sexualities, ethnicity, and race have been particularly attuned to the implications of method and epistemology. Why is this so? One reason is that they have been in communication with scholars in interdisciplinary studies and therefore have participated in the "turn to language" that took place in large parts of the social sciences and humanities in recent decades. They have taken part in the many epistemological discussions and critiques that were part of this movement. Moreover, being at the intersection of several disciplines made these scholars especially aware of possibilities beyond the canonical research approaches associated with psychology. They were ready to try out other ways of doing research, of thinking about psychology, and of creating psychological knowledge.

Aims of the book

New disciplinary developments inevitably are positioned, at least initially, in terms of their difference from the old discipline. The new psychologies of gender and culture are no exception; their proponents began by questioning much that was taken for granted in the discipline, from "method" to conceptions of the self, the psychological, and the social. Such disciplinary critique is indispensable to any scientific or professional endeavor (cf. Slife *et al.*, 2005; Wilkinson, 1988). In fact, critical interchange and debate have always been integral elements in building academic knowledge.

The history of psychology is one of pluralism and contestation – and change. Throughout its 130-year history, psychology has never been settled or unified, whether as an academic subject or as professional knowledge and practice (Koch, 1981; Richards, 2010). Surely nothing else is to be expected, considering the complex issues that its branches aim to cover, as well as regional variations between the countries where the discipline has developed. Debates and strife should not be avoided. Respectful debate helps scholars see where important fault lines run in their discipline's ways of creating knowledge and construing its subject. Such debate can also help researchers see where the important disagreements are, and which disagreements are less important. In this book, therefore, we want to encourage readers to critically scrutinize their discipline – and consequently also what we have written.

The fields and topics that can be included under the rubric "gender and culture in psychology" are many and far-ranging. In this book the reader will not encounter all of them. That would require far more than a single book. Our aims in writing this book are, instead, to acquaint our readers with some central theoretical and epistemological frameworks and methods that scholars in these fields have developed. We illustrate their use by describing examples of research and clinical applications based on them. We hope that these examples inspire readers to explore many more questions and topics.

A road map for reading

Chapter 2, "Categories and social categorization," examines some of the key social categories that are relevant to the study of gender and culture: sex and gender, ethnicity, race, social class, and sexuality. We discuss different ways of understanding the nature and uses of these categories, their inescapable complexity, and the interrelationships among them.

Chapter 3, "Laying the foundation," presents conceptual frameworks that are essential to developing psychological thinking and practices regarding the psychology of gender and culture. The chapter discusses definitions of culture, ideas about humans as meaning-makers, power differences in society and their implications for psychology, and ideas about knowledge and language.

Chapter 4, "Theories of gender in psychology: an overview," first briefly reviews the most common ways that psychologists have theorized gender. We then introduce theoretical propositions of culturally anchored psychologies of gender: thinking in terms of "doing gender"; femininities and masculinities as parts of cultural gender orders; identity and gender in cultural perspectives; theory about gender, power, and other asymmetries; intersectionality and gender; and gender and language.

Chapters 5, 6, and 7 set out the contours of a set of analytical approaches, conceptual tools, and research methods.

Chapter 5, "A turn to interpretation," introduces interpretative research traditions in psychology. It presents the points of departure for such approaches: what "interpretation" means in research, people's everyday meaning-making as built into local social contexts, and social contexts as parts of larger cultural systems. The chapter ends with a discussion of how all creators of knowledge – including researchers – exist in such cultural contexts, and how, consequently, all knowledge-production is influenced by social and cultural processes and forces.

Chapter 6, "Doing interpretative psychological research," describes some practices of interpretative research. We begin with a description of how interpretative researchers compose interviews and carry them out, and how they select research participants. We describe researchers' strategies for listening to their participants and for analyzing the participants' accounts. Finally, the chapter discusses the ethics of interpretative research, researcher reflexivity as a central tool for interpretative researchers, and the generalizability or trustworthiness of interpretative research.

Chapter 7, "Discursive approaches to studying gender and culture," presents discursive psychology as a theoretical and methodological framework for studying gender and culture. We begin with a short discussion of the contrasting meanings of the terms *discourse* and *discourses*. Then we review the development of discursive psychology and the major theoretical issues in using discursive methods to study gender. The second half of the chapter illustrates a number of discursive research tools.

The next four chapters – 8, 9, 10, and 11 – present examples of research that illustrate the ideas and approaches presented in the previous chapters of the book.

Chapter 8, "Gender and culture in children's identity development," presents research on children as they move from an identity as a child to an identity as a teenager in a multiethnic setting. The studies we describe highlight how this transition is shaped in accord with heterosexual templates, and how this shaping takes place in ongoing interactions in peer groups.

Chapter 9, "Identity and inequality in heterosexual couples," presents research on the practical and psychological complications of the encounters between the widespread acceptance of gender equality in the Nordic countries and the negotiations of everyday family life between members of heterosexual couples.

Chapter 10, "Coercion, violence, and consent in heterosexual encounters," presents research that explores the meanings and consequences of heterosexual coercion in the lives of women. The chapter focuses on the ways that cultural "givens" about heterosexuality set the terms for women and their partners to interpret heterosexual encounters, whether consensual or non-consensual.

Chapter 11, "Women's eating problems and the cultural meanings of body size," describes research on the gendered meanings of body size, eating practices, self-deprivation or dieting, and femininity for women in contemporary western, high-income societies. It explores how these meanings are related to eating problems that some girls and women experience.

Chapters 12 and 13 move into the domain of clinical psychology and psychological suffering. They turn attention to the language of the mental health professions and also explore power relations in those professions.

Chapter 12, "Psychological suffering in social and cultural context," critically examines the current practice of speaking about psychological disorders as if they were akin to physical diseases. The chapter points to several ways in which the "disease" metaphor is misleading. Psychological suffering, dysfunction, and deviance necessarily take their meaning from the cultural surround; at the same time, they imbue sufferers' actions and identities with meaning. The chapter also examines how, throughout history, psychiatric diagnoses have often served to reaffirm and justify the subordination of women, people of color, poor people, and colonial subjects.

Chapter 13, "Feminism and gender in psychotherapy," describes ways that feminists in the mental health professions have addressed the power relations in the mental health system. The chapter focuses on feminists' efforts to undo the power hierarchy in conventional therapist–client relationships, and feminist therapists resisting the systems of power in which they work. It also introduces narrative therapy, an approach that helps clients to observe and challenge the effects of ideological power in their lives.

Chapter 14, "Comparing women and men: a retrospective on sex-difference research," reviews sex-difference research in psychology. It then presents and discusses the results of contemporary psychological research about differences between women and men and girls and boys. In the latter portion of the chapter, we raise critical issues about psychological sex-difference research and the explanatory principles it most often uses.

Chapter 15, "Psychology's place in society, and society's place in psychology," reflects on the place of psychology and psychological experts in society today. As a prominent cultural institution, psychology both shapes and is shaped by society. This bi-directional relationship demands that psychologists engage in continual disciplinary reflexivity. We examine the contours of this critical self-scrutiny and introduce the growing critical psychology movement.

2   Categories and social categorization

What kinds of "things" are "women," "men," and gender? How can we best conceptualize these entities in order to produce good psychological knowledge? One way is to think about the "things" that women and men are as intrinsically different from each other. Other ways of conceptualizing women and men do not point to differences. Instead they focus on social hierarchies between men and women; that is, how men and women often are positioned unequally in the social structures they inhabit. Yet other ways of conceptualizing men and women and gender, such as those ways put forward by queer theorists and transgender theorists, reject entirely the idea of two distinct and enduring sex categories.

Sorting the world into categories is necessary in order to produce knowledge about anything. Knowers need to be able to say, for instance, whether two objects are similar or different. To be able to do this, they need to think in terms of categories. A category is a set of objects that share certain characteristics. "Dog," for example, is such a category. Knowers also need to be able to specify what differs between the categories that they have identified. For example, what features of the category "cat" distinguish it from the category "dog"?

The observation that people think in terms of categories may seem trivial. But the question of the origin and status of particular categories is far from trivial. For instance, where does the *category* "cat" come from, apart from actual cats existing at a certain moment? And what is the origin of a category like "attention deficit hyperactivity disorder" (ADHD), as apart from the set of behaviors it currently refers to? Furthermore, most readers would probably say that "cat" and "ADHD" are different kinds of categories, even if they cannot put their finger on exactly how "cat" and "ADHD" differ.

Are all categories kinds that exist independently of human observers or are some categories created by human observers for particular purposes? This question goes back in the history of philosophy at least as far as Plato and the Sophists, who debated the nature of categories. In the Platonic view, the world is divided into fundamental or natural categories that exist as categories whether humans know about them or not. In this view, categories such as "dog," "tree," "sex," and "race" are naturally existing and universal divisions of the world; they are said to denote natural kinds (Hacking, 1994). In this view as well, the task of science is to produce knowledge that gets progressively closer to reality by discovering these natural kinds and describing their true properties. Plato coined the phrase "carving Nature at its joints" to refer to this task (1972, pp. 265d–266a). These true properties are taken to be the inherent or essential meaning of the categories.

An alternative view, said to originate with another group of philosophers, the Sophists, is that the categories, assumptions, and metrics that people use to classify the world are not found in nature, but are human-made. This makes them *contingent*; that is, they are the product of humans' efforts to make sense of the world. Categories such as "mental illness" or "ADHD," for instance, are seen as created by humans and imbued with meaning by humans. More controversially, some have argued that the sex categories (man and woman) are contingent categories, not natural kinds. Humans with different sex organs existed in nature prior to the social distinctions drawn between them. Nonetheless, neither the social categorization of humans into two sexes nor the meanings given to these sex categories can be found in nature. The distinctions drawn between these categories and the meanings given to the categories both are matters of social negotiation. More generally, there is no reason to expect that any categorization scheme will be used everywhere or that any categorization scheme will stay the same forever. Nor is there reason to assume that when new categorizations replace older ones, the new categories are drawing closer to reality or nature (Hacking, 1994).

The contrast between these two opposing (and here simplified) ways of thinking about categories is pertinent to several of the topics discussed in this book. For instance, many gender scholars argue that the strict categorization of people into two sexes, and only two sexes, is not found in nature (Butler, 1990; Fausto-Sterling, 2000a). Instead, they argue that the meanings given to the sex categories are historically and culturally contingent. That is, the meanings have changed substantially over time, and they are not identical across all cultures. Critical race scholars have made similar arguments in relation to race. In contrast, psychology researchers have often accepted without question the popular view of the categories "man" and "woman" as natural ones with universal and unchanging meanings. Perhaps partly for that reason, the study of the societal and cultural meanings of human sex categories has often been relegated to the margins of psychology (Shields, 2008).

Sorting humans into categories has certain consequences that do not occur when sorting most nonhuman objects. That is, human categories are *interactive*. Humans usually are not indifferent to how they are classified. A person who is assigned to a certain category (such as "girl," "sissy," or "hyperactive") is inevitably influenced by the meanings that the category has in his or her social group. Conveying such meanings is one of the central tasks of socialization, whether by elders or peers. Through such socialization and by observing other people's reactions, individuals integrate these meanings into their experiences of themselves. Being subjected to a new categorization (for instance, receiving a psychiatric diagnosis) may lead people to develop new behavior, new feelings, and new ways of thinking about themselves. These new ways of being may in turn reaffirm and solidify the categorization. The philosopher Ian Hacking (1994) calls these circular processes "the looping effects of human kinds."

Using this general discussion as a background, we now turn to some categorizations that are central to everyday life, as well as to the study of gender and culture: sex and gender, ethnic group, "race," social class, sexuality, and sexualities. We also briefly introduce intersectional analysis.

Sex categories and gender categories

All known cultures give meanings to sex categories; these meanings serve to create and maintain social distinctions between women and men. Looking around the world today, we find that such distinctions and hierarchies are usually built into institutions such as the family, law, and religion. For example, in all known societies, men have more formal political power than women, and men generally earn more money than women. However, the characteristics that are claimed to distinguish the sexes are not uniform from one culture to another. Nor are the distinctions necessarily stable across historical epochs within a society. Furthermore, societies vary in the extremity of the distinctions they draw and the rigidity with which these distinctions are enforced.

In the late 1970s, feminist social scientists began using the word *gender* in addition to *sex* when researching women and men, and boys and girls. They did this in order to emphasize that a person's assignment to a particular sex category does not have a fixed meaning. Being a woman does not mean the same thing everywhere and in all historical epochs; nor does being a man. At the time, researchers took a sex category to be a biological given (though this has since been questioned); they wanted to highlight how the social meanings attributed to this biological given varied (Scott, 1986). Feminist scholars in psychology similarly introduced the term *gender* to point to the cultural, social, and psychological meanings that are given to sex categories in particular social settings (Unger, 1979). Feminist scholars borrowed the term *gender* from grammar, where it denotes a certain kind of noun, agent, or object. Most languages distinguish between feminine and masculine nouns and many also have neuter nouns. In short, "gender" in the grammatical sense is a system for sorting nouns into categories. Transferred to the field of gender studies, the term *gender* was originally used to propose a conceptual framework for thinking about the social sorting of people into different categories based on their presumed biological sex category and about how this sorting influences social life. Subsequently, gender scholars went further to dispute the naturalness and universality of the two-sex model assumed in these early versions of gender theory (Butler, 1990; Fausto-Sterling, 2000a). Cultural psychologists and anthropologists (e.g., Herdt, 1997; Reddy, 2005) have described social groups that use systems of categorization that distinguish more than two sex categories.

Ethnic groups, "races," and racialization

Over the past decades, as the human genome has been mapped, the notion of genetically distinct "races" of humans has become untenable. Although geneticists today agree that there are some genetic differences among humans of different geographical origins, the groups that have historically been called "races" are not genetically homogeneous. Put another way, there are no sharp genetic boundaries among different population groups. Instead, human genetic variation is a continuum across the world (Bonham *et al.*, 2005; Wang and Sue, 2005). The conclusions of genome researchers form a backdrop for a discussion of ethnicity and race. If races are not natural kinds, then there is no purpose in attempting to ascertain true differences between races. If we accept that the genetic variations among humans do not permit us to divide them into homogeneous and distinct racial groups, then we must ask instead why such divisions have been imposed. Throughout history, motives for dividing people into races have consistently had to do with distributing power and resources. The divisions are cultural inventions – products of meaning-making by people, just as other social categories are (Markus, 2008; Zuckerman, 1990).

Ethnicity is a term that is often used to denote boundaries between social groups. The terms *ethnicity* and *ethnic group* focus attention on how groups differ on such dimensions as language, cultural traditions, immigration history, and religious practices (Markus, 2008). Also, people who claim membership in an ethnic group generally claim the group's common meanings, values, and practices as their own. Claiming membership in an ethnic group, in other words, usually involves identification with that group and a sense of belonging to it. Members of ethnic groups often engage in expressive practices to mark their group membership. These practices include distinctive apparel, name choices, dietary preferences, bodily markers, residential patterns, and holiday celebrations. However, ethnic groupings are not immutable; their boundaries change over time, as do members' identifications. So too does the concept of ethnicity (de los Reyes *et al.*, 2005a; Peterson and Ålund, 2007; Smedley and Smedley, 2005).

Typically the terms *ethnicity* and *ethnic group* have been used to refer to minority groups within a society or a geographic region. The dominant group or majority group seldom designates itself as an ethnic group, even though according to the common definition of the term, it certainly is. This pattern tells us something about the implicit political meanings of ethnicity. Even though the formal meaning of the word is neutral, it is seldom neutral in actual use (Fine *et al.*, 1997; Perry, 2003).

From ethnicity to racialization: the invidious uses of "nice" words

The concept of *racialization* refers to social processes and ways of speaking that lead people to assume that certain qualities and traits are endemic to a particular social group. Robert Miles, an early proponent of the concept, offered this description of racialization: "[I]n certain historical conjunctures and under specific material conditions, human beings attribute certain biological characteristics with meaning in order to differentiate, to exclude and to dominate: reproducing the idea of 'race', they create a racialised Other and simultaneously they racialise themselves" (1993, p. 44).

Examining the social processes by which racialization takes place has been a central task for critical ethnicity researchers (Ålund, 2000; Burman and Chantler, 2005; de los Reyes *et al.*, 2005b; Frankenberg, 1993; Peterson and Ålund, 2007). For example, critical ethnicity researchers have drawn attention to politically charged ways of using seemingly neutral expressions such as "ethnic group." A group can be racialized without explicit mention of race. For example, Aleksandra Ålund (2000), an ethnicity researcher in Sweden, has argued that public discourse in Sweden puts forward a static view of immigrant groups that carries the seeds of racialization. In the mass media, ethnicity is regularly connected to immigrant "cultures," which are portrayed as alien, menacing, and consisting of immutable traditions. Ålund points out that the idea of permanence works to imbue certain ethnic groups with much the same negativity as "race." This idea creates a sense of an "us" versus an "other." Furthermore, because the "other" is portrayed as unchanging, such ideas come close to construing the other group as a biologically self-reproducing collectivity. This in turn opens the way for the racialization processes that Miles described.

Readers who are interested in the history of psychology's engagement with issues of race and ethnicity can find an excellent account in 'Race', racism and psychology: towards a reflexive history, written by the British historian of psychology Graham Richards (1997). Also, the American historian of psychology Jill Morawski (1997) details psychology's flirtations with the eugenics movement that flourished in the early twentieth century in the USA and western Europe. In addition, Elizabeth Cole and Abigail Stewart (2001), two American psychologists, offer an instructive account of how psychology might engage issues of race without inadvertently perpetuating invidious distinctions.

Social class

The term social class usually refers to the hierarchy of groups in a society, which is based on such factors as economic resources, education, occupational status, and factors such as political and economic interests. Being designated as a member of a particular social class means that one shares at least some attributes with other members of that class. However, exactly which attributes are in focus depends on the type of definition used. Indeed, social scientists have not agreed upon a way of defining social classes. "Working class," for example, may imply some attributes in one system of classification (for instance, not owning the means of production) and other attributes in another system of classification (for instance, having a relatively modest standard of living, but one above the poverty level).

In addition to differing definitions of what social class is, there are sharp national and regional differences regarding the salience of class for people's everyday identities. European social scientists have commonly regarded social class as an important analytical tool. By contrast, social scientists in the USA have tended to steer away from the use of social class as a category of analysis. Instead, they have studied specific features of social stratification such as educational attainment, occupational status, and income (Ferree, 2009; Lareau, 2003). Moreover, social class has rarely been a focus of theorizing or research by psychologists. Social class is seldom discussed in textbooks in social psychology, clinical psychology, and child development, or in clinical training. The lack of attention to social class is also reflected in the paucity of articles retrieved in searches of electronic databases of psychological research. In 2006, the American Psychological Association (APA) convened a task force to address issues of socioeconomic status in American psychology (APA Task Force on Socioeconomic Status, 2007). The task force noted a dearth of research about the social processes that maintain and justify social class differences, as well as a dearth of research about how class status shapes people's lives. The task force also lamented that the lack of attention to social class structure was rarely recognized as a problem by the psychologists whose work they reviewed.

Although psychologists have overlooked the significance of social class, there is good evidence that poverty is linked to diminished mental health. Epidemiological studies using self-report measures of psychological symptoms have shown that such symptoms are reported more frequently by individuals in lower socioeconomic groups than by others. In several countries, this connection has been found to be particularly strong for women (Swedish National Board of Health and Welfare, 2008, 2009; UK Mental Health, 2011). Furthermore, at least in western, high-income countries, the most debilitating conditions, such as schizophrenia and other psychoses, are more common among individuals living in conditions of deprivation. Some researchers sought to explain this pattern by what was called downward drift. This is the idea that these conditions and their debilitating symptoms led to decreased socioeconomic status and social problems for the individual (Dohrenwend *et al.*, 1998). Other researchers argued that the stresses and deprivations associated with low socioeconomic status serve to trigger mental disorders. Epidemiological studies carried out in Sweden have shown that a childhood in economically and socially strained conditions is a risk factor for schizophrenia and other psychoses (Hjern *et al.*, 2004; Wicks *et al.*, 2005). Of course, downward drift and social causation need not be exclusive processes; both could be operating.

Sexuality and sexualities

In most known societies, there are strong pressures to order society, and keep it ordered, into two sexes and two sexes only. Until recently, there has also been strong pressure to limit sexual relations to partners of different sex categories. Heterosexual relations were the only permissible form of sexuality; that is, the only form that had religious and civil sanction. As feminists have pointed out, this legitimate sexuality, heterosexuality, has tended to be overwhelmingly defined by men and to serve the interests and needs of men, rather than the needs and interests of both women and men (Gavey, 2005; Tiefer, 1991).

The study of human sexuality embraces many issues and spans a large terrain of human experience. It involves the meanings of biological sex, the number of sex categories, what kinds of people are permitted to have sexual relations and form intimate partnerships with each other, and which group or group member has the power to regulate sexual relationships and to define their meaning and content. Further, there are connections among these dimensions of sexual experience. One might ask under what conditions a society would construct and maintain strong systems to regulate the number of sexes. One might also investigate the circumstances that prompt societies to engage in rigorous policing to keep the two-sex model in place as the only "natural" one. One might also ask what social interests are served by forbidding same-sex sexual relations at various points in the life course or throughout the entire life course. And one might want to ask what societal interests are served by defining women's heterosexuality as subservient to men's sexuality. Questions like these are being posed by psychologists and other social scientists today. See, for instance, the writings by Bohan and Russell (1999), Clarke *et al.* (2010), Coyle and Kitzinger (2002), D'Augelli and Patterson (2001), and Herdt (1997).

Historians and anthropologists have accumulated extensive knowledge of the diversity of sexual practices, meanings, categorizations, and identities across different historical periods and different cultures. This body of work shows clearly that what some believed to be universal and natural behaviors are in fact contingent social practices. Worldwide, there are many societies in which more than two sexes are recognized, as well as societies in which it is recognized that individuals may change from one sex to another, whether in the course of physical maturation or by surgical means (Herdt, 1997; Kulick, 2005; Nanda, 1998; Reddy, 2005). Moreover, new evidence about the genes and hormones that determine "biological sex" has called into question the idea of only two biological sexes (Fausto-Sterling, 2000a; Jordan-Young, 2010). Biologically, it is possible to demarcate more than two sexes; the exact number depends on which criteria are used. Depending on the criteria chosen, a particular individual could be categorized as a member of a number of different sexes. The two-sex model, then, far from being grounded in immutable nature, is sustained by social, political, and cultural forces.

Heteronormativity

In many countries, ideas and values regarding same-sex sexual relations have changed substantially in recent decades. Legal and moral strictures have loosened as well. In many locales, people who do not identify as heterosexual have more rights and freedoms than they did even a decade ago. In popular culture, gay and lesbian entertainers are out of the closet; the lives of gay and lesbian people are the subject of dramas and sitcoms. The mental health professions have repudiated prejudicial views of homosexuality and bisexuality; homosexuality has been removed from official classifications of mental disorders. Sexual intimacy between same-sex adults has been decriminalized in many countries. In several countries, partnerships of same-sex couples are legally recognized and same-sex couples are legally permitted to adopt children. In some juris-dictions, marriages between same-sex partners are legally recognized.

Despite these important shifts, the idea that heterosexuality is the normative kind of sexual activity, at least for adults, remains ingrained in most cultures. This idea (and its social and cultural consequences) has been termed *heteronormativity*. Heteronormativity is a belief system in which heterosexuality and intimate relations between people of different sex categories are seen as the default and the natural state of affairs. Heteronormativity rests on a tacit assumption that virtually everyone is heterosexual (Kitzinger, 2001). All other forms of sexual expression and intimate relations are seen as exceptions to what is natural and, there-fore, requiring an explanation. Heterosexuality needs no explanation. It is seen simply as "the way things are" and as something neutral and natural (Kitzinger and Perkins, 1993). Consider, for example, how often it is taken for granted that "sexuality" and "family" refer to heterosexuality and male–female couple relations. In psychological theory and research, heteronormativity is still common; however, an increasing number of psychologists are challenging this view (Clarke *et al.*, 2010; Coyle and Kitzinger, 2002; D'Augelli and Patterson, 2001; Kitzinger, 2001).

Who defines heterosexual sexuality?

Norms prescribing heterosexuality not only render homosexuality unnatural. Throughout history, they have also served to hide and some-times "denaturalize" women's heterosexual sexuality. That is, hetero-sexual norms have typically been based on men's experiences and preferences. An example is the normative description of heterosexual activity known as the human sexual response cycle (HSRC), which was devised by two sex researchers in the USA, Edgar Masters and Virginia Johnson (1966). The American feminist psychologist Leonore Tiefer (1991) has shown that the template for the HSRC is men's sexual responses and preferences. For example, "sexuality" meant penetrative heterosexual intercourse. All other sexual activity was either regarded as "foreplay" or disregarded. Furthermore, reaching orgasm quickly was the measure of sexual adequacy. As Tiefer (1991) pointed out, the HSRC did not encompass the sexual experiences and activities that many women prefer.

Chapter 10 pursues some of these issues. The chapter highlights the work of Nicola Gavey, a feminist psychologist working in New Zealand. Gavey has explored how heterosexual norms enable individual men to impose their preferences and interests on individual women.

Intersectionality: the interrelationship of social categories

In real life, social categories never exist in pure form. There are no individuals or groups who are only gendered or classed or raced. To call attention to this complexity, Black feminist theorists in the USA coined the term _intersectionality_ (Crenshaw, 1991). Social identities or categories do not simply add on to one another. Instead, the categories inextricably intertwine with one another from the very outset, such that each takes its meaning partly from the other categories. Looked at from the perspective of an individual, what it means to be a woman (for instance) cannot be determined separately from other social categories. At the same time, these other social categories probably have different meanings for a woman than for a man, because she belongs to the category "woman." Put more generally, all social categories are continually given shifting meanings as the web of categories in which they are embedded shifts (Buitelaar, 2006; de los Reyes et al., 2005b; Ferree, 2009; Magnusson, 2011; McCall, 2005; Prins, 2006). Recently, some psychologists who study gender, ethnicity, and race have begun to explore the concept of intersectionality (Cole, 2009; Sex Roles special issue, 2008; Shields, 2008; Stewart and McDermott, 2004).

3   Laying the foundation

Before proceeding further, we need to put down a foundation for the topics we will take up subsequently. We provide brief discussions of several key ideas. These include culture, humans as meaning-makers, and knowledge as socially and historically situated. What do we mean by "culture" and what is its part in human psychology and social relations? How are meaning-making and language part of human experience, social relations, and cultural life? How is language related to culture, power, and meaning-making?

Culture and human psychology

Culture is an inextricable part of mental life. Culture must be seen as an inseparable part of people's psychological functioning, not something that can be added onto an individual. Seeing culture as *in* psychology has several consequences for psychological practice and research. Throughout this book, we describe many such consequences. In this section, we describe concepts and terms that are central to the ways of thinking about culture in psychology presented in this book. All of these ways share the conviction that meaning is central to human psychology. Moreover, meaning is unavoidably social; there could be no other kind of meaning (Mishler, 1979). No matter how private or unique a person's experiences may feel, meanings are not wholly created in an individual's mind, nor determined by biological drives. As soon as one invokes meaning, one has to begin to think about culture (Mattingly, 2008; Mattingly *et al.*, 2008). Meanings are based on a common or shared framework and a shared language. Such a shared framework is necessary if meanings are to be intelligible to others. Any psychological theorizing about meaning necessarily must take culture as one of its starting points.

Connections between meaning systems in society and individual psychology have been of interest throughout the history of psychology, although that interest has ebbed and flowed. Psychologists have thought about these connections in different ways. Some have simply carried out studies comparing people in one country to those in another, presuming that everyone who lived in a particular locale shared the same meaning system. Other psychologists have imported anthropological concepts and methods, which are geared to the study of culture, into their research. Others have redefined the relation between individual and society such that their research questions explicitly take culture into account (Kirschner and Martin, 2010; Rogoff, 2003). It is the latter two types of psychological theory and research that we take up in this book.

Defining culture

There are few terms in the social sciences that have been given so many, and such diverse, meanings as "culture." As we view it, culture is one of the conditions necessary for there to be such things as "persons" or "humans" or "humanity." Yet this condition is something that humans themselves produce. The cultural anthropologist Clifford Geertz has expressed this recursivity in the following quotation: "Believing . . . that man[1] is an animal suspended in webs of significance he himself has spun, I take culture to be those webs" (1973, p. 4). Because Geertz's thinking about culture has inspired many others, we look more closely at his statement.

The phrase "man is an animal" shows an appreciation of the importance of biology to human existence; it acknowledges that humans have much in common with other animals. The definition of culture as "webs of significance" calls forth an image of a complex and multidimensional network of local and global meanings that intersect and influence one another in a person's daily life. Humans, that is, humanity as well as individuals, are constantly suspended in these webs. This is what defines a person as human. There is no way of being outside culture and still being human. Humans are defined as *humans* by the webs of significance: A human animal without such a support system would not be human.

The image of individuals suspended in a culture as if in a web could be taken to imply that culture is outside individuals. However, as Geertz points out, it is humans themselves who have spun these webs of significance; thus, the webs are not outside at all. There is a fundamental recursivity of "culture" and "humans." Each is needed for the other to exist. Culture cannot exist without human beings and human beings cannot exist without culture. Culture at its very heart is something intrinsically human, and humans are intrinsically cultural beings.

---

[1] Today's readers will find it objectionable to use the word *man* to denote all of humanity. However, in 1973, when Geertz wrote this definition, this was still common usage.

Culture, then, can be seen as a web or universe of meanings that orders and gives shape to people's experiences and reality as humans. Culture makes experiences knowable in some ways but not in other ways. But culture is a set of meanings that humans themselves have created and continually re-create. Humans both perpetuate traditions and meanings and remake and change them. In order to fashion a personal identity and relate to one another, humans use the toolbox of possible meanings that culture provides (Haavind, 2002). Thus, culturally based interpretations of a certain action contribute greatly to the personal meaning of the action (Bruner, 1990; Geertz, 1973).

People as meaning-makers

Psychologists studying individuals in culture have a primary interest in meaning-making, particularly as it is part of everyday activity and as it is constituted by culture and cultural processes (Rogoff, 2003). People's meaning-making – both in communicating with others and in making their experiences intelligible to themselves – always draws upon sets of meanings that already exist. Therefore, to study meaning-making, psychologists must locate the individuals whom they study in culture. To speak of mental life – that is, meaning – we need to begin with culture, not with the notion of an individual standing in isolation from the social surround (Bruner, 1990; Mattingly *et al.*, 2008). Indeed, there is no such individual.

Ordinariness, deviations, and narrative

If culture is central to individual psychological functioning, how does culture shape mind? This is not a simple question and there have been many attempts to answer it. Let us follow the cultural psychologist Jerome Bruner through his recent discussion of the question. Bruner (2008) begins with an assumption that seems fairly easy to accept: To be a member of a particular culture means that one shares with the other members of that culture a number of ideas about what is ordinary and unexceptional. These ideas are supported by social institutions such as the family, the educational system, and religion, as well as by language and other shared communication tools. Such supports are of course "outside" each individual.

The sense of shared ordinariness among members of a social group is an experience that people find highly rewarding. It supports the uniquely human capacity for mutual understanding, which is a major part of what most people feel defines them as humans. Moreover, because the sense of shared ordinariness is so satisfying, breaches are discomfiting; they must be repaired. Daily life, of course, is not completely predictable. Social groups therefore need some means of handling departures from shared ordinariness; that is, instances when shared modes of thinking are not adequate to account for events and actions. Such "cracks" in the ordinary need to be made understandable, either by finding ways to accommodate them within existing modes of thinking or by finding ways to explain why one is not able to or willing to accommodate them.

One of the most common means for representing deviations is narrative. People tell stories about experiences that have created fissures in shared ordinariness. In these stories, cultural resources necessarily serve as both the framework and content. Narratives repair the fissures by using cultural conventions that make deviations understandable. Put another way, when members of a social group are confronted with an unintelligible or threatening event, they jointly devise a meaning that makes the event understandable. In Bruner's view of culture and psychology, culture is present in individual minds "through the conventionalization of experience into shared ordinariness, a conventionalization that makes place as well for rendering deviations from shared ordinariness into a comprehensible and manageable form" (Bruner, 2008, p. 35).

Cultural psychology

Psychologists who espouse ideas such as the ones we have just presented share a view that humans are active agents in their own lives. People make plans, develop intentions, and embrace values that they live out in the courses of action they choose. *Cultural* psychologists such as these are interested in people's own *reasons* for their actions, rather than developing *causal explanations* for certain behaviors. These psychologists see people's identities as constructed through narratives and narrating. Cultural psychologists also view humans as meaning-makers able to move flexibly among existing cultural conventions and resources. They also emphasize that people are always members of more than one social group. People move among different sets of cultural meanings when making meaning and narrating.

Cultural psychology is not a homogeneous field. Different theorists emphasize different aspects of the processes we have just described. We introduce the ideas of a number of cultural psychologists in several of the chapters that follow. For further reading about cultural psychology, we recommend the following texts: *The cultural nature of human development* by Barbara Rogoff (2003); *The sociocultural turn in psychology,* edited by Suzanne Kirschner and Jack Martin (2010); *Thinking through cultures: expeditions in cultural psychology* by Richard Shweder (1991); *Acts of meaning* by Jerome Bruner (1990); and *Cultural psychology: a once and future discipline* by Michael Cole (1996).

Who holds the power over meanings?

Does "power" belong in psychology? Yes. For psychologists interested in gender and culture, and perhaps for feminists in particular, addressing power is necessary. No matter what their approach, researchers need to take into account how those whom they study are situated in larger social systems that are suffused with power. If psychology is to formulate usable theories and effective therapeutic practices, power must be taken into account (E. Cole, 2009; Fox *et al.*, 2009; Goodwin and Fiske, 2001). Power issues – specifically, psychological aspects of power relations – are often discussed in the chapters that follow. In this section, we lay the groundwork for those discussions.

When people use the word *power* in everyday conversation, they usually refer to a force belonging to, or localized in, a certain person, group, or institution or in the state. In this usage, those who own power can direct their power against others who do not own power or who own less power. They can either force others to do something against their will or prevent them from doing something that they want to do. When one thinks about power in this way, an important task is to identify who owns the power. Another question is whether or not that ownership is legitimate. If not, it can be contested. For example, the state usually restricts the power to punish wrongdoers to the criminal justice system. Ordinary citizens may retaliate against another person for committing a crime, but they are not wielding legitimate power when they do so. Such "power-over" may be at stake in daily life, as when one person commits a violent act against another person, or one spouse restricts the other spouse to the confines of the household.

Often issues of power are not as easily deciphered as in the cases noted above. In daily life, it is not always clear who is the legitimate owner of power in a particular situation. Similarly, it is often not clear whether any power has been exercised, even though some people may be behaving as if it had been. Think, for instance, of how people may voluntarily engage in practices that appear self-injurious or self-defeating. If people are overtly forced to behave this way, it seems easy to say that they were subjected to power. But, if people seem to behave this way *voluntarily*, are they subjected to power? If we limit ourselves to power-over, or coercive power, it may not seem so. However, there are other kinds of power besides coercive power. Here, we examine some of the ways that scholars have conceptualized different kinds of power.

Dimensions of power

Many social scientists interested in power have adopted the tripartite definition offered by Steven Lukes (1974). Lukes, a political theorist, identified three dimensions of power.

The first dimension of power concerns the ability to make decisions that affect others even if those others object. Such power is often lodged in formal institutions such as the police, the military, psychiatric hospitals, or child welfare agencies. Parents of young children have such power over many aspects of their children's daily lives.

The second dimension of power is the ability to "set the agenda"; that is, to determine what can be talked about in public arenas and private life and what ways of talking about a topic are permissible. Power of this kind operates through both formal institutions and informal social processes. One of the consequences of agenda-setting power is that some topics or issues are never brought up for consideration. Power to set the agenda operates via influence, inducement, persuasion, and manipulation, as well as via direct coercion and force. State censorship is an example of the latter.

The third dimension of power, ideological power, is the power to shape people's ways of seeing the world, their meanings and interpretations, preferences and wishes. This power dimension is typically less readily discernible than the first two. It is typical of ideologies that they remain invisible; that is, people are unaware of them as ideologies. Because of the invisibility of ideology, ideologies are often experienced as "the way things are" and thus do not have to be explicitly invoked. Ideological power can lead people to embrace stances that are detrimental to their well-being or position in society. An example is the ideological power that leads many women to support laws and customs that discriminate against women as a group.

Power and knowledge

Michel Foucault, a French historian of science and philosopher, put forward another influential theory of power at around the same time as Lukes was writing. Foucault, who originally studied psychology, was by his own account particularly interested in how societies through the course of history have induced people to regard themselves as certain kinds of human beings (Foucault, 1983). Inevitably, power issues and the relations among power, knowledge, and identity (or subjectivity, as Foucault preferred to call it) became important parts of his study (Foucault, 1965/1988, 1975/1991, 1979, 1986). Many psychologists who are interested in identity and power, along with the vicissitudes of how people develop knowledge about themselves, have been inspired by his writings.

The word "subject," as Foucault used it, has a double meaning. First, it means being a subject in the sense of "tied to one's own identity by a conscience or self-knowledge." Second, it means being subjected to someone else's control (Foucault, 1983, p. 212). For Foucault, the inextricable connection between being a subject and being subjected to external control is the central issue to be explored and understood. How do state power and social power work to form self-knowledge? For Foucault, studying the operations of power required new scholarly tools. Foucault therefore developed a number of analytical concepts. He argued, for instance, that, in contemporary societies, certain kinds of knowledge (but not other kinds) about oneself are made available to individuals and made to seem necessary. This knowledge, according to Foucault, is intrinsic to the ability of modern states to govern their subjects without recourse to direct physical coercion. In this view, power exercised by the state in modern societies is not so much about coercing or prohibiting certain behaviors (though it sometimes is) but about enabling and guiding certain desires and forms of conduct.

Free individuals within governed collectivities

By inviting and guiding individuals to want certain outcomes, modern states exert "totalization power" without seeming to do so (Foucault, 1983, p. 221). As Foucault pointed out, no one explicitly forbids individuals to go against the grain, but everyday life is shaped in such a way that going with the grain appears to be the best option or even the only one. Even more, individuals experience that option as their chosen option; that is, as a choice that expresses their own personality and personal preferences. Even when nearly everybody in a group makes the identical choice, it still feels like a matter of personal will and preference. Parents who have observed their fifteen-year-olds being rebellious and expressing their own personalities by wearing clothes that are identical to the clothes of every other fifteen-year-old in the community may appreciate these arguments. This simultaneous individuality and conformity (or totalization) is what Foucault meant by "totalizing power." He saw it as the political genius of modern societies, because power operates on individuals but remains invisible to them, leading people to embrace their subjection as freedom.

Normalization processes and disciplinary power

Foucault's concept of normalization is of special interest to psychologists. (Normalization) refers to the processes by which a particular way of life (or a way of being a person) comes to feel natural: as *the* way, with all other ways seeming deviant. This way of being becomes a source of pride, self-worth, and pleasure; it is experienced as self-fulfilling. Normalization takes place through what Foucault called disciplinary power. This term points specifically to the power of "the ordinary" (or the taken-for-granted) to discipline individuals (Foucault, 1975/1991; Gavey, 2005). Such disciplinary power operates through social institutions such as education, medicine, work, law, marriage, and religion, as well as through the social institutions of the mental health professions (Rose, 1989, 1996).

In modern societies, disciplinary power has become less open and explicit. Increasingly, it has come to involve self-surveillance and voluntary conformity. Today disciplinary power often takes the guise of guidelines for how people ought to live, guidelines that promise fulfillment, authentic living, happiness, and mental health. When we consider this kind of power, it is not surprising that people willingly seek to comply with such standards. This points to an important aspect of disciplinary power. It is not only constraining or restrictive; it is also productive. That is, it produces desires: meanings, practices, and identities that people want to embrace.

Power/knowledge and self-regulation

Normalization and disciplinary power work through knowledge. For instance, in a particular society, only certain kinds of knowledge about what it means to be a human being are made available. This knowledge seems sufficient, right, true, and morally correct. Its exact content varies over time and between cultures. When people take up such right knowledge, it comes to seem natural to them to want to align themselves with its prescriptions. The ensuing self-regulation and self-surveillance are, according to Foucault, distinctive features of modern life (Foucault, 1980).

Foucault's work has had a profound influence on scholarship in the humanities and social sciences for several years. Foucault's thinking, which is multifaceted and much debated, has been interpreted in many ways. Among psychologists who have made use of Foucauldian thought are discursive psychologists such as Margaret Wetherell, poststructural psychologists such as Nicola Gavey, and narrative therapists such as Michael White and Stephen Madigan. Drawing on various facets of Foucault's work, they have studied justifications for "soft" racism (Wetherell and Potter, 1992), the cultural scaffolding of rape (Gavey, 2005), and practices of social control that produce personal distress and dysfunction (White, 2007). We explore the research programs of some of these writers in later chapters.

Knowledge as social artifact

In 1966, Peter Berger and Thomas Luckmann published *The social construction of reality: a treatise in the sociology of knowledge*. They argued that what people regard as real depends largely on social consensus rather than on empirical validity. In their view, knowledge is a social product. Berger and Luckmann's work was part of a long line of philosophical inquiry into both the nature of reality and the processes by which people know reality. They wrote at a time when these issues generated intense debate among scholars. As sociologists (rather than philosophers or natural scientists), Berger and Luckmann were not concerned with the ultimate nature of reality, but rather with the social processes by which knowledge about what is real is developed, warranted as true, and maintained over time.

The social construction of reality presaged subsequent developments in the sociology of knowledge, feminist theory, ethnomethodology, social constructionism, post-structural thought, and discursive psychology. Most generally, these diverse lines of thought share two broad goals: first, to show that taken-for-granted concepts in everyday life and scientific thinking are contingent on the events and circumstances of their time and place; and, second, to examine in close detail the social and cultural processes by which knowledge is formed and views of the world are produced and naturalized.

What does it mean to say that knowledge is a social artifact? It means that it is not possible to achieve objective knowledge about the world, in the sense of reading off facts directly from the world. People's observations of the world do not simply mirror what is "out there." They are always re-presentations in which language plays a central role. Multiple re-presentations are possible because people have broad repertoires of linguistic expressions to draw on. People's linguistic and conceptual categories determine what they know about the world. These concepts and categories are not inherent in the nature of things; they are products of exchanges between people. Furthermore, people's knowledge of the world is not disinterested; it is laden with cultural, moral, political, and emotional meanings. Knowledge is the outcome of negotiation on both interpersonal and cultural levels. There are often disagreements about what is to be accepted as knowledge and about which categories and constructs are valid (Hacking, 1995). Moreover, negotiations about such matters are often carried out in circumstances of inequality.

Constructionism in psychology

The term *social constructionism* was introduced into academic psychology in the mid-1980s (Gergen, 1985). Psychologists have continued to pursue constructionist ideas and their applications to social research, to methodological critique in psychology, and to psychotherapy. A number of feminists in psychology, as well as psychologists interested in sexualities, have taken up the idea that what we take to be reality is a product of social negotiation (Bohan, 1993; Bohan and Russell, 1999; Hare-Mustin and Marecek, 1988; Marecek *et al.*, 2004; Unger, 1989). Very often, feminist psychologists have been interested in using the analytic lens of social construction both for social critique and for critical scrutiny of psychological knowledge and practice. Within conventional psychology, theories have often been built on the notion of a solitary, bounded individual who stands apart from the social and cultural surround. Constructionist theories of gender move beyond that notion and instead embed the individual fully in ongoing social life.

Before we describe constructionist perspectives in feminist psychology, we take a moment to sketch a bit of background. For many psychologists, concepts such as roles and socialization have seemed adequate to account for gendered patterns of behavior. Others have found these concepts to be insufficient. For example, they found that the construct of "role" (as in "sex role" or "gender role") was too specific and too limited to capture the pervasiveness of gender imperatives and the multiple ways of enacting them. Moreover, the notion of a sex role originated in theories that advocated complementary male–female roles as a means to achieve harmonious marriages. "Role," therefore, did not easily lend itself to theorizing inequality, power, and subordination. Speaking in terms of roles served to depoliticize gender and conceal male–female hierarchy. Neither "role" nor the related concept "norm" could be used analytically to account for women's and men's social condition, critics argued. Roles and norms needed to be explained by the aid of other concepts (Holter, 1992).

Some feminist researchers also objected to the idea that gendered behavior is a matter of socialization. The idea that gendered behaviors are a matter of training seemed to place too much emphasis on early learning. In fact, few behaviors learned in childhood carry directly into adulthood. Moreover, these researchers criticized socialization theorists for setting their sights on small slices of social life (families or play-groups, for example) without taking the larger societal and cultural context into account.

Both role theory and socialization theory were criticized for often portraying people as robots who had no recourse but to conform to social imperatives. This picture did not square with observations of everyday life in which improvisation, irony, and subversion occur along-side conformity. Moreover, role theory and socialization theory could not account for the life experiences of many – including many gender scholars – who willfully flouted at least some gender conventions and openly rebelled against normative expectations. Many scholars who sought to theorize psychological gender therefore abandoned these ways of thinking and embraced constructionist ideas instead. Of particular importance, these ideas offered a way to bring societal and cultural patterns into theorizing about individual psychology. We discuss these lines of thinking in Chapter 7.

Making language an object of study

Language shapes thinking; that is, language does not simply reflect inner mental activity. Language enables and limits what these inner activities can be. Language is not just "about" things in the world, but it also sets the frame for how these things can be understood (Wetherell et al., 2001). This means that language is far from neutral. Language practices are always situated within societal and cultural fields; to a great extent, these determine the possible meanings of what is said. Local meanings are always bound up with larger social processes.

There is a field of psychology, discursive psychology, that focuses on language as a social and cultural activity. Some discursive psychologists study the dynamics of conversations and other spoken discourse. Others scrutinize texts of interviews or conversations in order to trace the impact of cultural presuppositions. In Chapter 7, we describe the principal goals and methods of discursive psychology. In subsequent chapters, we discuss several research programs that have drawn on the ideas and methods of discursive psychology.

The historical and cultural specificity of knowledge

If knowledge is a product of ongoing social negotiation, then it is specific to its historical and cultural setting. What is accepted as true here and today may not be accepted as true in another place and time. This is especially true for knowledge about the social world. In other words, the durability and the truth status of a certain piece of knowledge (including a psychological theory or concept) are determined not solely by its empirical validity but also by a number of social processes. These processes need to be scrutinized in both historical and psychological terms (Smith, 2007). An example of such scrutiny is feminists' scrutiny of the male-centered worldview that prevailed through much of the history of psychology. That worldview, along with a tacit acceptance of the subordination of women as natural, led to an array of biased scientific claims about women's nature (Chesler, 1972; Horney, 1967; Weisstein, 1971; Woolley, 1910). Feminists argued that this knowledge was more a reaffirmation of stereotypes than a depiction of the experiences of women.

Social artifacts are not ephemeral or easily changed. Those who argue that knowledge and meanings are social products do not argue that knowledge and meanings are malleable or easy to change. Far from it. Indeed, once concepts congeal as truths and acquire the weight of social consensus, they often are impregnable. Once in place, knowledge and meanings create conditions for social action and interaction. One example is how shibboleths about femininity and masculinity have influenced interpretations of biological research data. Anne Fausto-Sterling (2000a) has pointed out how scientific observations and ideas about bodily processes are filtered through cultural notions about gender. Meanings of masculinity and femininity almost inevitably influence what it is possible for both laypeople and experts to see and say about "biology" and the bodily processes concerned with sexuality.

4 Theories of gender in psychology: an overview

In this chapter we give a brief overview of the ways of thinking about psychology and gender that have been developed in recent decades. We begin by sketching the most common ways of conceptualizing gender in psychology. We then discuss some feminist critiques of these ways of understanding gender. Then we turn to current feminist thinking about femininity and masculinity, the production of gender in daily life, gender asymmetries in power, and intersectionality.

Setting the stage

Since the early years of academic psychology, researchers have been interested in finding out what (if anything) distinguishes men's and women's mental life. This interest has continued to the present day. In part, of course, the persistent interest in questions of male–female difference stems from policy debates regarding equality between the sexes, family organization, and other crucial social issues. When psychologists have searched for differences between men and women, they have usually turned their sights toward traits, abilities, and emotions. They have conceived of these as personal characteristics and examined whether certain characteristics were prevalent in women as opposed to men, or vice versa. In Chapter 14, we take up research on such differences in detail.

Psychologists have also had a strong interest in the origins of sex differences. Some researchers search for biological explanations of observed behavioral differences. They look to hormonal differences, neurochemical differences, or differences in brain structure and function. Such biological differences are then invoked as the causes of observed sex differences in behavior. Such explanations are often reductionist; that is, they claim that what happens on the physiological level fully accounts for what happens on the psychological level. Reductionist accounts, in other words, reduce psychology to biology (Robinson, 1995). Biological explanations usually are phrased as though they were valid for all humans, regardless of cultural background, historical epoch, or social categorization.

Many other psychologists have instead looked for evidence that differences in early experiences or upbringing might create specific patterns of psychological differences between women and men. Psychodynamic thought offers several examples (Chodorow, 1978; Erikson, 1968; Freud, 1905, 1952, 1963). Social learning theories, such as those put forward by Bussey and Bandura (1999) and Martin *et al.* (2002), also posit that differences between men and women are due to external influences in childhood ("nurture"), not biology ("nature"). In both theoretical frameworks, the differences established in childhood are seen as stable traits and abilities that reside inside the individual and cannot readily be changed. Like biologically oriented researchers, socialization researchers have often made universal inferences about "men" and "women" from differences they observed between the specific groups of men and women whom they studied (Hare-Mustin and Marecek, 1994; Marecek, 1995a, 1995b).

As we discuss in Chapter 14, psychological researchers interested in differences between women and men have often assumed that abilities, traits, and emotions can be fruitfully studied without taking into account the meanings attributed to them in different situations or contexts. Such assumptions were more common earlier than they are today, and they were not limited to research about male–female differences. For instance, a great deal of social psychological research was conducted on young, white, male college students, but conclusions were drawn about all humans. This practice was heavily criticized by early feminist psychologists as *androcentric*. That is, the research centered on men's experiences and interests and took them to represent all human experiences and interests. Such one-sexed studies of "general human psychology" rarely used women as subjects (Crawford and Marecek, 1989). An analysis of psychology journal articles showed that when researchers used all-female (versus all-male) samples, they were more likely to provide a justification for a single-sex sample and to point out that their results could not be generalized to the other sex (Ader and Johnson, 1994). Similarly, samples of people who were not white, and of people who were not heterosexuals, were rarely taken to represent the population of humans in general (Guthrie, 2004; Mays, 1988). When members of such groups were studied, the goal was to learn about issues that were seen as specific to them, such as low academic achievement, unsafe sex, or teenage pregnancy.

The power of situations

Many feminists in psychology have criticized psychologists for being preoccupied with possible intrinsic differences between men and women, but disregarding the different circumstances in which men and women live.

First they investigated whether psychology's claims and findings about men and women were universally valid (Maccoby and Jacklin, 1974). If the findings were not universal, then what accounted for them? Feminist psychologists studied the effects of social expectations, situational demands, and social rewards and penalties. They found ample evidence that these social conditions produced gendered behavior (Haaken, 1988; Sharps et al., 1994; Sherman, 1978). Moreover, many activities and behaviors elicited different responses from others depending on whether they were performed by a woman or a man (Deaux and Major, 1987). Researchers also studied how onlookers made different interpretations of behavior, physical attributes, and skills depending on the sex category of the person whom the onlooker observed. Such social gendering patterns were observed across the life span and across many different domains, including infant temperament, behavior in corporate boardrooms, scholarly essay writing, and teenagers' dating behavior. For example, a number of studies showed that the physical characteristics, temperament, and activities of an infant (sometimes referred to as Baby X) were judged and recalled differently depending on whether onlookers believed Baby X was a boy or a girl (Seavey et al., 1975; Sidorowicz, 1980).

These lines of feminist research moved the explanatory locus from the inside of the individual to the interpersonal surround. The researchers highlighted the power of local situational variations, social expectations, and social rewards and penalties. Such forces, they showed, can influence people's behavior in such a way that women and men behave according to gendered expectations. The research also showed that because of such expectations, a certain social situation may not be the "same" situation for a woman and a man. Sometimes the "same" actions performed by a man or by a woman may be perceived as different actions. Research within this "situational" framework has produced many important findings showing the extent of situational demands and their power to create gendered patterns of behavior. This field of research continues to flourish, accumulating more and more evidence of the thoroughgoing power of the social environment. The research has lent itself to activist projects, such as programs to eliminate sex-role stereotyping in school classrooms, activism against sexual harassment, and challenges to sexualized portrayals of girls in popular culture (e.g., Lamb and Brown, 2006; Sadker et al., 1994).

Toward a cultural psychology of gender

Although the research on the power of situations has produced important knowledge, it does not provide the complete picture. In much of the research, expectations and norms are presumed to be located in cognitive schemas, attitudes, and beliefs. Little attention is paid to tracing the origins of these expectations and norms to wider contexts. When psychologists stop at this point, their theories risk "psychologizing" phenomena that are social and cultural in origin. They also risk framing people as "cultural dopes," that is, as automatons who cannot help but march to the tune of situational demands (Garfinkel, 1967, p. 68). Situational approaches have also been criticized for accepting uncritically the categories "man" and "woman" as they are conventionally conceived. In the eyes of the critics, the categories themselves and their social and cultural origins need to be interrogated.

The approaches we describe below address these limitations. Above all, they take into account how the meanings of sex categories are continually negotiated – for example, in close interactions, in institutional frameworks, in state policies, and in mass media. These negotiations are of interest to psychologists because they serve to regulate people's conceptions of themselves and their actions, as well as interactions between people. The approaches go beyond proximal situations to examine cultural and political systems of meaning and power. Researchers assume that any phenomenon, no matter how local, is always formed and given meaning within the larger social and cultural context. Researchers also assume that language – as the primary medium of social interchange – plays a key role in giving meaning to phenomena and in social negotiations about meanings. These approaches do not presuppose that "man" and "woman" are *a priori* categories or natural kinds. Rather, they take the creation and upholding of the two-sex model as a subject of investigation. They also take gender – that is, the meanings given to the sex categories – as a subject for investigation. In this view, the sex categories and the meanings that they are given in a particular society are not only about local situational demands. They are part of and dependent on larger cultural patterns (West and Zimmerman, 1987, 2009).

Gender has to do with how individuals *perform* sex categories in everyday life. The expression "doing gender" is often used to denote such performances. "Doing gender" most often involves performing oneself in a way that enables one to pass as an acceptably feminine or masculine person (Butler, 1990; Fenstermaker and West, 2002; Lorber, 1994). However, people also "do gender" by *not* conforming to the norms of acceptable masculinity or femininity. This is so because their behavior, conforming or not, inevitably is interpreted in terms of societal gender norms.

People do not "do gender" in a social and cultural vacuum. In most settings, there are shared rules about how gender is to be enacted. Such demands and rules are the raw materials – the cultural resources – from which personal meanings of gender are fashioned (Wetherell, 2007, 2008). Usually these rules need not be expressed openly because people are quite knowledgeable about the boundaries that define the acceptable behavior of members of each sex category. In fact, this tacit knowledge is an important part of what it means to be a competent member of a culture (Garfinkel, 1967). By striving to pass as acceptably masculine or feminine, individuals further legitimize the accepted meanings of the sex categories. The behavior becomes proof, to the actor as well as to onlookers, that this is what it means to be a man or a woman (Connell, 1995; Gulbrandsen, 2006a; Wetherell and Edley, 1999).

Can people stop doing gender or refuse to do gender? If researchers find that women and men are becoming more similar, does this mean that people are no longer doing gender? No. Let us take a hypothetical example of a workplace in which male and female employees have the same educational background and the same profession. And let us say that a researcher finds no differences between women and men in patterns of communication (an aspect of behavior for which researchers typically find sex differences). The researcher would not conclude that the employees were no longer doing gender. Rather, the researcher would conclude that communication was no longer a prime locus of the local gender order. As long as sex categorization remains an important form of social stratification, people will have reason to inscribe themselves in their appropriate category. People will continue to do gender as long as the social stratification of people according to sex categories remains decisive for their individual fates (Butler, 1990).

Femininity and masculinity

If the meanings of femininity and masculinity are not fixed once and for all, but shift with societal and cultural change, then it is pointless to search for enduring differences (or similarities) between people categorized as women and men (Hare-Mustin and Marecek, 1994; Weatherall, 2002a). Rather, femininity and masculinity need to be explored as cultural manifestations. Although femininity and masculinity are often experienced as personal traits, they are better conceptualized as manifestations of the local gender order. Femininity, for example, can be conceptualized as a set of normative ideas and cultural resources held in place through social and cultural negotiations. The ideas and resources are usually fairly stable over time but far from immutable. Conceptualized this way, femininity designates a repertoire of actions and characteristics that are appropriate and even natural for individuals categorized as female. Femininity therefore is located in the interactions and actions that have been given feminine meanings, not in the minds or bodies of individual women (Currie *et al.*, 2006, 2007). Masculinity, of course, is an exact parallel (Edley and Wetherell, 1997; Wetherell and Edley, 1999).

Psychologists who view femininity and masculinity as parts of the gender order pursue a distinctive research agenda. For instance, they are interested to learn about the local processes by which certain ideals of femininity and masculinity are created and maintained. They might also study the processes by which people come to feel that living up to the social requirements of their sex category is an authentic expression of their inner selves. Put another way, these scholars study the processes by which people internalize the cultural imperatives of femininity and masculinity such that they are experienced as "the way I really am" or "the way I want to be." In addition, these scholars study how people resist and change the imperatives. We briefly explore these issues in the next section.

Gendered identities: mastery, appropriation, and change

In recent decades and in many parts of the world, there have been dramatic changes in the ways that people conceive of men and women. Feminist movements and other liberatory movements have protested against gender imperatives. Many women and men have on occasion defied some social norms or flouted certain gender imperatives. Despite the regulatory force of gender, individuals and groups have sometimes developed a critical consciousness and mobilized for change. How has this happened? And how is it that sometimes change has seemed impossible? Let us begin by noting that in most situations in everyday life, there are several possible ways of acting. And there are also usually several ways of thinking about one's actions. Some of these ways are likely to be more culturally favored than others.

Sociocultural psychology offers two concepts that are helpful for thinking about identity processes and sex categories. Many sociocultural psychologists have studied how children learn new skills. They focus not only on learning an ability, but also on how possessing an ability comes to form a part of the learner's sense of self (Wertsch *et al.*, 1995). The concepts of "mastery" and "appropriation" refer to two sets of processes involved. "Mastery" refers to the state that a person has reached when he or she can perform a certain task well enough to satisfy others and herself or himself. "Appropriation," on the other hand, refers to the process by which the mastery of a skill becomes part of a person's self-image (Rogoff, 1995, 2003; Wertsch, 1997). To appropriate a skill means that performing this skill has become an expression of who the person is (Gulbrandsen, 2006a; Haavind, 1998, 2002).

Not all skills that are mastered are also appropriated (that is, become part of the self). The cultural meaning of a skill always contributes to the meaning that the skill comes to have for an individual. One element of cultural meaning is the connection of the skill to various social categorizations, such as sex category, social class, age, generation, and ethnicity. Such cultural connections influence whether or not the skill will be appropriated into an individual's sense of self (Thorsen and Toverud, 2002). For example, people have traditionally expected it to be naturally easier for women to master abilities that are socially defined as feminine; furthermore, they expect women to reach a higher level of mastery of such abilities. However, traditionally, society has also afforded women more opportunities for mastering these feminine abilities and granted them more social rewards for doing so. Indeed, these social patterns are so strong that it is impossible to say whether or not women are inherently specialized to master "feminine" skills. These arguments, of course, apply equally to men and "masculine" abilities.

Such cultural meanings have consequences for identity, that is, the appropriation of different abilities. Let us take an example. Imagine that a boy and a girl have mastered "relational abilities" equally well. In western societies, the meaning of these abilities is likely not the same for a girl as for a boy. "Relational abilities" have been strongly marked as typical of women and are often taken as an expression of feminine personality traits or even female hormones. A girl who masters relational abilities likely receives different feedback from adults and peers than a boy. For example, she will be praised more than a boy, and she might also receive fewer questioning or downright negative responses. If a girl consistently receives confirmation from important people that "relational abilities" are expected of her as a girl, she will eventually begin to experience being relational as an expression of who she is as a girl. A boy showing the same degree of mastery would not receive affirmation from adults and peers that his relational abilities are part of who he is as a boy. This would mean that relational abilities contribute to the girl's experience of herself as feminine, but do not contribute to the boy's experience of himself as masculine. And this, in turn, would make it less likely that a boy who had mastered relational abilities would appropriate these abilities as part of his identity as a boy (Magnusson, 2006).

Appropriation is seldom all-or-none. There is often slippage and leakage. For instance, people do not always appropriate all the abilities they master, even when the abilities may be culturally appropriate for their sex category. Many women can recall that, as children, they were pushed to master a "feminine" skill but they did not feel as if that skill was a part of themselves. One might say that they "went through the motions" but their "heart was not in it." That is, they knew how to perform, but they did not identify themselves as the kind of person to whom these skills belonged. They did not appropriate the ability as an aspect of their identity. Many men can recall similar experiences.

Power, gender, and psychology

Sex category is a prime category for distinguishing among people and ranking them. Across the world, sex category serves as one of the most important bases for distributing resources, privileges, and status within society. Although distinctions between the sexes are more pronounced in some societies than in others, there are no known societies in which sex categorization makes no difference. Power, privilege, and resources tend to be inequitably distributed between men and women, whether in workplaces, leisure activities, religious institutions, or intimate hetero-sexual relationships. Overall, men have more power than women, although, of course, it is not true that *all* men are more powerful than *all* women. Sex category is thus tied to power. Should psychological theory and practice take such power issues into account? Yes, according to feminists and other critical psychologists.

The argument that gender scholars should study power is rooted in the women's movements of the 1970s. Those movements highlighted inequities in all the aspects of power that we described in Chapter 3. Men's coercive power over women has been a main focus of feminist activists. Coercive power is the ability to inflict one's will on others even if those others do not agree. Such power was the target of the large-scale, public "speak-outs" organized by the women's movement in western, high-income countries. These speak-outs broke the silence about men's sexual violence and other kinds of violence against women and children (Gavey, 2009). In Sweden, for example, massive protests against the Government Committee on Sex Crimes (Swedish Department of Justice, 1976) forced the government to withdraw its proposed rape legislation. The protesters criticized the committee for basing its work on a male-centered view of women and hetero-sexuality, and for presuming that men had sexual rights to women's bodies.

In the same period, women's groups in many countries started shelters for battered women. This volunteer shelter movement stood as a criticism of the healthcare system and the mental healthcare system, as well as the criminal justice system and the law. Women and children who had been the victims of the coercive power of men were often not taken seriously when they turned to the criminal justice system, the healthcare system, and the mental healthcare system for help. Often women and children suffering from the consequences of physical and sexual abuse were diagnosed as mentally disturbed rather than as reacting to violence and abuse (Carlsson, 2009; Herman, 1992). It is not surprising that many activists became deeply skeptical of mainstream health services and also of clinical psychology. Feminists criticized these systems for neglecting gender-linked coercive power.

Prior to the 1970s, the training of mental health professionals about psychological distress and about psychotherapeutic treatment largely omitted mention of men's violence against women, rape, and sexual assault, and the sexual abuse of children. When these issues were mentioned, they were described as rare occurrences and as having inconsequential effects (Rush, 1980). Moreover, the psychotherapeutic literature often described women (both those who were victims and those who were mothers of victims) as complicit in or inviting the man's violent acts (Bergman, 1988; James and McKinnon, 1990). This neglect of coercive gendered power leads us to Stephen Lukes's (1974) second dimension of power, the ability to "set the agenda." The ability to set the agenda involves controlling what can be talked about and how people are allowed to talk about it.

Sharon Lamb, an American feminist psychologist, explored some linguistic practices by which gendered power was kept off the agenda of mental health professionals. Lamb (1991) analyzed how researchers publishing in professional mental health journals wrote about men's violence against women. She found several ways in which those researchers engaged in what she termed "linguistic avoidance" of men's violence against women – and particularly the linguistic avoidance of men's responsibility for such violence. The avoidance strategies included using euphemisms ("the incident") for such acts and using passive verb constructions (e.g., "the patient was hit in the face by a fist" and "the incident happened").

Feminists also argued that many traditional psychotherapists had actively kept power off the agenda in their work with clients. For example, many therapists remained unaware of the prevalence and consequences of violence and sexual abuse, and ignorant about gendered power issues. Until recently, such gaps in knowledge did not seem incompatible with the ethics of their professions. Many therapists skirted the subject of violence (for example, by failing to ask couples in marital therapy whether their fights were physical as well as verbal) and evaded questions of men's responsibility for their violent actions (Hare-Mustin, 1978, 1980). Feminists in the mental health professions demanded that the psychotherapeutic professions – especially those that worked with couples and families – put violence against women, the sexual abuse of women, and the sexual abuse of children on their agenda. Critique and activism in psychology have led to dramatic changes in psychological theories and practices. Today, the subject of intimate violence and the development of treatments to help victims are given considerable attention by the psychotherapeutic professions. Interventions for perpetrators are under development. But psychologists' knowledge of the antecedents and consequences of gendered violence is far from complete, and there are still many controversies and gaps in knowledge and therapeutic practice. See, for instance, Gavey (2008), Gavey and Schmidt (2011), Haaken and Reavey (2010), and Lamb (1999).

Ideological power – Lukes's (1974) third dimension – must also be very much part of psychology's investigations. Ideological power is the power to shape people's ways of seeing the world, their meanings and interpretations, their preferences and wishes. Scholars today often refer to ideological power by Michel Foucault's term, *disciplinary power*. Cultural ideologies "discipline" people by portraying certain ways of understanding themselves and comporting themselves as desirable and fitting (Foucault, 1975). For instance, ideologies of gender specify particular practices as desirable ways of being as a woman or a man. When people strive to achieve these particular ways of being and acting, they likely feel no sense of being coerced or compelled. Disciplinary power that sets out the good or correct ways of being a person emanates from many sources, including scientific pronouncements by psychologists. The knowledge and practices of psychologists have become a prominent form of disciplinary power in contemporary western societies (Rose, 1989, 1996).

Asymmetries, differences, and thinking from the outside

Contemporary societies are characterized by asymmetries between men and women that have consequences for individuals as well as for groups. Here are a few examples. Men and women are often treated differently when they do the same thing, as, for instance, when they have identical jobs. When a woman performs a job, she usually gets paid less than a man who performs the same job. Men have more freedom of movement than women in many societies. Women are more often the victims of sexual violence than men; men are more often victims of street violence. Using such asymmetries as starting points for thinking about individual behavior is a radical departure from conventional psychological theorizing. It means thinking about the individual "from the outside," not from the inside. Thinking from the outside means assuming that such asymmetrical gender orders are not kept in place by intrinsic differences between women and men. Instead they are sustained from the outside, above all, by ongoing social negotiations. Thus, it is gender orders and the negotiations within them that maintain the ideology of intrinsic differences between men and women. In other words, cultural ideologies about *intrinsic* psychological sex differences are produced by *extrinsic* gender orders.

For psychologists who think from the outside, the question is not whether or not there are "real" psychological differences between women and men. Such psychologists begin at the outside and argue that if a society is organized to uphold strict distinctions between people in different sex categories, then that society will inevitably promulgate ideologies about psychological and other differences between men and women. The issue is not whether these ideologies are correct or incorrect. Researchers who think from the outside argue that emancipatory research about sex and gender must go beyond efforts to correct erroneous ideas about differences or similarities between women and men. If a researcher were to find evidence of such differences in a society that ranks men and women differently, it would not be possible to know whether such differences were intrinsic to men and women or were the product of the gender order (Hare-Mustin, 1994; Morawski, 1994).

Thinking intersectionally about psychological gender and identity

In Chapter 2 we introduced the concept of intersectionality. Here, we reiterate that gender is never just gender. What a person's sex category means to her or him and to others is always influenced by other salient categories of identity, such as social class, ethnicity, race, and sexuality. Even if social categories are conceptually separable, they are not separable in social reality (Buitelaar, 2006; Ferree, 2009; Prins, 2006). Sex category is always involved in mutually constitutive relations with other categorizations, from which it cannot be meaningfully teased out. Because of this irreducible complexity, extracting categories one by one for study can be no more than a starting point; it cannot provide direct access to any inherent characteristics of the world (Walby, 2007).

For intersectionality theorists, social categories are contingent and dynamic; that is, they take meaning in relation with one another, and they are created in specific and contingent historical processes. Positing this view of social categories has implications for psychological theories of gender, as well as for psychological theories of personal action and identity. One of the most important implications is the importance of the situatedness of who and what are being studied. Intersectionality does away completely with the idea of a generic woman or man, let alone a generic human being. Some intersectionality theorists further argue that people are not just *subjected to* categorization. An individual is also always *becoming a subject*; that is, shaping herself or himself as an active agent and as the source of his or her own thinking and acting. Consequently, category markers (such as "woman" or "white") are not just labels that position individuals in social hierarchies. They are also resources that afford positions from which to understand and narrate oneself, as well as to act (Prins, 2006). Identity in this view is therefore not just a matter of being positioned by a set of social categories; it is also a matter of narrating and understanding oneself and acting in relation to these categories (Buitelaar, 2006).

Language and gender

The language that people use makes certain meanings of gender available to them (Speer, 2005; Weatherall, 2002b). Often this takes the form of constraint. Only a certain number of meanings of being a woman or a man are available in a particular setting. Furthermore, in many cultures, there have been no meanings available to a person outside the sex categories "woman" or "man." Language practices play an important part in setting and upholding restrictions on categories.

The language environment that young children enter as they learn to speak is saturated with words and expressions for the locally accepted ways of understanding what boys and girls, or women and men, do, say, and think. These words carry information about what is good and proper for members of each sex category and what is not. The local patterns of language are shaped by the larger culture. In both local and global settings, it is likely that language is gendered in problematic ways. Think about the large number of pejorative words for "girls," "girly behavior," and "girl stuff" that young children are immersed in daily. These words and expressions are a large part of what is available to children to make sense of people as gendered beings. Individual children do not invent these words, of course; rather, the words originate in the larger language community.

Language practices are a central focus for psychologists who study gender. We take up the topic of language throughout the book, especially in Chapter 7.

5   A turn to interpretation

In Chapter 3, we presented some conceptual bases shared by researchers who regard people as intentional, reflective, self-knowing, and culturally situated. These researchers have found the tools and practices of conventional academic psychology (such as experiments, quantitative scales, questionnaires, and statistical hypothesis testing) to be ill-suited for answering the questions they want to ask. In place of conventional tools and practices, these researchers use interpretative methods; that is, methods that take meaning as a central focus for psychological investigation. Often the expression "qualitative methods" is used to denote these approaches, but we prefer "interpretative methods," an expression that points explicitly to the researcher's analytical work and to the view of humans as meaning-making.

The foundational assumption of interpretative approaches is that meaning-making is central to individuals, as well as to social life and culture. Interpretative approaches focus on individual meaning-making, as situated in cultural contexts. In other words, researchers attend to the meanings people give to the flow of events, activities, and relationships in their lives. Researchers attend as well to the ways that such meanings form the basis for action. Interpretative researchers also try to answer questions about where meanings come from and about how people make social meanings into their own or sometimes resist them.

We first discuss what interpretation is in the context of psychological thinking and research about gender and culture. Then we sketch a brief history of interpretative research. We go on to look at how researchers situate meaning-making in social settings and cultural contexts. Finally, we point to some unsettled issues that confront interpretative researchers.

What does "interpretation" mean in research?

In every kind of research, interpretation is a central part of the researcher's task. That is, every researcher has to find ways to make sense of the data that he or she has collected and then to express that sense in words that can be understood by others. Interpretation is thus not an activity that is confined to what we here are calling interpretative research (Denzin, 1998). In contrast to the bulk of psychological research, interpretative researchers rely on people's own words (for instance, in interviews or conversations) to find out how they make a particular event or situation meaningful to themselves. Therefore, interpretative researchers have an additional interpretative task. They have to translate people's talk about their experiences – talk that is not couched in the concepts that researchers use – into terms and concepts used by the research community (Smith *et al.*, 2009). Interpretation in this sense is often about analyzing research participants' narratives in order to identify patterns in individuals' meaning-making and to make these patterns comprehensible to readers. Clifford Geertz put this succinctly when he described his goal as an interpretative researcher:

The trick is not to get yourself into some inner correspondence of spirit with your informants... The trick is to figure out what the devil they think they are up to... [A researcher] does not, and in my opinion, largely cannot, perceive what his informants perceive. What he perceives, and that uncertainly enough, is what they perceive 'with' – or 'by means of', or 'through'... or whatever the word should be. (1983, p. 58)

Researchers have no means of discovering participants' "real" experiences. As Geertz says, what researchers are able to know is what people perceive "by means of." Therefore, interpretative researchers do not aim to place themselves inside the skin of their participants. Their goals are instead, for instance, to find out about participants' ways of understanding their experiences – that is, the presuppositions and worldviews that guide how they think, talk, and feel. Interpretative researchers come to know this by examining closely ordinary ways of talking about everyday life. When people talk about their experiences, they use everyday words and expressions that feel natural in their local contexts. Such words are usually taken as "the way things are." These words rarely match the vocabulary of researchers, because researchers' concepts are intended to draw inferences beyond the local settings. In other words, researchers must listen to words and expressions that have local taken-for-granted meanings and then reframe those meanings in terms of theoretical concepts that have wider meanings. The analyses in interpretative research therefore typically move from close-up accounts of narratives that give detailed descriptions of specific events to more generalized accounts of what a set of such narratives are *examples of* (Becker, 1998).

Interpretative researchers hold that this reframing ought to be done in ways that do not allow the researcher's preconceived concepts to govern or distort the participants' meanings. Instead, the researcher's theoretical concepts should become anchored more firmly in the everyday lives of the participants as the analysis proceeds. Not surprisingly, interpretative researchers are skeptical of standardized questionnaires and of scales with fixed response alternatives (e.g., "strongly believe," "somewhat believe," etc.) in which meanings are preconceived. They prefer to study people's own talk and to observe how people create meanings on their own terms.

The history of interpretative research

Although interpretative research is unfamiliar to many psychologists today, its history stretches back to the beginning of the discipline. The idea that psychology should study humans as meaning-makers situated in culture was in the minds of some of its founders. In academic psychology's first decades, approaches that enabled such study were seen as an intrinsic part of psychologists' practices (Cole, 1996; Danziger, 1990). However, early in the twentieth century, academic psychologists in many European countries and North America largely abandoned interpretative approaches in favor of such practices as experiments, quantitative procedures designed for "measuring" the mind, and forced-choice questionnaires (Hornstein, 1988; Richards, 2010). In line with large parts of natural science, psychology in those days took as its *raison d'être* the measurement, prediction, and control of human behavior (Morawski, 1988). Although interest in people's ways of making sense of their experiences never disappeared completely from psychological research, it waned considerably. Psychologists with such research interests were seldom in the mainstream. Explicitly interpretative approaches did not die out completely, however. An example is the "cognitive revolution" of the late 1950s. In its initial stages, the cognitive revolution emphasized such issues as people's plans, intentions, and meanings. It therefore offered a stark alternative to behaviorism, which was then the dominant paradigm (Bruner, 1990; Mattingly *et al.*, 2008). Another example is research on psychotherapeutic processes, in which researchers draw on different interpretative approaches in order to make inferences about mechanisms of therapeutic change (e.g., Crits-Christoph *et al.*, 1993; Rennie, 2006; Silberschatz, 2005; Stiles and Angus, 2001).

Although interpretative approaches fell out of favor in much of academic psychology, they have flowered in other social sciences – anthropology, education, sociology, and gender studies, as well as in literary analysis. Researchers in these fields have developed several new interpretative approaches and methods. Also, in many parts of the world, there has been a sharp increase in the number of psychology researchers who have turned to interpretative approaches. These researchers have benefited from cross-fertilization with the other social sciences (Mattingly *et al.*, 2008). They have also developed interpretative approaches specifically for addressing psychological questions (Andrews *et al.*, 2008; Camic *et al.*, 2003b; Crossley, 2000; Freeman, 2010; Kirschner and Martin, 2010; Richardson, 1996; Tolman and Brydon-Miller, 2000).

Meaning-making always takes place in a social context

Researchers who study humans as meaning-makers do not conceive of those they study as bounded and free-standing individuals. People do not arrive at their understandings and meanings by private thought. Rather, people's knowledge of the world is always a social product, which they express in the language of the surrounding culture. Nor do people speak from or into a void; they always make meanings with reference to an audience (Bruner, 1990). Often this audience is composed of listeners who are actually present. It may be, for instance, one's classmates in school or the interviewer in a research project. Speakers anticipate and get different kinds of responses from different audiences. These different responses lead speakers to refer to different memories and ideas and to use different vocabularies. In so doing, speakers make different meanings and may even draw different moral conclusions. Sometimes the audience is a group (such as a political party or interest group) that is not physically present but whose ideas and interests are known to the speaker (Bakhtin, 1981; Rosenwald and Ochberg, 1992; also see Chapter 7). Then, of course, speakers receive no overt response. A culturally competent person, however, has sophisticated ideas about the likely responses of others and takes those responses into account in the meaning-making. The audience might sometimes be an imagined group whom the narrator does not know. As we write this book, for example, we are imagining its readers and trying to adjust what we say to meet readers' needs as knowers.

Interpretative researchers want to know how talk and other forms of language function in social life; they also look for the material consequences of language use. For instance, researchers often ask how meanings are created, reaffirmed, and changed as conversations unfold. Or they may be interested in how certain ways of talking and certain meanings work to increase group solidarity or to shore up or diminish a speaker's status in the group. Researchers also sometimes examine which words and terms are available to a speaker (or to a speech community) and how these words make some ways of thinking possible and make other ways impossible. They also might look at how a person's position in an interaction may make some kinds of speaking more accessible and other kinds less accessible to that person. They might also study how people use language to position themselves and one another in conversations and, by doing so, create or uphold asymmetries and hierarchies among themselves.

Individual meaning-making is always situated in cultural systems

Interpretative researchers see culture and mind as inseparable; culture is not something that is added to individual psychology. Individuals' meaning-making always takes place within, and is shaped by, local inter-actions and larger cultural systems (Mattingly, 2008; Quinn, 2005). People's ways of making sense of their experiences are socially structured through local interactions and culturally informed through larger systems of shared meaning. This means that people's activities, as well as their ways of making sense of these activities, are different in different cultural locations. People are who they are in relation to the self-understandings that are culturally available to them, although they may sometimes alter or resist these self-understandings. For many interpretative psychologists, the variations and cultural specificity of people's ways of making sense of themselves is a central research interest. (See, for instance, Bhatia, 2007; Diamond, 2006; P. Miller *et al.*, 2002; Phillips, 2000.)

Cultures provide meanings to their members, but they also restrict the range of meanings that a member of the culture can give to an event or experience. Well-established cultural meanings are often experienced as "the way things are," not as one of many possible ways of understanding things. In other words, the dominant cultural meanings have become so ingrained that it is no longer apparent that they are interpretations. This makes it difficult to discern the power that these cultural meanings have to shape and restrict thought. It is only when something happens to contest culturally sanctioned meanings that the cultural restrictions on meaning-making become visible.

Researchers' knowledge is always perspectival

If humans are meaning-makers who are socially and culturally situated, then it inevitably follows that psychology researchers too are situated knowers. Researchers see what they see from a particular angle of vision that is shaped by living in a particular time and place. All knowledge, including scientific knowledge, is perspectival (Haraway, 1988; Harding, 1986; Jordan-Young, 2010). Researchers cannot help but bring to their work pre-reflective understandings and explicit convictions, concerns, and viewpoints that are shaped by their cultural locations and disciplinary allegiances, as well as the historical moment. Theories and research are always developed by people, and people always have investments in particular worldviews or theoretical models. Researchers, for instance, belong to intellectual communities that have allegiances to particular ways of thinking about and doing research (Fleck, 1935/1979). Scientific knowledge cannot be seen as separate from the academic contexts and larger societies in which it is produced, or from the personal histories of the researchers who produce it.

If researchers' knowledge is perspectival, then it is crucial to acknowledge and examine the processes and forces that shape the production of knowledge. Both the researcher and the participants have interests that contribute to their interaction in the research situation. Researchers may not be aware of all the interests that draw them to a particular topic and that inform the interpretations they make. Moreover, participants' interests often do not coincide with those of the researcher. Whether the interests of researchers and participants coincide or not, the research project is a joint enterprise of constructing knowledge (Wilkinson, 1988). However, researchers and participants are asymmetrically positioned in that enterprise. Researchers nearly always have the final say about what is contained in a research report. Interpretative researchers argue that it is important to reflect on the varying perspectives and interests in play throughout the research process. Such reflexive analyses offer researchers opportunities to deepen their thinking about the topic of study. Chapter 6 explores reflexivity in research, while Chapter 15 raises issues of reflexivity that go beyond specific projects.

A focus on reasons and interpretations

To highlight some of the main features of an interpretative stance in psychology, we can briefly compare this stance to the stance taken by most researchers in academic psychology. Let us ask, for instance, what kinds of knowledge laboratory research usually produces and whether such knowledge is anchored in people's everyday meaning-making activities. Derek Edwards, a discursive psychologist working in the UK, voiced his thoughts on this matter: "[O]utside of the lab (and perhaps inside it too), meaningful human actions are simply not organized on a factors-and-variables causal basis. It could be that experiments do not *reveal*, but rather *make it so*, that human actions can be fitted to predictable causal formats" (1997, p. 4).

Thinking in terms of variables and factors implies that knowledge is best obtained by looking for *causes* of people's behaviors and experiences, often described in terms of mechanisms proposed by the researcher. Examples of such mechanisms are cognitive dissonance, self-esteem, and insecure attachment. In this view, the causes are thought to be determinative, even though the person may be unaware of them. The task of a psychological researcher is to discover the causes of behaviors and experiences. Could it be, as Edwards asked, that such causality-oriented theories do not reflect the ways that people function psychologically in daily life? Maybe people's everyday psychological functioning is not built up from variables that produce changes in one another in predictable causal chains. If that is so, when psychologists "discover" causal patterns, it may be that the design of their experiments limits them to finding such causal chains. Many interpretative psychologists believe that factors-and-variables research in psychology produces limited knowledge about people's everyday lives (Slife *et al.*, 2005; Spackman and Williams, 2001; Yanchar, 2011). These psychologists favor a move away from thinking in terms of *causes* of behavior and *explanations* for behavior; they have moved instead toward thinking in terms of people's *reasons* for their actions and their *interpretations* of their experiences. For a similar discussion of research practices in developmental psychology, we refer readers to Susan Engel's (2005) *Real kids: creating meaning in everyday life*.

Where and how do interpretative researchers look for knowledge?

Interpretative researchers usually leave the laboratory in order to study people in close relation to their ordinary daily life experiences. Moreover, interpretative researchers usually set aside procedures such as surveys, tests, and standardized assessments. Such procedures predetermine what issues and questions are relevant; they also constrain participants to respond to the alternatives chosen by the researcher. The meanings that the participants themselves make of their lives are lost unless they happen to coincide with a questionnaire item. In such research, the researcher sets the boundaries around what participants can express and what kind of knowledge can be produced. This inevitably means that large parts of people's experiences are lost. Whether or not these restrictions are problematic depends on the aims of the research. For an interpretative researcher, placing such restrictions on participants is profoundly problematic.

As we will see in Chapter 6, interpretative researchers prefer to gather rich and unstructured talk in which individuals use their own words to bring meanings into being. These researchers see the study of such talk as the best way to capture the psychological reality of human experience (Billig, 1987, 1991; Haavind, 2000; Polkinghorne, 1990). When the focus is on reasons and interpretations and on how people make sense of their experiences, it is necessary to study people's everyday language and language use. Interpretative researchers study, for instance, naturally occurring conversations, conversations among focus group participants, and narratives produced in response to open-ended questions in interviews. Such ordinary talk "does work": it is the means by which people handle their lives (Billig, 1991). Researchers who adopt an interpretative stance have a number of different ways of conceptualizing talk and language. All, however, agree that the study of rich and unconstrained talk is pivotal to understanding lived experience. Now we turn to the research practices used by interpretative researchers.

6 Doing interpretative psychological research

How do interpretative researchers do research? In this chapter, we move from the general principles described in Chapter 5 to show how those principles shape research practice. We first give an overview of the contemporary landscape of interpretative research. Then we describe how interpretative psychological researchers go about gathering and assembling the conversations, stories, or texts they intend to analyze. We give some examples of how interpretative analyses proceed. Then we discuss some of the ethical complexities that arise when researchers study people's everyday lives. We end with a discussion of reflexivity, that is, systematic reflection on the process of the research.

The landscape of interpretative research

Interpretative researchers study people as reflective, intentional, meaning-making actors. Researchers from many fields use interpretative strategies in their work, including discursive researchers, narrative researchers, phenomenological researchers, and psychodynamic researchers, as well as cultural and psychological anthropologists. What these approaches have in common is a goal of understanding how research participants engage in making sense of themselves and of the world and how they portray themselves to others. The studies usually rely on rich talk – that is, talk that is not constrained by detailed questioning or fixed response alternatives (Marecek, 2003).

Because people's narratives, meanings, and identities are never produced wholly inside a person's head, interpretative studies are typically situated in the social realm. Some interpretative researchers – those who do fieldwork, participant observation, or ethnography – spend substantial amounts of time with the people they study during which they typically observe, converse about, and sometimes take part in their daily activities. For example, researchers have studied workers on the assembly lines of global garment factories, recorded on-the-job conversations between nurses and doctors, videotaped families' dinner table conversations, and observed teachers and students in classrooms.

Other interpretative researchers elicit conversations by carrying out one-on-one interviews with research participants or by bringing groups of participants together for interviews, focus group discussions, or other kinds of semi-structured or unstructured conversations. One example, which you will read about in Chapter 9, is a study that one of us (Eva) did, in which she analyzed three-way conversations between an interviewer, a husband, and a wife about how the couple organized their everyday lives and shared housework and child-care. Another example is a study by the USA-based researchers Neill Korobov and Michael Bamberg (2004), who brought together small groups of adolescent boys for free-flowing conversations about themselves and their activities.

Yet other interpretative researchers have experimented with moving beyond rich talk to use methods such as photo-elicitation or photo-voice. This involves asking participants to take photographs that depict their ideas about a certain topic or issue and then interviewing the participants about the images (see, for instance, Staunæs, 2005; Wang and Burris, 1997). Some research projects rely on rich talk that is not elicited by the researcher. For example, Ikunga *et al.* (2009) studied online conversations in an internet chat room set up for people searching for a partner with whom to commit suicide. Another example is Crawford's (2004) analysis of a television program featuring the pop marriage counselor John Gray, the author of *Men are from Mars, women are from Venus* (1992), in discussion with couples about proper gender roles in marriage. Interpretative researchers in psychology and other disciplines have gathered and analyzed all these forms of talk as well as others.

Interviews and interviewing in interpretative research

In the field of psychology, interviews are used for research purposes, for clinical assessments, for personnel evaluations, and in counseling and psychotherapy. The term *interview* thus encompasses several types of interaction. Interviews in interpretative research are designed to generate rich talk. They differ in a number of ways from the structured interviews favored by survey researchers. The purpose of interpretative interviews is not to amass factual information from a large number of people as efficiently as possible. Instead, interpretative researchers use interviews to elicit the narratives, meanings, worldviews, and presuppositions that participants use to make sense of the world. For this purpose, interviews are unsurpassed. As Naomi Quinn, an American anthropologist, put it, "[I]nterviews can provide a density of clues to cultural understanding that is virtually unobtainable in any other way. This is largely because interviews frame the interviewee's task as one of communicating what he or she knows to the interviewer" (2005, p. 7).

Narratives, rich talk, and interview guides

In interpretative research, the goal of interviewing is to elicit rich talk, stories, and reflections from research participants. Interviewers engage participants in a conversation that is informal and fluid, not a series of unconnected, question–answer interchanges. Moreover, the form of interpretative interviews grants considerable control to the person being interviewed. Although the interviewer usually follows an interview guide, the guide does not serve as a script. That is, it does not contain a list of questions that must be asked in a uniform way or in a uniform order. The interviewer may change the order of topics or skip questions entirely, depending on what the participant has already said. Interviewers adjust their language and speaking style to what works best in a particular interview. Interviewers are not obliged to ask all participants exactly the same questions. This gives participants the latitude to tell their stories in whatever ways they want, with the words of their choosing, and with whatever details they choose to include. Often interviews in this format are referred to as "semi-structured" interviews.

Creating a good interview situation

Interviewers bear the responsibility for creating an interpersonal situation in which participants are able to contribute full, rich, and unconstrained accounts. Rapport is one key to obtaining rich interview material; privacy and guarantees of anonymity and confidentiality are also crucial. The interviewer's demeanor and actions, as well as what she or he says, need to accommodate participants. To be effective, interviewers need to adjust their language and speaking style to match the participant's speech patterns. They need to avoid language that distances them from their participants, such as using jargon, overly formal style, or technical terms. Adopting a style of speaking and a vocabulary akin to those of the participant helps to convey both that the interviewer is interested in what the participant is saying and that the interviewer understands it as the participant intends. Of course interviewers should not hector their participants. The aim is, after all, to create an environment of acceptance, respect, and openness that enables each participant to tell a full story.

How to ask questions in interviews

The interview guides for semi-structured interviews often contain relatively few main items (perhaps as few as six). These items may take the form of requests for narratives about a particular topic (e.g., "Tell me about …"). Sometimes specific questions are asked, especially when the interviewer wishes to probe or follow up a particular event and experience. For instance, the researcher may ask questions about when, where, or how particular events occurred. Such questions help participants tell their stories. Inexperienced interviewers often benefit from having an interview guide with possible follow-up questions spelled out, even if they do not use all the questions or ask them verbatim.

Follow-up questions, sometimes called probes, are important parts of semi-structured interviews. Questions that probe such details as when or where events took place help to keep the conversation going and encourage interviewees to flesh out their stories. Expansion questions are also important. One type of expansion question asks an interviewee to elaborate further on a topic that he or she has already begun. For example, "Can you tell me more about X?" Another type of expansion question redirects the interviewee's attention toward a new aspect of a topic. This includes questions such as "What was that like *for you*?," a question that prompts interviewees to reflect on their experience of an event rather than factual details. Such follow-up questions help participants to fill out their thoughts and stories about a topic. They also enable interviewers to ensure that the interview covers the ground they hope to cover.

People's stories about their experiences serve as an entree into how they construe their relationships and situations. To elicit such stories, interviewers usually avoid asking head-on, terse, close-ended questions. The form of a question usually sends a signal that people should respond in kind; a terse, close-ended question usually prompts a participant to provide terse, close-ended, and, perhaps, guarded answers. Direct questions sometimes elicit answers that are at odds with what people reveal in fuller, less-structured narratives. Blunt questions may, for instance, sometimes arouse participants' concerns about portraying themselves or their social group in an undesirable light. Direct questions may also violate cultural or familial taboos about what can be disclosed. Furthermore, because direct questions are formulated by the interviewer in advance of knowing the participant, they may be phrased in language that is outside the participant's frame of reference. These are problems that researchers have noted time and time again, especially in research about topics that are culturally sensitive or taboo.

A well-known example of such "question effects" comes from survey research on rape and sexual assault (e.g., Koss, 1985). Researchers have noted that a substantial proportion of women who have had sexual encounters that meet the legal definition of rape or sexual assault do not label those encounters as such. These women have been called "unacknowledged rape victims." When such women are asked a direct question about whether or not they have been raped, they answer no. However, when they recount their sexual experiences freely, they describe situations of violence, coercion, and intimidation that meet legal definitions of rape or assault (Gavey, 2005; Koss, 1985; McMullin and White, 2006; Phillips, 2000).

Similar "question effects" were evident in a study of gender dynamics in a large transnational corporation in Sri Lanka that one of us (Jeanne) did (Marecek *et al.*, 2009). In the study, women managers and executives were asked about a variety of aspects of their experiences on the job. At one point, the interviewer asked directly if they had ever experienced sexual harassment at work. Not one of the forty participants said yes. In their narratives about their everyday work experiences, however, many women mentioned experiences of sexualization that they found disturbing, including receiving vulgar emails, facing large posters of scantily clad women in hallways and conference rooms, enduring male colleagues' comments about the size of female workers' breasts or buttocks, being asked to "try out" bras and panties, and being "pawed" by drunken male coworkers at obligatory office parties.

A third example comes from Al-Krenawi and Wiesel-Lev's (1999) study of Bedouin women's attitudes about female circumcision. The women's responses to a survey instrument containing close-ended questions with fixed response alternatives seemed to indicate that they accepted genital surgery and did not connect it to negative effects. During semi-structured interviews, however, when the women spoke to interviewers in their own words, they portrayed a far less benign situation and described a number of distressing and disturbing psychological and social consequences of the procedure.

A final example comes from a study of women employees in large organizations in Sweden. In this study, Eva found that when she asked women employees explicit questions about gender inequality, they tended to give answers that were in accord with dominant views in these organizations. The general tenor of these answers was that there was no inequality. However, when the same women offered free narratives about their everyday experiences in the organizations, the narratives incorporated rich material about gender and inequality. This material opened the way for other interpretations of events that were less benign than the official ones (Magnusson, 1998).

All these research examples reveal stark contrasts between answers to direct questions and the reflections and information that participants bring forward in response to an open-ended request for a story or recollection of events. This is not to say that such stories are always truer than other accounts. But the rich talk that less structured formats draw from participants enables interpretative researchers to develop fuller and more complex accounts of social phenomena.

Historical truth and narrative truth in interviews

Interviews are valuable research tools for interpretative researchers but, like any other means of gathering data, they do not guarantee "true" depictions of reality – that is, what some have called historical truth (Spence, 1982). Like any form of conversation, interviews yield meanings that are always jointly constructed by the conversation partners. Interviewers, even if they were to remain nearly silent, are always present as partners in the conversation. What a research participant says and how he or she says it are always shaped in some way by the interviewer's presence. For example, participants may adjust their accounts to accommodate an interviewer who is an outsider. On the one hand, they may leave out things that they assume that the interviewer is unable to understand, such as traditions that are specific to a particular social group. On the other hand, they may presume that the interviewer has knowledge that he or she does not have. Participants may skim over important aspects of their experience, believing that those aspects are common knowledge. In both circumstances, interviewers do well to assume a "not knowing" stance and to ask follow-up questions, even when the participants' narrative may seem self-evident.

Refining the questions and topics as you go

In interpretative research, interview procedures and lines of questioning may change in response to what a researcher observes and learns in the course of conducting interviews. In fact, interpretative researchers expect that their research questions will be refined as the study proceeds and they learn more. Often they reformulate their research questions and even devise entirely new ones. In many instances, interviews will uncover topics that the researcher could not see *a priori*. Such topics may be invisible to the researcher and to participants because there are no readily available words for an experience, or because the experience is so mundane that it remains unseen.

The USA-based sociologist Marjorie DeVault (1990) has explored how interviewers can develop questions that open up invisible or "unsayable" topics. DeVault also describes how researchers can find the traces of "unsayable" topics in what people say. The work of the Britain-based sociologist Elizabeth Stanko (1995) provides an example. Stanko had noticed how the risk of being a victim of sexual assault seemed to be taken for granted by many women, so much so that the steps they took to protect themselves had become routine and invisible, and thus "unsayable." To open up this topic in her research interviews, Stanko asked women to tell her about "things we do to keep safe." By wording her request this way, Stanko enabled participants to recall and describe a broad array of daily activities, vigilant stances, and self-imposed restrictions on their movements and actions, all of which they undertook in order to be safe.

The participants in interpretative research

Interpretative researchers choose participants carefully, keeping the purpose of their study in mind. They take care to recruit participants who are able to contribute in meaningful ways to the topic at hand. For example, a researcher may recruit participants who share a common social location (e.g., middle-class teenage boys) or who have had a common experience (e.g., recovering from breast cancer or caring for a relative with Alzheimer's disease). Participants may also be selected because they have different vantage points on a specific social field such as a workplace or a high school. For example, in her study of a psychiatric crisis unit, Lorna Amarasingham Rhodes, an anthropologist working in the USA, shadowed and interviewed the psychiatrist in charge, the nursing staff, social workers, psychologist, attendants, and medical students – workers at all levels of the staff hierarchy (1995).

Interpretative research usually involves fewer research participants than laboratory experiments or questionnaire research. Often interpretative researchers do not set a specific number of participants prior to beginning the study. Instead, they may continue to recruit and interview individuals until the input of additional participants does not seem to yield new information or concepts. These ways of selecting and recruiting participants may appear haphazard or biased. But they are actually deliberate strategies that are built upon the logic of interpretative research. We take a moment to explicate the rationale behind the selection and recruitment procedures that interpretative researchers use.

The grounds for selecting participants

Interpretative researchers do not aim to produce parametric statements about a population. For instance, they do not intend to describe the average behavior of a certain category of people or to uncover law-like cause–effect relationships that are presumed to pertain to all humans. Therefore, there is no point in recruiting a group of participants who are presumed to constitute a random sample of a population. Instead, as we said above, interpretative researchers select individuals who have something to say about the topic of the research. This points to a crucial feature of interpretative projects: interpretative researchers aim for rich talk. Rich talk enables the researchers to discern cultural meanings and symbol systems, the ways in which meanings shape people's actions, judgments, and feelings, and how people bring those meanings into play in interchanges with others in order to accomplish certain goals. If certain meanings and the ways of deploying them are indeed shared among members of a culture, then intensive study of a small group of culturally competent individuals will reveal them.

Selecting and engaging participants

How do interpretative researchers go about locating and recruiting participants? One common way is to begin with a written invitation or solicitation (e.g., a letter, a newspaper advertisement, flyers, or an email solicitation). Another common way is chain referral, in which participants are asked to suggest other potential participants. Chain-referral methods (which are informally called "snowball sampling") are useful for locating participants from a small network of individuals or participants who are likely to be known to one another but who may keep their identities hidden (such as people employed in the sex industry or parents with adopted children from a particular country). Chain referrals are also useful when the endorsement of former research participants might be helpful in persuading others to participate.

When inviting participants into a study, interpretative researchers often steer away from highly specific descriptions of the purposes of their research. Instead they use relatively general descriptions of the goals of the research and the topics of the interview. Preliminary communications about the research topic set in motion the participants' thought processes and memories before the interview takes place. By setting a broad frame for the interview, a researcher will not constrain participants to narrate their experiences in a certain way. A broad frame might enable participants to narrate their experiences in ways that go beyond conventional frames of reference (Charmaz, 2006). For example, considerations of this sort were important to the Canadian psychologists Suzanne McKenzie-Mohr and Michelle Lafrance (2011) when they set out to interview women about their experiences of clinical depression and the aftermath of rape. McKenzie-Mohr and Lafrance wanted to avoid placing rape victims and depressed women inside the medicalized framework within which they are usually treated. How, in their words, could they "invite participants to talk with us without prefiguring the stories that could be told" (p. 54)? Lafrance chose to recruit participants by indicating that she wanted to speak with women who had "experienced times of depression in their lives and who no longer experience these feelings." Her letter added that some women "may use the word 'recovery' to describe their experience of getting out of depression and others may refer to it in other ways" (p. 54).

Listening, reading, and analyzing

Because interpretative researchers often come upon new topics, themes, and meanings while they are collecting data, data collection is not wholly separate from data analysis. In fact, the analytic process starts when interviewers adjust their topics and ways of asking questions in accord with what they are hearing. A researcher's reflections on what she hears in an early phase of data collection may lead her to alter the later phases of the data collection. Additional questions or additional follow-up questions may be added to the interview guide in order to learn more about an emerging topic. Or what a researcher learns from one set of participants during the early phases of a project may lead her to expand the study to include another set of participants. Such deliberate changes in procedure are instances of what the sociologist Howard Becker, one of the most respected interpretative researchers in American sociology, calls "think[ing] about your research while you are doing it" (1998, p. 1).

Interpretative researchers approach the analytic process with comparatively general topics and concerns in mind, not with specific hypotheses or narrow questions. Researchers also often do not have *a priori* analytical categories in mind; if they do, those categories are provisional and open to revision. When researchers steep themselves in verbatim transcriptions of participants' stories and accounts, they usually see old concerns in a new light, and perhaps see wholly new topics and questions as well. They may also find that participants have ways of conceiving of a category that are quite different from the way the researcher conceives of it. Or, participants may organize their knowledge and meaning-making around categories that are entirely new to the researcher.

For example, Jeanne and Matthew Oransky studied boys' friendships by interviewing middle-class teenage boys in the USA (Oransky and Marecek, 2009). They found that these boys (even boys who had been victimized) described taunting, bullying, and crude practical jokes as ways that boys "helped" one another to "harden" and to learn to be able to "take it like a man." The boys' interpretation of these abusive and hurtful behaviors were quite different from the standard ideas about "bullying" and "bullying prevention" that circulate through the psychological and educational literature.

Analyses, rereading, and searching for patterns

In the analysis phase of a project, researchers read and reread transcripts, and extract passages from the transcripts that pertain to topics or themes of interest. They then read extracts pertaining to a single topic or theme and systematically compare them to one another until they see a pattern. Researchers usually do this reading and comparison over and over, because the patterns may be refined as the analysis proceeds and a fuller picture of the whole emerges. As the analysis continues, the researcher identifies patterns or commonalities and eventually summarizes each commonality with a descriptive label. The next step is to tie these labels to existing theoretical constructs within the same field.

We illustrate the analytical process with a description offered by two psychologists, Jonathan Potter and Margaret Wetherell:

[A]nalysis involves a lot of careful reading and rereading. Often it is only after long hours of struggling with the data and many false starts that a systematic patterning emerges. False starts occur as patterns appear, excitement grows, only to find that the pattern postulated leaves too much unaccounted, or results in an equally large file of exceptions. (1987, p. 168)

At that point the researcher will have to start her sorting anew. There are no automatic routines in interpretative analyses. As the American psychologist John Dollard put it many years ago, "the primary research instrument would seem to be the observing human intelligence trying to make sense of the experience" (1937, p. 18). A researcher's subjectivity necessarily comes into play in the analytical process because researchers must make use of their cultural knowledge and experiences to interpret their research data. This, of course, means that a researcher could (and often does) approach an interview or even a short conversational exchange from different angles and could arrive at multiple interpretations. These interpretations may all be equally valid and justified. They are different because they reflect different research concerns.

Many interpretative researchers have stressed that although interpretative strategies ought to be suited to the researcher's questions, they should primarily be formed around characteristics of the research data. These researchers argue against assembling a toolbox of rigidly specified analytical procedures. Jonathan Potter and Margaret Wetherell, for example, objected to the idea that research methods are neutral, all-purpose tools. They disavowed the goal of "perfecting a cast iron methodology" (1987, p. 179). In Potter's (1996) view,

> Indeed, it is not clear that there is anything that would correspond to what psychologists traditionally think of as a 'method'... The lack of a 'method' in the sense of some formally specified set of procedures and calculations, does not imply any lack of argument or rigour; nor does it imply that the theoretical system is not guiding analyses in various ways. (pp. 128–129)

Interpretative researchers argue that the credibility of research results (what is sometimes called validity) is not about showing that one has followed certain prescribed procedures or techniques. Doing that is not enough. A project in which the researcher has followed the methodological rules but asked trivial questions and conducted superficial analyses is not good research. This, of course, does not mean that interpretative researchers are careless about credibility. On the contrary, they address credibility both in the research process and in their reports, as we will discuss below. In fact, reports of interpretative research often present verbatim excerpts from the interview material and show the reader in detail how some analyses were carried out. Such reporting practices give readers insight into how analyses have been done and enable readers to make their own interpretations.

The ethics of interpretative research

Because interpretative research is grounded in real-life experiences, everyday identities, and everyday settings, it inevitably opens up ethical questions that do not face researchers who study behavior in laboratory situations or who use questionnaires or standardized tests. When researchers ask respondents to tell about their real-life experiences, they need to be prepared to face ethical (and perhaps legal) dilemmas. For example, when Jeanne and her colleagues interviewed urban teenagers in the USA about their knowledge of contraceptives, they were confronted with one such ethical quandary. A number of these boys and girls had incorrect information about preventing pregnancy and sexually transmitted diseases. In many cases, the misinformation placed those who were sexually active at risk. But providing the children with information about contraception and safe sex would have violated the terms of the researchers' agreement with parents and school officials. Neither one had given permission to provide sex education to the young participants (Flaherty *et al.*, 1983).

Another ethical concern is raised when a researcher comes to realize that she has been "too good" at helping participants talk freely and they have revealed more than was prudent. Eva had this experience when she conducted a study in which she interviewed participants several times over the course of four years. In the later interviews, some participants remarked on how easy it had been to confide in her during the interviews. They told her that they had revealed more to her than they had intended. How should learning that some participants had acted against their better judgment affect a researcher's behavior? In this situation, Eva decided to remove some of the interview material from the analyses (Magnusson, 2000a). Although good interviewing involves facilitating people to tell their stories, it is not necessarily about leading participants to reveal more than they ought to.

When researchers elicit stories about activities, identities, and relationships in participants' lives, they gain information not only about the participants who tell the stories, but also about others who figure in those stories and sometimes about easily identifiable social groups. How do researchers decide what should be revealed and what needs to remain unsaid in order to prevent possible reputational harm or condemnation? One example is a report published by researchers in Sri Lanka on the experiences of sex workers in garrison towns adjacent to the country's war zone. The national press condemned the researchers as unpatriotic for daring to say publicly that soldiers were customers in the commercial sex trade. This was seen as impugning the reputation of the armed forces and disgracing soldiers' honor. The goal of the researchers had been to bring to light the risky conditions that the sex workers faced, not an exposé of military sexual behavior. The researchers had a self-evident responsibility to protect the anonymity of the sex workers who were research participants, but did they also have a duty to protect the public image of the armed forces as a collective entity?

The USA-based psychologist Lisa Fontes (2004) faced a similar decision when she wrote about men's violence against women in families in Colombia. Would her research report serve to stigmatize the community and to reinforce Euro-Americans' prejudices regarding "macho" Latino men? (Fontes, 2004). A similar dilemma faced the feminist scholars who first wrote about intimate violence in lesbian couples. They worried that their research reports – no matter how carefully they were framed – would

64 Doing interpretative psychological research

contribute to negative views of lesbian women and lesbian relationships (Holmberg *et al.*, 2005; Ristock, 2003).

Some feminist researchers have discussed the ethical concerns that arise when relationships between researchers and participants produce unintended expectations on the part of the participants. For instance, researchers may inadvertently create false expectations of a friendship that will extend beyond the research interview into the future (Gluck and Patai, 1991; Oakley, 1981; Stacey, 1988, 1995). Another set of false expectations may arise when researchers invite participants to comment on drafts of research reports or even to contribute to writing them. Such invitations may inadvertently create the impression of equally shared control over the research process or over what is reported. However, ultimately, the researcher bears both the responsibility for and the authority over the research reports.

Interpretative researchers are not the only researchers who encounter these kinds of ethical issues. But it is interpretative researchers who have focused attention on the issues. They have also made them an important part of planning and doing research.

Reflexivity in research

Researchers inevitably bring traces of their experiences into their research. These traces include the researchers' historical and social locations and cultural backgrounds, as well as the social identities (based on class, gender, age, and ethnicity) that constitute who they are. Researchers' ways of observing and interpreting the world are further shaped by the language available to them. Bearing this in mind, interpretative researchers have called for researchers to deliberate closely on the process and products of their work. Sue Wilkinson, a prominent British psychologist, has argued that reflexive self-awareness is a mandatory part of the research process: "[O]ne is obliged to acknowledge the continuity between the psychological processes of the researcher and the researched, and to accept that they are necessarily engaged as participants in the same enterprise – a dialogue of knowledge construction" (1988, p. 495).

Reflexivity encompasses a broad range of considerations about the research process. Wilkinson (1988) identified three kinds of reflexivity: personal reflexivity, methodological reflexivity, and disciplinary reflexivity. Carla Willig (2008) added epistemological reflexivity. Here we discuss personal, methodological, and epistemological reflexivity, as well as reflexivity in interaction. Disciplinary reflexivity, which we discuss in Chapter 15, moves beyond reflecting on the processes involved in conducting a specific research project.

Personal reflexivity

A primary condition for personal reflexivity is that researchers acknowledge that they are an active presence at all stages of their research. Personal reflexivity involves reflecting on the ways in which one's values, experiences, interests, beliefs, political commitments, and social identities shape the research. Decisions about the conduct of a study are not solely a matter of dispassionate scientific judgment; they are also shaped by a researcher's personal history, social identity, value commitments, and experiences. These factors inevitably shape the choices that researchers make regarding research topics, theoretical frameworks, procedures, and interpretations of the data (Finlay and Gough, 2003). Moreover, a researcher's social identity and educational background invariably influence the material that a participant brings forward. Such aspects of identity can have profound effects both on what participants choose to say and on the researcher's ability to understand what they mean.

By systematically reflecting on their position, motivations, and interactions with participants, researchers may arrive at crucial insights that shape the direction of the research and the interpretation of the findings. Such reflections may prompt researchers to consider alternative interpretations of the data that they might otherwise have overlooked. This type of reflexive analysis is integral to interpretative research, and it is often presented explicitly in research reports. When researchers acknowledge their histories and subjectivities, readers have the opportunity to reflect on the connections between a researcher's identity and what he or she studies, and on how the researcher's personal and professional standpoints might have affected the research process. Readers might also be spurred to reflect on how their own identities and personal and professional standpoints shape the way they read the research report.

Methodological, procedural, and epistemological reflexivity

Interpretative researchers are self-conscious and deliberative about their methods, perhaps because they often are breaking the mold of conventional psychological research. What is more important, interpretative researchers hold that the methods that researchers use determine the types of answers they get to the questions they pose. In this book, we have described various methods for studying gender in "real time" and real life. These methods answer questions about gender as a set of meanings and relationships that are continually reproduced and contested – what people do, not what men and women are. Studying gender in this way involves studying the many ways in which cultural ideologies and meanings operate in everyday experiences and how such meanings harden into forms that are difficult to change. For these topics, which are relatively new to psychology, reflexive consideration of research projects can help shape new and innovative methods. Such reflexive consideration can also help researchers discern which research methods improve knowledge about gender issues and which do not.

Epistemological reflexivity requires researchers to scrutinize the categories they employ and the methods and procedures they use (Willig, 2008). What part do the methods of research play in shaping or even creating what researchers take to be the evidence? What assumptions has the researcher made prior to designing the research and carrying it out? How might those assumptions have affected the outcome? How has the form of the research question constrained the possible answers? How have the design of the study and the analysis of the data shaped the findings? How could the research question have been investigated differently? To what extent would this have given rise to a different understanding of the phenomena under investigation?

Reflexivity in interaction

Interpretative researchers have identified yet another aspect of reflexivity, one that has both methodological and ethical implications. Researchers' interactions with research participants are not close-ended, one-way, information-gathering sessions. Interviews, focus groups, and other activities may have repercussions beyond providing data. Participating in research may change participants' understanding of themselves. Indeed, what transpires in interactions with researchers may sometimes lead to changes in participants' lives outside the interview. Feminist interpretative researchers have described a number of examples of this.

Lisa Diamond, an American psychologist, was interested in learning about how young women developed and affirmed a sexual identity (Diamond, 2006). She interviewed a cohort of young women several times over a ten-year period, using an open-ended interview format. In the course of these interviews, many of the participants spontaneously offered their thoughts about the consequences of participating in the study. Some of the young women told her that taking part in the interviews had led to changes in their subsequent sexual identities, experiences, and activities. For example, some women reported that reflecting later on Diamond's questions had prompted them to see early same-sex friendships and other interactions (such as "crushes" on camp counselors) in a new light – as early premonitions of same-sex erotic interest or romantic attraction to women. Moreover, some women reported that they had changed their actions and ways of thinking about their sexuality as a result of participating in the interviews. This back-and-forth movement between interview and lived life poses a dilemma for researchers who seek objective truth about psychological development. Were the later revised reports that a young woman created about her developmental history more true or less true than the ones she had reported earlier? Do narratives that people tell about past experiences inevitably recast those experiences in the terms set by the present perspective of the speaker? Lisa Diamond discusses these questions and their implications for conventional psychological research methods.

Eva's (1998) study of working women, which we discussed previously, uncovered another type of back-and-forth movement. The participants in her study, which involved several one-to-one interviews over four years, were coworkers. Eva came to know that the participants discussed their own and one another's interviews in the intervals between the interviews. Among other things, they discussed Eva, her questions, and her manner of interviewing. Some of the participants then reported these conversations to Eva in subsequent interviews. Eva had to take into account how these kinds of loops influenced her project. Ultimately, this led her to another study that explored this back-and-forth movement from several angles (Magnusson, 2000c; Magnusson et al., 1998).

Trustworthiness and generalizability in interpretative projects

Often psychologists who are unfamiliar with interpretative research read reports of such research projects with interest and even pleasure, but then express some puzzlement. How could such particularistic accounts, with their close attention to historical and social situatedness, be "psychology"? How could they contribute to refining and extending general knowledge? With their small, purposive samples, what could such studies say about the population at large or about humanity? In the absence of validated instruments and measures or standardized experimental manipulations, how could one know if the results were valid? (Andenæs, 2000).

Like all researchers, interpretative researchers care about the accuracy and credibility of their results. They therefore take several steps to test the accuracy of their results. For instance, interpretative researchers, like all researchers, compare their results and interpretations with other studies of the same or similar topics and groups of people. Some interpretative researchers also check back with the research participants (or people from the same community or social group as the participants) as to whether they have understood the participants' accounts correctly and whether they have grasped the dynamics of the social setting. For instance, in one study, Eva gathered participants in small groups to read and discuss the initial reports of the findings. These discussions yielded valuable comments, including ideas about how to write the final research reports (Magnusson, 1998).

In presenting the results of projects, interpretative researchers take steps to make the material and the interpretative process visible to readers. Verbatim excerpts from interviews or other interactions usually figure importantly in published reports of the research. This enables readers to see for themselves at least a part of the evidence for the researcher's inferences. Researchers also include detailed descriptions of the relevant aspects of the backgrounds of the participants and of the research setting. They give careful descriptions of the data-collection process (including reflections on how the researcher's persona and behavior might have affected the data that were collected) and step-by-step accounts of the analytic process (Haavind, 2000; Magnusson, 2000a).

Generalizing beyond a research project

Interpretative research usually does not produce parametric statements about populations (e.g., "Two and half times as many women as men are diagnosed with clinical depression") or law-like generalizations in the form of cause–effect relationships (e.g., "Deprivation of micronutrients in infancy leads to lower performance on intelligence tests in early childhood"). Nonetheless, interpretative research can produce knowledge that is useful and applicable beyond the immediate setting in which it was generated and that contributes to theory development. The generalizations drawn from interpretative research are not statements about individuals and populations, but rather generalizations about cultural meanings and social processes. A project might draw conclusions about the shared presuppositions or repertoires of ideas that frame the ways that members of a culture talk about and think about an issue (for example, about gender equality or about immigration or about gay marriage). Bringing such presuppositions or cultural repertoires to light and naming them enables researchers and the concerned public to be more alert to, and sensitive to, related instances in other arenas.

For researchers, interpretative projects bring forward constructs that may serve as sensitizing devices in adjacent areas of research (Blumer, 1969; Russell and Bohan, 2006). Such sensitizing devices can spur further research questions, in a process that leads to wider theorizing. Moreover, for researchers who work across cultures, identifying the presuppositions of other cultures that are counterintuitive may serve to "denaturalize" the presuppositions held by the researcher, a process that Richard Shweder has called "thinking through" cultures (1991). Making tacit presuppositions visible can enable psychology as a discipline to become more self-knowing and reflexive. It may also contribute to social policy debates and public discussions of an issue. Furthermore, especially in the context of public debates, it may foster self-knowledge and help people to reflect on their own lives.

7 Discursive approaches to studying gender and culture

Many psychologists interested in questions about gender and culture embrace discursive psychology, the subject of this chapter. We open the discussion of discursive approaches with an examination of the terms *discourse* and *discourses*. Then we present some central theoretical concepts in discursive psychology, focusing on the ideas of critical discursive psychologists. Finally, we describe a number of tools that discursive psychologists use to analyze talk and social interaction.

Discourse and discourses in psychology

The word *discourse* comes from the Latin *discursus*, which originally meant "running to and fro" but eventually came to mean "conversation." Over time, the word has been used in several different ways, not least by scholars. In this section, we describe the two meanings used most frequently by discursive psychologists. They are usually indicated by *discourse* in the singular and *discourses* in the plural.

Discourse and psychology

Discourse (in the singular) refers to speech and other language practices. The term is used by researchers who have turned to language-focused research methods in order to study social interaction. They are interested in the details of conversations because social interaction is largely carried out through the use of language. The general question they ask is, "What are the detailed conversational processes by which people, as competent members of their cultures, 'do' their everyday lives in interaction with one another?" For example, some researchers are interested in the details of conversations that serve either to reaffirm or to challenge gendered social patterns, especially gendered power relations and social identities.

Discursive researchers usually focus on what people accomplish or intend to accomplish through language. This way of working with spoken discourse has its origin in the methods that ethnomethodologists and conversation analysts have developed (Edwards, 1997; Garfinkel, 1967). For their analyses, the researchers record and transcribe conversations, also noting details such as the length of pauses, emphases, voice volume, variations in tone, nonverbal expressions such as laughter and humming, and instances of parallel speech and interruptions.

Some feminist psychologists who embrace this kind of discursive psychology have examined questions to do with gender, sexuality, inequality, and prejudice. They have studied how shared understandings of these topics emerge through talk. They also study how certain choices of words or ways of speaking help speakers to achieve their interaction goals in a conversation (Kitzinger and Peel, 2005; Speer, 2005; Stokoe, 2004; Weatherall, 2002a, 2002b). Simplifying somewhat, we can say that researchers with this focus are interested in the details of how people use discourse – that is, language and conversation – to achieve their goals.

Discourses and psychology

The term *discourses* (in the plural) traces its origins mainly to Michel Foucault's historical and genealogical studies of formations such as "the medical discourse" or "madness" (Foucault, 1965). Foucault offered varying definitions of the term *discourses* in works written at different times. So have the researchers who followed him. We define *discourses* as cultural patterns of meaning – that is, shared ways of understanding a phenomenon in a culture or subculture. Discourses are not a single individual's idiosyncratic ways of seeing the world; they are products of processes shared by members of the culture. Discourses contribute to creating and maintaining social institutions (such as the family and the military) and social identities (such as man, white person, and feminist). In an oft-quoted statement, Foucault described discourses as "practices that systematically form the objects of which they speak" (1969/1994, p. 47). In other words, discourses do not merely denote things: They also provide ways of speaking about them and understanding them, as well as rules for using words. A certain discourse makes it possible, or even necessary, to understand a phenomenon in one particular way and impossible, or at least very difficult, to understand it in any other way. In this sense, a discourse can be said to create or construct that phenomenon as a particular kind of object. That is, the phenomenon did not exist as that particular object prior to the discourse. An example of this meaning of "discourses" can be seen in a study by the British feminist psychologist Wendy Hollway. Hollway (1989) identified three contemporary discourses of heterosexuality: a discourse about the male sexual drive as unstoppable, a discourse about women's sexuality as focused on achieving a lasting relationship, and a permissive discourse about sex as "free." According to Hollway, these discourses combine to position women as sexually submissive and they preclude a genuinely emancipatory discourse of heterosexuality and women's desire. Simplifying somewhat, researchers focusing on discourses often explore what a certain discourse enables people in a certain position to know about themselves and others. In other words, what does a discourse contribute to people's identities?

The analysis of *discourse* and the analysis of *discourses* have different theoretical origins; they focus on different aspects of social life. Each leaves some aspects of social interaction unstudied. Therefore, we argue that it is useful for discursive researchers to be familiar with both perspectives, even though their work may emphasize one of them (Edley and Wetherell, 2008; Wetherell, 1998).

What is discursive psychology?

Discursive psychology is part of the late twentieth-century "turn to language" in the social sciences, which focused on language, signifying practices, and meaning-making. In psychology, this "turn" was influenced by social constructionist thinking, which had its origins in sociology in the 1960s and came into social psychology, feminist psychology, and critical psychology in the 1980s (Gergen, 1985; Hare-Mustin and Marecek, 1988; Wetherell, 2007).

Discursive psychologists see language as a site of action. Their major analytical interest is exploring what people achieve by their talk and how social settings influence what can be achieved (Edwards and Potter, 1992). Everyday language and talk is the main arena for exploring these issues. To quote Margaret Wetherell, a feminist discursive psychologist, discursive psychologists study "the publicly available social practices which constitute the psychological" (2007, p. 664). In this view, people's mental activities are never entirely individual. People's identities, for example, are their versions of the culturally available ways of understanding themselves; identity therefore is simultaneously personal and anchored in the social. Discursive psychologists have criticized conventional cognitive psychologists for ignoring those aspects of human thought and emotion that are anchored in everyday interactions, conversations, and collective sense-making (Billig, 1991; Edwards, 1997). Discursive psychologists argue that such social activities are central in shaping individual thinking, identity, and subjectivity.

Thinking and talking

Discursive psychologists argue further that mental life is largely rhetorical and argumentative (Billig, 1987). They see human thought and emotion as produced and maintained in daily interactions such as conversations. Because cultures are hardly ever homogeneous, there are usually several discourses or cultural "voices" present in a person's everyday life; these discourses leave traces in the form of inner "voices" (Edley, 2006). Thinking can thus be seen as engaging in arguments – not with people in one's surroundings, but with the inner voices for which the mind is the meeting place (Billig, 1998). Thinking (or speaking) in one voice inevitably means thinking or speaking instead of or against other voices (Billig, 1987).

We illustrate these ideas by examining how the discursive psychologist Michael Billig (1991) reinterprets attitude, a concept that has been central to social psychology. When a person expresses an attitude, he or she does at least two things. First, the person expresses something personal; the attitude indicates something about the individual attitude-holder. Second, by expressing an attitude, the person locates himself or herself in a social field of meanings or controversies. An attitude, then, is never only personal or individual; it also makes reference to other people's opinions or positions. To fully understand a person's expressed attitude, one needs to know about the array of attitudes that he or she is relating to (for instance, taking exception to). Therefore, the practical meaning of an expressed attitude can never be understood solely from the lexical meanings of the words used. The attitude's meaning is always determined by the social context in which the words are spoken (Billig, 1991).

It is easy to observe that people's speech is social. People address their utterances to other people and the utterances often are responses to others' opinions and arguments. Sometimes the utterance is in agreement with and strengthens the other person's opinion, and sometimes it disputes or undermines that opinion. Discursive psychologists argue not only that people speak socially but also that people think and feel socially. The same socially anchored strategies that speakers employ in spoken discourse serve as the building blocks of everyday thinking. Therefore, as Michael Billig claims, private thoughts have not only the same content as public arguments but also the same structure (Billig, 1991). Thinking can be seen as an inner dialogue or argumentation between socially anchored opinions. Thoughts, even though not spoken aloud, are nonetheless often addressed to other people (or to their opinions and arguments).

Because of the correspondence between thinking and talking, discursive psychologists argue that those who are interested in studying everyday thinking have much to gain by studying everyday talk (Seymour-Smith and Wetherell, 2006). Indeed, if thinking were not discernible through talk, it would be impossible for children to learn to think. If people's thought processes were hidden inside their minds and not discernible in their speech, young children would have nothing explicit to guide their learning. How could the customary ways of thinking in a culture be disseminated to its new members? (Billig, 1991, 1998, 1999).

Critical discursive psychology

Critical discursive psychology is a strand of discursive psychology that is concerned with how talking and thinking reflect cultural patterns and ideas as well as proximal interactions. Researchers who study both the proximal and the cultural aspects of discourse often study power issues and the contested meanings that sustain social differences and inequalities (Wetherell, 2007). Typically, their studies combine close analyses of the details of language and interaction with attention to larger discursive patterns in society. In Chapters 9 and 10, we give examples of this approach.

Critical discursive psychologists argue that humans are simultaneously agents who produce talk and interaction and products of discourses and interactions that shape and constrain who they are and who they can become (Billig, 1991; Wetherell, 1998). Individuals make use of discourses and other cultural resources for their own purposes, but they are also being written into discourses (Edley, 2001). Discourses set boundaries that are difficult to transgress. Critical discursive psychologists attend to this duality in their theories and analyses. This enables them to take into account both the historical and cultural patterns that shape and limit people's talk and the local talk and interaction that may transform such patterns (Edley, 2001; Wetherell, 1998).

Let us consider how critical discursive psychologists analyze the action orientation of talk. By action orientation, we mean that people's talk does more than convey bare facts. Talk accomplishes other ends. Think of a conversation in which one person describes an event to another person. Suppose the event is a conflict between two other people. The way that the conflict is described is likely to communicate the speaker's evaluations of the two people involved (e.g., who was right and who was wrong; who behaved well and who behaved badly). A critical discursive approach takes the analysis further. It asks, for example, who has selected the evaluations that are communicated by the description.

Should we see the speaker as freely choosing certain descriptive terms in order to achieve a certain rhetorical effect? Or should those choices be seen as largely determined by societal discourses? For a critical discursive psychologist, the choice of certain terms and the actions that people's talk accomplishes are related both to the individual's interests in the local conversational context and to larger historical and societal contexts. When people talk, they use words and concepts that exist in the surrounding culture and that existed prior to a particular speaker's use of them. Usually, such cultural patterns supply more than one possible way of talking – and thinking – about an event. By using one way rather than another in a conversation, people are able to establish their own and others' positions, as well as the outcomes of the interactions. Critical discursive psychologists see individuals as agents who make choices. At the same time, however, not all people have access to all options and all resources. Access to individual freedom and power depends on one's life circumstances, which in turn depend partly on one's social identity and material and cultural resources (Edley, 2001). The study of such inequalities, especially inequalities related to gender, has been a special interest of feminist researchers (Edley and Wetherell, 2008; Magnusson and Marecek, 2010).

Feminism, discursive psychology, and sex differences

Unequal gender orders are constituted by pervasive cultural ideologies that link psychological abilities and traits to sex categories and that hold those linkages to be intrinsic and permanent. In other words, discourses of intrinsic differences between men and women are used to justify segregation and unequal treatment. Cultural ideas of stable, sex-linked traits contribute to prevailing discourses of femininity and masculinity as "difference." These discourses offer ways of speaking and thinking about women and men that make it difficult to think about them in any way other than as "different."

For a critical discursive psychologist, what is important is not whether discourses of differences reflect truth or falsehood. What is important is that these discourses provide the available categories for attending to and thinking about what women and men do. Insofar as "sex-difference" ideas form the framework that organizes how people think about men and women, it is no surprise that popular psychology pundits and psychological researchers often frame their explanations of men's and women's behavior in terms of "difference."

Since the early twentieth century, feminist scholars have claimed that psychology – as an academic discipline, in therapeutic practice, and in popular media – has played a prime role in upholding the cultural ideology of the sexes as different (Hare-Mustin and Marecek, 1988, 1990; Magnusson, 2003; Rutherford *et al.*, in press). By uncritically accepting the discourses of femininity and masculinity that prevail in western culture, psychology promulgated notions of intrinsic differences between women and men; these notions went far beyond what research findings justified (Bohan, 1993; Hare-Mustin, 1994; Hare-Mustin and Marecek, 1994; Maccoby and Jacklin, 1974). We discuss psychological research on sex differences in detail in Chapter 14, "Comparing women and men."

Language, action orientation, and meaning

Discursive psychologists are interested in several functions of language. First, people use language to represent experiences, including interactions, social categorizations, and identities. They also tell stories and give accounts of their experiences. Second, language is action: People do things with their talk. Descriptions, for example, are slanted in such a way that they add evaluative dimensions beyond the bare facts. Studying language and conversation as a discursive psychologist means studying language in use in everyday talk and interaction (i.e., in action), rather than as a formal system. Language, especially ordinary talk, is a central arena for working through psychological and relational concerns (Potter, 2005). In conversation (including conversations that people might carry on in their heads), people make their thoughts and feelings intelligible to themselves and others. They create identities for themselves, they account for their actions, and they are also called to account by others (Seymour-Smith and Wetherell, 2006). Third, language is productive and formative: The language available for everyday talk is suffused with culturally anchored meanings that were present well before a particular speaker entered the scene to speak or listen. These meanings are the resources that speakers have at their disposal.

Power to control language is real power: Language, discourses, and cultural meanings have material consequences (Weatherall, 2002a). Consider a ubiquitous example: In settings where there are pervasive discourses of male–female difference and numerous linguistic expressions that emphasize such differences, there are invariably hierarchies that rank men higher than women. Such hierarchies are part of a social order in which men differentiate themselves from women by enacting particular bodily and behavioral standards of masculinity (Connell, 1995, 2002; Edley and Wetherell, 2001).

Against this background, feminist discursive psychologists emphasize the gendered dimensions of language and other everyday interactions.

They study, for instance, how asymmetrically gendered meanings emerge in conversations and the consequences of the conversational processes for the participating individuals. Many also study the connection between local gendered meanings and larger societal patterns. For instance, they examine how language use has historically been shaped to favor men over women, and to favor men of privileged social classes over men and women of lower social classes. In sum, feminist discursive psychologists study how gendered language patterns not only reflect but also actively reproduce social inequalities (Gavey, 2005; Speer, 2005; Weatherall, 2002a).

Personal order and the "stickiness of identity"

One of the unsettled issues in discursive psychology is the question of whether people have enduring personalities. The cultural traditions of western societies and most of the psychological theories in those societies presume that people have an inner character or personality that largely determines how they will act throughout their lives. Nigel Edley, a British discursive psychologist, has referred to these folk psychologies of personality as the "stickiness of identity" (2006, p. 602).

Scholars who work in discursive traditions approach questions of character and personality in a different way than either folk psychologies or conventional psychological theories. They begin by acknowledging that, at least in contemporary western societies, people's everyday experience of themselves is one of being someone who is particular and unique and who has an enduring identity. For an individual in such a society, such a way of experiencing oneself comes naturally. People expect themselves and other people to act more or less consistently over time, and they usually feel that they themselves are consistent. To be inconsistent or erratic is commonly regarded as a sign of mental disturbance. Discursive psychologists take these notions of enduring identity and personal consistency as culturally anchored beliefs, ones that, like culture more generally, are mediated through language. They further argue that an individual's identity or sense of self is discursively organized. In other words, if members of a culture expect that people have stable personalities, people will interpret their experiences as indicating a stable personality. This discursive organization of personal identity has far-reaching consequences for subjectivity and for people's ways of being social actors (Wetherell, 2007). Some discursive psychologists even argue that if it is normative and seemingly natural that individuals have stable personalities, then it is not necessary for psychologists to invoke unconscious structures and processes or other kinds of "inner psychic furniture" to explain behavior (Edley, 2006, p. 606).

Cultural expectations, as well as everyday interaction patterns and language practices, have thoroughgoing effects on people in many areas of life. Therefore it seems likely that they may have similar effects on individual identity (Wetherell, 2005). Discursive psychologists, as we have seen, conceive of interactions as social sites where people create meanings. Similarly, they conceive of individuals – who constantly create personal meanings – as social sites. It follows that there is no personality that resides inside the psyche. To elaborate further, the term *social order* refers to patterns and forces in society and culture. Analogously, the term *personal order* refers to patterns and forces involving the individual. When researchers investigate the social order, they study the history of institutions and interactions, as well as the procedures that regulate them. When researchers investigate the personal order, they study the activities, resources, and history of the individual (Wetherell, 2007). In daily life, individuals engage in many activities that aggregate over time into characteristic patterns and styles. Eventually, these patterns – for example, a person's tastes, preferences, and moral standards – come to serve as that person's guide for how to carry on in life. The concepts of mastery and appropriation, which we described in Chapter 4, serve as one model of how activities can come to be felt as expressions of one's personal identity. Discursive psychologists are continuing to develop these ideas about personal order. For those interested in reading further, we recommend works by Nigel Edley (2006), Brendan Gough (2004), Susan Speer (2005), and Margaret Wetherell (2003, 2005, 2007, 2008).

Doing discursive research: some analytical tools

Discursive psychologists typically analyze discourse – whether in the form of spontaneous conversations, facilitated conversations such as focus groups or interviews, or written texts such as news reports, journal articles, or online communications. In what follows, we briefly describe some of the analytical tools that enable discursive researchers to explore meaning-making practices and identity practices.

Ideological dilemmas

The concept of "ideological dilemma" builds on the view of human thought as rhetorical and argumentative (Billig *et al.*, 1988). People live their everyday lives by a set of ideas – their lived ideologies. Lived ideologies are composed of the ideals, beliefs, values, and practices for handling ordinary life that are present in the person's cultural setting. Cultures are rarely homogeneous or totalitarian; instead, they are contradictory and therefore dilemmatic. Because of this, people's lived ideologies are usually not coherent or well integrated. Ideological dilemmas arise in circumstances in which individuals are forced to confront the inconsistencies or contradictions in their lived ideologies – for example, when they have to reach a decision.

To illustrate the analytical use of ideological dilemmas, let us take the example of how people often talk about gender, gender equality, and individuality today. Many western high-income societies are suffused by the ideology of liberal individualism, which contains assertions such as "we are all humans"; that is, there is a uniform nature shared by all human beings. Liberal individualism also strongly asserts that "we are all individuals"; that is, there is infinite human variation that makes each individual unique. Looked at closely, these two assertions contradict each other. Moreover, in discussions about gender equality or sex discrimination, a common-sense assertion is that it is important to acknowledge the differences between men and women. This assertion contradicts the assertion that "we are all human" and the assertion that "we are all individual," both of which are gender neutral. These three widely shared "lived ideologies" in relation to gender equality not only contradict one another, but they also lead to contrary ways of thinking about gender-equality politics. The first two assertions – of a common human nature and of individual uniqueness – suggest that differences between men and women should not be in focus. The third assertion argues that people must always be understood as either male or female and that differences between the sexes must be taken into account (Billig et al., 1988, pp. 124–127).

In everyday life, contradictory assertions and ideologies coexist but the potential dilemmas often remain hidden. For instance, a speaker may express contrary ideologies about gender equality at different points in a single conversation without becoming aware of their incompatibilities and the dilemmas that those incompatibilities pose. Eva readily observed this tendency when she analyzed the arguments in favor of gender equality made by Swedish politicians (Magnusson, 2000b). Many of the politicians drew on different (and contradictory) ideologies about gender equality in different parts of their speeches without acknowledging the contradictions. The politicians sometimes argued from an individualist position (for instance, that couples must be allowed to decide for themselves who will take care of young children) and then shifted to an argument based on a sex-difference ideology (for instance, that women have nurturing abilities that men lack) without commenting on the contradictions between the ideologies.

Analyzing texts or conversations to locate ideological dilemmas is a useful strategy for "unpacking" collective common sense. Locating and analyzing ideological dilemmas is also useful when studying individual narrators' stories and deliberations. When people tell about their lives and experiences, they regularly draw on mutually incompatible arguments and values. For example, participants often give contradictory accounts in different parts of an interview without noticing the contradictions. Such inconsistencies and contradictions need not be taken as evidence of lying, confusion, or subconscious conflict. Rather, participants draw upon different lived ideologies in order to address the different topics and life experiences that they take up during an interview. Using the analytical tool of ideological dilemmas enables researchers to explore this.

Interpretative repertoires

An interpretative repertoire is a lexicon of terms and metaphors that people draw on to characterize and evaluate actions and events (Potter and Wetherell, 1987). Interpretative repertoires consist of related sets of words and terms that are familiar to and well understood by members of a particular group. Indeed, knowing a group's central interpretative repertoires is a prime indicator that a person is a member of that group. The concept of interpretative repertoire is closely akin to the concept of a discourse, but the term *interpretative repertoire* emphasizes its link to talk and social interaction. Analytical approaches that examine interpretative repertoires are based on the observation that when people give accounts or tell each other stories, they often enhance their credibility by referring to common sense or the "facts" about the topic. These facts are things that "everybody knows" and takes for granted. In everyday life, common sense is usually organized into repertoires or sets of interpretations or explanations about the topic under discussion. An interpretative repertoire offers a coherent way of talking about and thinking about an event or object. It is a way that is well known among members of a particular social group. Cultures are never homogeneous, however, and so there are likely to be several interpretative repertoires relevant to a certain topic, some of which will be incompatible (Gilbert and Mulkay, 1984). Conversations can be read as exchanges of "quotations" from several repertoires (Edley, 2001; Reynolds *et al.*, 2007).

Interpretative repertoires serve as building blocks that narrators use to compose stories about their actions or their identity. Repertoires are thus resources for people's meaning-making. Researchers study the particular repertoires that speakers use to position themselves in conversations, how conflicting repertoires become reconciled in conversations, or how one repertoire comes to take precedence over others. When analyzing conversations, discursive psychologists focus on two characteristics of interpretative repertoires. The first is that people use repertoires locally; that is, to accomplish various conversational goals when interacting with others. For instance, people may refer to a certain repertoire to enhance their own (or someone else's) credibility, status, or standing in a social interchange or to diminish another speaker's status or credibility. The second characteristic is that repertoires – even seemingly local ones – are part and parcel of societal meaning-making. A repertoire that contributes to a person's standing locally may simultaneously serve to promulgate positive images of a group to which the person belongs or to promulgate negative images of a group to which the person does not belong (Edley, 2001; Wetherell and Potter, 1992). This function of repertoires has been observed in research studies of conversations about marginalized ethnic groups (Wetherell and Potter, 1992) and homosexuals (Russell and Bohan, 2006).

Subject positions

Human meaning-making always occurs within a matrix of the different discourses or repertoires that constitute social life. These systems of meaning make available different subject positions. Think about a conversation. In a conversation, different speakers are usually taking different stances or roles. The term *subject position* denotes the stance that a certain conversation offers to a speaker. In other words, a subject position is a conversational "place" that makes possible certain ways of speaking and acting. In any social situation, a range of possible subject positions is available; these are in place before a particular person enters into the situation and before any conversation occurs (Mouffe, 1992). When an individual enters a social situation, he or she is not completely free to choose a way of speaking and acting. Rather he or she will be expected to fit into one of the culturally prepared subject positions.

Individuals in different social categories typically have access to different sets of subject positions. These subject positions often involve asymmetries in status and power connected to gender, class, ethnic categorization, and other social categorizations (Davies and Harré, 1990). For example, a sole woman in a group of men has a different set of subject positions available to her than does a sole man in a group of women. Perhaps such differences help explain why men who enter professions in which most members are women quickly advance to managerial positions, while women who enter professions in which most members are men may find it difficult to advance at all.

Critical discursive research is not confined to examining subject positions solely in the local setting. Rather, researchers take into account the larger societal, political, and historical forces that inflect local interactions. Every conversation has a historical context (Wetherell, 1998). Such historical contexts and discursive histories have been of special interest to feminist researchers. For example, they have studied how sociopolitical asymmetries between the categories women and men have contributed to sustaining dominant–subordinate relations between women and men in heterosexual couples (Dryden, 1999; Gavey, 2005; Magnusson, 2008a, 2008b).

Research on subject positions is two-pronged. On the one hand, researchers study how subject positions are constituted from larger social and ideological discourses. On the other hand, they study how certain subject positions enable individuals to accomplish interactional goals (Edley, 2001). Investigating "troubled" and "untroubled" subject positions is part of the latter research program.

Troubled and untroubled subject positions

In a particular situation, people will find some of the available subject positions congenial and comfortable or *untroubled*. Other positions will be uncomfortable or *troubled* (Edley, 2001; Wetherell, 1998). Of course, this will differ for different people. And, of course, the same individual may find a position troubled in one conversation but untroubled in another. Think of a husband and wife who are describing their child-care arrangements to an outsider. Given contemporary cultural expectations and social arrangements, it is likely that the woman will feel more comfortable positioning herself as a "carer" – the one who naturally gives priority to child-care and works part-time – rather than a careerist who wants to work long hours and not be encumbered by child-care. For a woman, the second position is probably more troubled than the first (cf. Magnusson, 2006). In everyday interactions, people usually aim to shift out of troubled positions into less troubled ones. These shifts produce variations or even contradictions in people's accounts of themselves in the course of a conversation. That is, people may tell different stories about the same topic or they may restory the same event with different elements, different emphases, different emotions, and different interpretations in different parts of a conversation.

Subjectification, self-regulation, and productive power

A subject position not only enables an individual to assume a stance in a conversation but also, simultaneously, constrains the individual to assume the ways of being and behaving prescribed for that position. The term *subjectification* denotes the process by which positions offered to a person in an interaction both enable certain identities and regulate behavior. The term draws on Michel Foucault's writings on subjectivity and power, which we introduced in Chapter 3 (Wetherell and Potter, 1992). The process of subjectification involves two stages. First, a person becomes subject to certain kinds of knowledge about what members of his or her social category are like or ought to be like. For instance, a boy may come to know what is typical of boys in his peer group. This knowledge constitutes the boy's image of what it means to be a boy like himself. If a boy comes to recognize these ways of being and acting as normal, natural, or morally correct for members of his peer group, he will usually want to adopt them. In this way, knowledge about a particular social category influences people's visions of themselves. Such knowledge invites them to adopt socially valued ways of being that are associated with that category. No coercion or external control is needed (Foucault, 1980; Wetherell and Potter, 1992). Foucault used the term *productive power* (in contrast to coercive power) for this kind of process. That is, people desire to regulate their actions in accord with social dictates, but the desire is felt to come from within themselves. Thus, self-regulation is felt to be freely chosen.

Identity practices: constructing one's individual psychology

The term *identity practices* refers to talk in which people speak about themselves in psychological terms – for example, in terms of identity, personality traits, character, emotions, and goals. Discursive psychologists see such psychological terms as cultural resources that are available for people within a particular cultural and historical setting (Wetherell, 2007, 2008). Individuals constitute their mental lives and their self-images through the use of such culturally anchored terms. Identity or character is constituted by the recurring sets of identity practices that a person has held on to for a long time (Wetherell, 2007; Wetherell and Edley, 1999).

Every culture offers an array of self-presentations or identities that are recognizable to its members. When a member of a cultural group adopts a self-presentation from this array, however, this always occurs within a local context, such as a conversation. Therefore, a self-presentation is culturally anchored and yet also molded to local demands and expectations. Those expectations vary between conversations or between participants in a conversation. Moreover, one person's self-presentation may be challenged by another person. This may place the first person in a troubled subject position, prompting her to maneuver a rhetorical escape. In short, identity practices are not only ways to describe oneself but also ways to perform oneself as a certain kind of person.

An example may make this clearer. In a study of heterosexual couples in the Nordic countries, Eva found that all the men who contributed only minimally to housework and child-care in their families took recourse to two specific identity practices during the interview conversations (Magnusson, 2006). First, they described themselves as men who were not easily influenced by others (perhaps especially not by their female partners). Second, they described themselves as people for whom it was natural and acceptable to prioritize other things before housework. Being difficult to influence and following one's own priorities rather than cooperating to achieve collective goals are self-presentations that fit nicely into a certain kind of traditional masculinity in the Nordic countries. Because these men were able to present themselves as such men without being upbraided by their partners, we may assume that this kind of masculinity was accepted and perhaps normative in their social settings. Portraying themselves in this way did not place these men in a troubled subject position.

Accountability management

We have noted that speakers move between troubled and untroubled subject positions in the course of conversations. Not surprisingly, people prefer untroubled positions to troubled ones. Speakers have numerous linguistic devices for managing conversational situations such that they do not end up in a troubled position or find themselves unable to get out of one. *Accountability management* is a term for managing conversations in such a way that the individual presents a good face or remains in an untroubled position (Buttny, 1993; Edwards and Potter, 1992). An example may help to clarify this. Most people are motivated to avoid being seen as having ulterior motives or being dishonest. In a heated debate between adversaries who accuse each other of dishonest dealings, the issue of honesty versus ulterior motives is likely to be openly verbalized. When politicians debate, for example, each typically accuses the other of misleading the constituency by falsely promising benefits or of misrepresenting facts. In political debates, we expect speakers to be aggressive and contentious, to exaggerate, and to twist each other's arguments in order to maintain or regain their credibility. In most other settings, however, people maintain their credibility by a range of conversational devices that are less direct and confrontational. Accountability management is an important aspect of what people accomplish with language in their daily lives and consequently an important feature of their psychology (Horton-Salway, 2001).

People engage in accountability management whenever it seems needed. That is, speakers engage in it when they have a cause to uphold or a position to maintain or in response to a threat to their prestige or character. For a researcher, then, observing that speakers are using credibility-enhancing rhetoric signals that they have something to defend or that they want to argue against something. Accountability management is not always successful, however. Because the techniques are well known to members of a social group, speakers and listeners are familiar with them. Not only are they proficient in using them, but they are also proficient in scuttling others' use of them. In a conversation, one speaker's effort at accountability will often be countered by another speaker. Derek Edwards and Jonathan Potter (1992) have written extensively about accountability management and described in detail specific rhetorical techniques.

From theories and methods to research illustrations

In previous chapters, we discussed key concepts and frameworks for the psychological study of gender, paying particular attention to theoretical frameworks that enable researchers to study gender in cultural and social contexts. In this chapter, we have described several practices and methodological tools for investigating gendered lives situated in cultural and social contexts. The remainder of the book shifts from theory and method to research and practice. In the next four chapters, we describe four research programs that have made use of the frameworks and practices we have been describing. We aim to show in concrete detail how these theories and frameworks lend themselves to empirical work. We also offer an assessment of the powers and limits of these research practices. We have chosen four topics that have been well studied by feminist researchers and that have been key issues for feminist protest and activism. These topics are sexual violence and coercion in heterosexual encounters, the heterosexualization of girls as they cross from childhood to adolescence, women's struggles to achieve equitable sharing of family labor in heterosexual couples, and the cultural politics of women's preoccupations with weight, body size, and eating practices.

8   Gender and culture in children's identity development

For cultural psychologists and discursive psychologists, there is no such thing as just "a child." What it means to be "a child" is always dependent on both the immediate context and the larger context. Moreover, many psychologists who are interested in gender issues prefer to talk about "boys" and "girls" rather than "children." In most societies, a child's sex categorization plays a decisive role in his or her life, although its specific influences depend on the local situation. In this chapter, we describe research by cultural psychologists concerning such influences on girls and boys as they move from childhood to young adulthood.

Cultural psychologists and discursive psychologists who study children and childhoods have been especially interested in children's identity development and social development. Such psychologists take it as given that the ideals and developmental goals for children are organized and negotiated within specific societies and historical epochs (DeLoache and Gottlieb, 2000; Gulbrandsen, 2006a). They have investigated the cultural logics of childrearing, asking what kind of child do different cultures and subcultures strive to produce. Such researchers often compare different social groups or different cultures, or they study the socialization of boys as compared to girls.

Research on children's development in societies other than those in western Europe and North America has led to pointed criticisms of theories that posit universal processes of development (Greene, 2003; Rogoff, 2003). Even if there are features of biological development that are common to all children, many elements of children's lives are specific to time, place, and sociocultural context. These contextual elements are often powerful enough to alter biology. For instance, economic, social, and cultural factors play a determining role in a child's nutritional status, which in turn affects the developing brain and later intellectual development. This illustrates how context can influence biology and also psychology. Contemporary developmental research points to the importance of contextual factors even in children's earliest development, including development before birth. Environment and biology often act in concert, such that environment influences biology, which in turn alters the basis for further influences of the environment (Fox and Rutter, 2010; Kagan, 1998; Sameroff, 2010).

Some researchers have pointed out that many universal claims about children's development have been based on studies of children in western, high-income countries, most of whom were white and from middle-class families (Burman, 1994/2008a, 2008b; Henrich *et al.*, 2010; Lareau, 2003). Moreover, in the early days of psychology, research subjects were often boys. As a consequence, developmental patterns that were the outcome of normative practices in the western, middle-class families were presented as universal scientific truths about children. Today researchers know that many such developmental patterns are not found in societies or social groups other than the one in which they were originally found (Rogoff, 2003).

In the next section, we present ideas about child development that cultural psychologists have brought forward. Then we discuss research about children's paths from childhood to young adulthood. In this research, the focus is on how cultural influences shape girls' movement into early adulthood. Specifically, the research examined the impact of cultural templates of femininity on girls' identity development, as well as on peer group relations among girls. We end the chapter with a brief description of similar research about boys' identity development.

Thinking about children's development in gendered and culture-specific contexts

Cultural psychologists who study children attend to the meaning and impact of specific life circumstances. Such attention to context yields pluralistic accounts of both the process of development and of developmental outcomes. Cultural psychologists and cultural anthropologists have shown striking differences in developmental trajectories across the world. For example, parents in western, high-income societies do not expect 5-year-old children to be able to take care of their younger siblings nor do they give them opportunities to learn how to do this. In parts of the world where it is common for children as young as 5 to be childminders, cultural ideas about the capabilities of 5-year-olds are consonant with such practices (Rogoff, 2003). Such culture-bound differences suggest that children's development should be understood as localized in the *context*, not mainly in the child (Greene, 2003; Miller *et al.*, 2002; Shweder *et al.*, 1998; White and LeVine, 1986). In the words of Sheila Greene, a child psychologist in Ireland, "the child is developed by the context rather than development being intrinsic to the child" (2003, p. 26).

Many developmental psychologists study the roles that children themselves play as active participants in their development. Such research builds on *transactional models* of development that figure children not only as active and changing, but also as actively shaping their environments (Sameroff, 2010). This includes influencing the important people in their lives, such as parents, teachers, siblings, and peers. Transactional models of development draw attention primarily to the *processes* of psychological development and secondarily to outcomes of development (such as developmental stages). The latter have usually been the focus of developmental psychologists. Many developmental psychologists who have adopted feminist, cultural, or discursive frameworks have embraced transactional models.

Transactional models posit a view of children in context that corresponds closely to cultural psychologists' view of humans as simultaneously embedded in culture and continually reproducing culture. Barbara Rogoff, who is both a developmental psychologist and a cultural psychologist, characterizes development as "a process in which people transform through their ongoing participation in cultural activities, which in turn contribute to changes in their cultural communities across generations" (2003, p. 11). In this view, children cannot be understood without considering them within the context of which they are a part. At the same time, that context cannot be understood without taking the child into account (Gulbrandsen, 2006a).

Girls making themselves into teenagers in multiethnic Oslo

Now we turn to a study that followed boys and girls from the age of 12 to the age of 16. The project was conducted in Oslo, Norway, and was headed by two cultural psychologists, Hanne Haavind and Liv Mette Gulbrandsen. These researchers were interested in how children develop themselves through their participation in social activities with their peers. As children shape their development, they create possibilities and limitations for themselves and others in gender-specific and culture-specific patterns. It was this aspect of development that Haavind and Gulbrandsen wanted to study. These two researchers conceived of development as the strategies that children undertake to "make themselves bigger," not merely as something that just happens to children. These strategies are specific to a particular local context. That is, children develop themselves in the terms set by the local culture, including the gender expectations in that culture (Gulbrandsen, 2003; Haavind, 2003). Moreover, they develop themselves primarily through ongoing negotiations with peers and close adults.

The researchers followed 32 children (18 girls and 14 boys) from the same school, conducting seven interviews with each child over roughly 2 years. The initial interviews took place when the children were between 12 and 13 years old, and the last interview, when they were between 14 and 15 years old. In a follow-up study, the researchers asked the children to participate in another interview when they were about 16 years old. Sixteen children accepted this invitation. In yet another follow-up, ten of the children were interviewed again when they were 18 years old. All in all, the project spanned a 7-year period.

The school was located in an ethnically mixed neighborhood in Oslo, the capital of Norway. About half of the participants were white and of Norwegian ancestry; the other half were born in, or had parents from, Eastern Europe, South Asia, or North Africa. This immigrant and ethnic diversity is a fairly recent phenomenon in Norway. The children's religious affiliations were diverse, as were the social and economic conditions of their households. For the most part, children of Norwegian ancestry came from households with a somewhat higher economic standard.

The interviews were in the format of a "life mode interview," an approach developed by Haavind (1987) and elaborated by Andenæs (1996) and Gulbrandsen (1998). The interviews were loosely structured around the everyday activities and interactions that each child narrated. An interview typically began by asking a child to tell about what had happened during the previous day. In this way, the interview assumed a structure and a time format that was familiar to the child. Moreover, the interviews were organized around the specific events and experiences that the child chose to talk about, not around topics that the researcher had selected in advance. The interviewer asked follow-up questions to clarify the child's story and to encourage the child to reflect on the events that he or she had recounted. These follow-up questions were important because much of what the children spoke about was self-evident to them but not always understood in the same way by the interviewer. Typical topics in the interviews included the children's daily activities and social interactions, their interests and emotions, and their understandings of themselves and one another (Gulbrandsen, 2006a).

By conducting a series of interviews over time, the researchers were able to study how the children's stories developed. The interviewers asked the children to recall and comment on events and experiences that they had described in previous interviews. By comparing narratives from interviews at different points in time, the researchers could study how the children's perspectives on their experiences changed over time (Gulbrandsen, 2003; Hauge, 2009b).

To analyze the interviews, the researchers used qualitative content analysis to identify major themes in the children's narratives. They also used discourse analysis in order to examine the tentative and vague notions expressed by the children about what it meant to be a grown-up person (Gulbrandsen, 2006a). Discourse analysis enabled the researchers to take into account the nuances, contradictions, and inconsistencies in the children's stories and anchor those features in the cultural setting surrounding the children. Such anchoring, as Gulbrandsen (2003) notes, is one of the strengths of discursive methods. These analyses also enabled the researchers to throw light on tensions between dominant and marginalized discourses in the children's narratives.

Now we turn to the outcomes of the study, focusing in particular on the portions of the project that concerned girls.

From little girl to teenager: heterosexuality as normative development

One of the researchers on the project, Liv Mette Gulbrandsen (2003), was interested in how the girls understood and managed the transition from being a "little girl" to being a teenage girl. She asked how the girls in the study made the transition from being 12-year-olds to being 15-year-olds. Gulbrandsen was especially interested in how this transition was gendered and in the specific meanings of gender available to the girls. If girls wanted to create personal "ways forward" that fit into their culture, what were the cultural codes they needed to heed? How did the girls in their peer groups rework these codes into functional local versions? How did ethnic background and social class shape the ways in which girls managed the transition to being a teenager? Were there commonalities among different social groups or only differences? What social and personal processes did the girls engage in as they made their movements toward being teenage girls? What skills did girls need to master to make these movements successfully? What was signified for the girls by appropriating these skills? Let us see how Gulbrandsen answered some of these questions.

To analyze the narratives, Gulbrandsen drew on both sociocultural and constructionist formulations. She conceptualized development as "patterns of change that are culturally recognized because they project individuals and social fields 'forward'" (Gulbrandsen, 2003, p. 115). In noting that such patterns must be culturally recognized, Gulbrandsen highlights that what is regarded as development is not universal, but is connected to the dominant meaning systems of a culture. Even though one meaning of "development" may be dominant, there likely are other meanings that are connected to what are sometimes called subjugated discourses. Gulbrandsen focused first on the consequences of different kinds of forward movement (or development) for girls as individuals. She next focused on the interpersonal plane and explored such aspects as how girls' "forward movements" were negotiated among peers.

Gender-related and age-related meanings that were dominant in the majority culture of Norway figured prominently in the girls' narratives. These meanings shaped most of the content of the narratives, as well as the ways in which the girls spoke about growing up and about their projected future goals. At the age of 12, all the girls were already well versed in these meanings. The stories they told about their own and other children's activities and relationships fit into what Gulbrandsen called a "heterosexual complex" (2006a). This observation echoed other research showing that the image of the heterosexual couple and the gendered positions associated with it become more and more central to girls as they move into later childhood. Other studies of girls in the Nordic countries and elsewhere have reported similar patterns (Ambjörnsson, 2004; Haldar, 2006).

Framed by heteronormativity

Gulbrandsen (2006a) used the concept of heteronormativity to frame her examination of how girls negotiated the expectation that they assume a culturally acceptable, heterosexual feminine position. Heteronormativity refers to the institutions, structures, relations, and practices that maintain heterosexuality as uniform, natural, and universal (Clarke *et al.*, 2010). These structures and practices are so pervasive that they escape conscious reflection, even though they organize everyday experience. In her analyses, Gulbrandsen studied how heteronormative expectations inflected the girls' narratives about becoming teenagers. She identified an overarching heteronormative discourse that organized the narratives that all the girls gave about becoming a young teenager. Regardless of social class or ethnic background, every girl's efforts "to make herself bigger" centered on making herself heterosexual in an acceptable manner. However, this transformation was not accomplished in the same way for all. The girls' social positionings determined both what constituted appropriate heterosexuality and the way that expressions of heterosexuality were evaluated by a girl's peers. Gulbrandsen describes groups of girls – such as "popular girls" and "ordinary girls" – whose experiences illustrate cultural variations of heteronormativity.

"Popular girls"

Girls used the term "popular girls" to refer to an informal group of girls that formed around the time that girls were moving from primary school to secondary school; that is, among girls who were 12 or 13 years old. The popular girls were seen (by themselves and others) as enacting the dominant or "best" form of girlhood. Many girls aspired to become members of this group. Membership in the group shifted over time, but at any one time all the girls agreed about which girls were popular girls. They also agreed about what activities were required to be one of the popular girls. Exploring romantic relations with boys was essential, as were wearing tight-fitting, fashionable clothes, using makeup, and carefully styling one's hair. Using language, gestures, and body movements that were thought to be more like those of grown-up women was also required. It was important to reject outright "childish" activities, such as wearing loose-fitting clothes and playing. As a girl transformed herself into a popular girl, it was important that her new way of being be perceived as an expression of her "real self." The ideal of the popular girl closely resembled the contemporary ideal of white femininity in Norway and other western, high-income countries. This included both being autonomous (that is, self-determining) and being attractive to men. The ideal popular girl was simply being herself. Moreover, it was *because* she was seen as just being herself and not striving to achieve popularity or femininity that she would be attractive to boys.

In their endeavors to be or become popular, girls drew on the dominant heterosexual codes in their surrounds. The girls themselves were not the originators of these codes nor of the relations of power embedded in the codes. Nonetheless, the girls who succeeded in becoming popular held dominant positions among their female peers. Moreover, the local version of the heterosexual codes that the girls (and their male peers) produced in their daily interactions became a central part of the girls' emerging understandings of themselves and others (Gulbrandsen, 2006a).

Even though most girls were not popular, the popular girls served as the reference point for all girls, including girls who talked about themselves as ordinary or "not popular." Even girls who rejected the views and behaviors of the popular girls could not ignore them. Those views served as the yardstick against which all the girls were measured. Not surprisingly, every girl did not have the same chance of attaining the status of popular girl. Most of the popular girls were white and of Norwegian ancestry; in contrast, the ordinary girls came from a greater variety of backgrounds.

"Ordinary girls"

Some girls actively exempted themselves from the heterosexualized practices that the popular girls adopted. They chose instead other positions such as tomboy (Gulbrandsen, 2002). However, being a tomboy became a difficult position for a girl to maintain once she reached the age of 12 or so. Some other "ordinary girls," particularly Muslim girls, chose not to dress or behave like the popular girls. Nonetheless, the Muslim girls were as intent on achieving heterosexual femininity as the popular girls were. However, their femininity was expressed in a different way, as we shall see below.

The Muslim girls hailed from many regions of the world, including the Middle East and North Africa. Despite their varied national backgrounds, they constituted a distinct subgroup of the ordinary girls. Regardless of their ethnic ancestry or skin color, the Muslim girls set themselves apart from the popular girls by their clothing and social habits. However, their pursuit of heterosexualized femininity was just as avid as that of the popular girls. For most of the Muslim girls, becoming a teenager required adopting more modest forms of dress and more modest self-presentations, as well as segregating themselves from boys. The expectations that girls would adopt these practices came from their families and religious communities. These expectations became more stringent as girls grew older.

Two themes were prominent in the Muslim girls' narratives about their clothing and demeanor. One pertained to the symbolic meanings and significance of age. For example, when girls spoke about wearing a headscarf, they spoke about it in relation to the movement from childhood to adulthood. Although the exact age at which a headscarf became mandatory varied, headscarves always signified a more grownup status. The second theme was that wearing a headscarf and other traditional clothing was emblematic of a femininity that was tied to the gender order of their local Muslim communities. Once a girl was no longer a child, the code of femininity required her to wear clothes that would not arouse men's desire and would not compromise her honor. Modest clothing and demeanor were also a necessity if a girl hoped to be viewed as suitable for marriage. Thus, for Muslim girls, as for the girls of Norwegian ancestry, the transition from girl to teenager was a transition to appropriate heterosexuality.

The invisible dominant heteronormativity and ethnification

Whether popular or ordinary, Muslim or non-Muslim, all the girls whom Gulbrandsen studied were positioned within a discourse of heteronormativity as they became teenagers. None of the girls reflected on this or spoke about it in an explicit way. Nonetheless, the radically different requirements of heterosexual femininity had important implications for peer relations and increasing ethnic differentiation. The girls' different ways of moving forward produced increasing segregation among them. This segregation was based on differences in clothing and feminine beauty practices, such as hairstyling and makeup. It was also based on differences in consumption practices, such as shopping. The segregation was also a byproduct of differences in social practices. The popular girls sought out opportunities for mingling with boys while the Muslim girls avoided them. As the girls grew older, the popular girls became more dominant. Their ways of making themselves older were the ways that were valued by the majority of the girls and deemed to be the most advanced and up-to-date. Moreover, these ways mirrored the culture at large and therefore needed no justification. The Muslim girls' ways of making themselves older and their forms of heterosexual femininity were not taken as natural in the school setting; therefore, they needed justification. In short, the popular girls held the privileged position of being the arbiters of all girls' ways, including the Muslim girls' ways. All of these practices led the girls to segregate more and more as time passed (Gulbrandsen, 2006a).

The later teenage years: bodily practices
and normative heterosexuality

Another member of the research team, Mona-Iren Hauge, focused on the set of interviews that girls provided when they were moving from junior to senior secondary school; that is, when girls were roughly 16 years old (2009a, 2009b). Hauge studied the meanings of the body evident in the girls' ways of doing femininity as they progressed through their teens. She asked how bodily practices marked girls as no longer children but teenagers. In listening to the girls' narratives, Hauge used Margaret Wetherell's (1998) strategy of examining "troubled" and "untroubled" subject positions in relation to a particular discourse. (We described the analysis of troubled and untroubled subject positions in Chapter 7.) Hauge examined how certain practices placed girls in either troubled or untroubled positions vis-à-vis the dominant discourses of appropriate femininity.

We describe the results of two of Hauge's analyses (2009a). In the first analysis, Hauge observed that, as girls grew older, particular bodily practices shifted from being untroubled to troubled because others' readings of their bodies changed. As long as a girl was regarded unequivocally as a child, she was expected to be involved in activities related to play and her body was read as sexually innocent. Being a girl who no longer played was a way that a girl could demonstrate that she no longer possessed a childish body. This was true for all girls, irrespective of their social group. When girls – especially those who were popular – entered adolescence, they abandoned bodily practices connected to childish play. This functioned both as a way of rejecting the childish body and its connection to innocence and also as a way of setting the popular group apart from other girls. Moreover, for the popular girls, these changes were accompanied by a gradual shift from having boys as friends to being limited to having boyfriends.

Hauge's second analysis asked how the possibilities for accomplishing untroubled feminine positions differed for girls of different ethnic backgrounds and how these possibilities were connected to bodily sexual practices. For the white Norwegian girls, the trajectory of moving toward an identity as a "decent" heterosexual young woman was clearly spelled out. It consisted of a series of relationships with boyfriends that were increasingly prolonged and increasingly physically intimate. The ideal of sexual intimacy was that a girl would engage in physical intimacy when she felt she was "ready" for it, not because a male partner pressured her into it. This trajectory of sexual practices was so normalized and "untroubled" that the girls did not have to defend it or argue for it. It was simply the way teenagers did things.

The trajectory of the white Norwegian girls stood in sharp contrast to the way for Muslim girls to achieve "untroubled" positions as decent young women. As we described above, Muslim girls were expected to assume more modest ways of dressing, more circumspect ways of behaving, and more distant relations with boys as they moved into adolescence. In the eyes of white Norwegian girls, the Muslim girls appeared childish because they did not appear to be moving into young womanhood. The Muslim girls saw things quite differently. In the interviews, some reflected on the differences between themselves and the "popular" girls. Privately, they judged the behavior of the popular girls as improper and described them as "boy crazy" (Hauge, 2009a, p. 301).

Making oneself into a "bigger" boy or a young man

It is not only girls and young women who must navigate cultural expectations regarding becoming a young adult. There are also cultural ideologies of masculinity and normative ways of "becoming a man." A number of studies have used approaches of discursive and cultural psychology to ask questions about how boys "make themselves bigger." These studies include works by Michael Bamberg and Neill Korobov (Bamberg, 2004; Bamberg and Korobov, 2004; Korobov, 2004, 2005); Nigel Edley (2001); Stephen Frosh, Ann Phoenix, and Rob Pattman (2002); Matthew Oransky and Jeanne Marecek (2009); and Margaret Wetherell (Wetherell and Edley, 1998, 1999).

An example of discursive research on boys is a project carried out by Michael Bamberg and Neill Korobov, two USA-based developmental psychologists (Korobov, 2004, 2005; Korobov and Bamberg, 2004). The researchers were interested in how the boys interacted with one another in group conversations and made use of local norms of male heterosexuality to make themselves bigger and more mature. Bamberg and Korobov held ongoing discussions with small groups of boys from public schools in Worchester, Massachusetts. The discussion groups had an adult man as a facilitator. Focusing on boys who were roughly 15 years old, Bamberg and Korobov examined the kinds of talk that the boys used in order to portray themselves as heterosexually competent and mature in accord with the norms of their peer group. One prominent aspect of the boys' conversations involved indicating emphatically that they were not homosexual, but without appearing to be homophobic or heterosexist. As Bamberg and Korobov point out, the group conversations nonetheless included implicit expressions of homophobia as well as forms of talk that implicitly privileged heterosexuality as the normal and preferred sexuality. These patterns of speaking persisted even though the boys repeatedly professed to be progressive in their views.

For Korobov and Bamberg, the "developmental imperative" to appear sexually mature that besets contemporary American adolescent boys is best seen as "an ongoing discursive project that requires a careful nego-tiation of different ideological dilemmas" (2004, p. 488). They argued that mastering the discursive tools required to manage conventional masculinity is a significant component of adolescent boys' maturation. Korobov and Bamberg urged developmental psychologists to attend to this aspect of gender socialization because "this is the subtle level where hegemonic masculinity lurks" (p. 488).

Finally: young women, young men, and heterosexuality

The studies we have described highlight how girls and boys confront heterosexuality and heteronormativity as central dimensions of identity in the transition from child to young adult. It is striking that sexuality in the daily lives of girls and boys is so self-evidently heterosexuality. Boys and girls alike seem to be facing the same overarching developmental task: to achieve a heterosexual identity in the terms set by their social group. But that is where the similarity ends. For the girls in the Norwegian studies, transforming themselves from childish gender neutrality (or occasionally, tomboyishness) to adolescent femininity required assuming an appearance and demeanor that young men would appreciate and find sexually appealing. For boys in the US study, transforming themselves from childish gender neutrality to adolescent masculinity demanded developing a body and demeanor that other young men would not construe as homosexual or girlish; the ideal of heterosexual masculinity did not require making oneself attractive to young women. Here we can see two contrasting faces of heteronormativity. For girls, it is femininity focused on being attractive in the eyes of boys; for boys, masculinity focused on being manly enough, as judged by other boys. Note that what these have in common is that both require that individuals subject themselves to the judgment of males.

9   Identity and inequality
in heterosexual couples

The Nordic countries (Denmark, Sweden, Norway, Finland, and Iceland)
are known as the most gender-equal countries in the world. This is true
for governmental policies, the labor market, and education, as well as for
family life. National politics and government policies reflect a long-
standing commitment to reduce inequality in the number of men and
women in political bodies and in powerful positions in workplaces and
other organizations. The state is also committed to reduce inequalities
and asymmetries in spheres of life such as the care of small children,
access to and payment for paid work, and access to healthcare, as well
as to reduce women's risk of sexual victimization. These aspirations have
been accompanied by many practical governmental policies and other
measures to achieve equality, as well as by an overarching ideology
about what the good life for women and men should look like. However,
some spheres of life have changed more quickly than others. Life in
families composed of a man and a woman and their children seems to
be especially slow to change. For instance, although fathers and mothers
now have equal rights to paid parental leave to care for their small
children, the overall pattern in the Nordic countries is that women use
most of the days of parental leave. In 2009, for instance, Swedish fathers
used only 22 percent of the total available paid parental leave days
(Swedish Social Security Agency, 2010). Also, although nearly as many
women as men work outside the home, women usually have the overall
responsibility for the household and child-care, and they do substantially more of the housework and child-care than men do (Statistics
Sweden, 2010).

Why is it that even in the Nordic countries, where national ideologies
strongly promote such change, movements toward equality in family life
are so slow? To learn more about the dynamics of change and resistance
to change, feminist researchers have studied how different conceptions
of parenthood, in conjunction with ideologies about equality, femininity,
and masculinity, influence women's and men's ways of understanding
themselves as parents and partners (Aarseth, 2008; Bekkengen, 2002;

Bengtsson, 1985, 2001; Dryden, 1999; Eriksson, 2003; Holmberg, 1993). The researchers have been especially interested in the cultural discourses that shape how men and women think and feel about themselves as mothers, fathers, spouses, partners, and workers. Eva has studied the dynamics of these discourses in the everyday life of families composed of a man and a woman who live together and have children together (Magnusson, 2006, 2008a, 2008b). In this chapter, we describe the parts of Eva's work that focus on the contradictions between ideologies of gender equality, on the one hand, and contemporary notions of the good life and the good ways of being a woman and a man, on the other hand.

Heterosexual family life and individual identity projects

Eva's project involved men and women in Denmark, Finland, and Sweden who lived together and were raising children together. A main focus of the study was how these women and men think about themselves and their partners – as women and men, as partners, as fathers and mothers, and as paid workers – and how they talk together about this. Many heterosexual couples in the Nordic countries today strive to establish and maintain equality in their relationship. Others resist such change. In this project, listening to couples' joint stories about such strivings and such resistance gave insights into everyday meanings of gender and how these meanings were woven into larger social and cultural patterns.

The analytical framework for the project was critical discursive psychology, which we described in Chapter 7. That is, the analyses examined the couples' narratives through dual lenses. The analyses were based on theories and analytical tools that looked beyond the individual and the couple in order to take larger societal dimensions into account. The analyses also focused on the details of how the women and men told about their ways of organizing their everyday lives. Mundane activities and negotiations about these activities are sites for much of men's and women's identity work as partners and parents. Narratives about these activities and negotiations – especially narratives in which a woman and a man jointly take part – offer opportunities to explore a couple's ways of performing gender, as well as their strategies for maintaining an image of themselves as a good couple.

Studying couples' narratives about equality and everyday life

In this research project, thirty heterosexual couples with children were interviewed. Of these couples, ten each were from Denmark, Finland,

and Sweden. The couples were selected to match the modal family: a man and a woman who were biological parents of the children whom they were raising. The couples were selected through a modified chain referral method, in which the researchers used their own friendship networks to contact couples with whom they were not acquainted, but who fit the distribution of characteristics that the study aimed for. In this way, the researchers achieved similar distributions of educational levels, ages, number of children, and children's ages, as well as residential patterns (large cities, towns, rural communities) across the three national samples. The participants were white and of Danish, Finnish, or Swedish ancestry. In most couples, both partners worked outside the home; in a few cases, one partner was a student. The ages of the participants ranged from 30 to 45 years; the children's ages ranged from 5 months to mid-adolescence. Most couples had more than one child. All the parents were the biological parents of their children.

All the interviews were conducted in the couples' homes. They were audio-recorded and transcribed verbatim. Both partners were present throughout the interview. The interviews were semi-structured with open-ended questions about practical issues in the daily organization of life and about decision-making and responsibility related to these matters. The couples were also asked to describe in detail an ordinary working day. (For a discussion of such "life mode interviews," see Andenæs, 1996; Haavind, 1987.) They were also asked who was responsible for each of a number of common household and family tasks.

Three analyses were undertaken. The initial analysis was a thematic analysis, undertaken to identify recurring patterns in the content of the interviews as well as to examine differences in how women and men used culturally available discourses. Next was a discursive analysis that explored the relation of the themes to cultural and political rhetoric on gender issues. A third set of analyses was carried out on the interaction sequences in some parts of the interviews, in order to explore the couples' strategies for "doing gender" in these conversations (Braun and Clarke, 2006; Magnusson, 2000b, 2006). Three central topics emerged in the analyses: talk about gender equality and inequality, the gender division of practical parenting tasks, and the internal limits and boundaries that couples set in their daily lives.

Themes of equality and inequality in Nordic couples' talk

The theme of equality and inequality emerged in couples' accounts of who did what in the household. In a third of the couples, the woman was responsible for nearly all the practical tasks, including child-care.

In another third, the partners shared the tasks equally. In the remaining third, the woman was responsible for most, but not all, of the tasks. These quantitative differences were linked to differences in the way couples described their relationships.

There were systematic differences between the narratives of couples who did not share family work and those who shared equally. The couples in which women did nearly all the work consistently reported that they had had no discussions about how to allocate tasks in their households. "It had come about naturally" was a common expression. The couples reported that conflicts were practically absent from their daily lives; furthermore, they spoke as if conflict was to be avoided if at all possible. The preservation of peace and quiet at home was spoken of as a paramount concern. Several of the couples used derogatory terms to describe other couples who (according to the speakers) quarreled continually to achieve equal sharing. Such quarreling was described as both unnecessary and dangerous to the relationship. The couples who shared equally offered a sharp contrast. They talked about housework and child-care in terms of fairness and as topics for negotiation. They described a history of negotiations that had often escalated to conflicts. They portrayed these conflicts as benign and as something to be expected. In some couples, the negotiations were ongoing, although most had found an equilibrium that both parties regarded as fair and that worked for them. Among the couples who had an in-between distribution of housework and child-care, most told of more or less constant conflict over sharing housework and child-care. Nearly half of these couples described the conflicts as unpleasant and potentially destructive.

The couples in which women did nearly all the housework and child-care spoke as if it were self-evident that men were more oriented toward paid work and women were more oriented toward child-care and housework. No such ideas were brought forward in the narratives of the equally sharing couples. The same patterns emerged in the narratives about leisure activities: The couples in which women did nearly all the housework and child-care spoke as if having access to leisure outside the home was self-evidently a right (or, in some accounts, a necessity) for the man but not for the woman. No such ideas were brought forward in the interviews of the equally sharing couples.

Most of the couples talked about the wife as more knowledgeable about household matters than her husband, although some couples dwelt on this expertise more than others. Among the equally sharing couples, however, attributing special expertise to women had little consequence for distributing responsibility for household tasks.

Parenthood, fatherhood, and motherhood

All the couples in the group had children and therefore all had been faced with decisions about using the paid parental leave provided by the state. In almost all couples, the father as well as the mother had taken some parental leave. In a quarter of the couples, the men took substantially more leave than the national average in their respective countries, but no man took more leave than his partner. When these couples talked about their motives for sharing the paid parental leave, they usually described practical circumstances that had made it seem like a good idea. Only a few mentioned an ideological commitment to equal sharing. Among the remaining three-quarters of the couples, the woman had taken all or nearly all the paid parental leave. These couples talked as if this were natural; it was not something that had required discussion or deliberation.

The couples in which women did nearly all the housework and parenting talked about parenthood in distinctly gendered terms. They described the work of parenthood, especially caring for young children, as primarily a mother's task. This view was taken for granted: It was neither discussed nor questioned, even when such an arrangement caused practical problems for the woman, such as difficulties of fitting her paid work schedule to the day-care schedule. Some couples discussed what minimum daily "dose" of the father's presence in the home was required for a child. It is worth noting that those couples did not discuss how large or small a dose of the mother's presence was necessary; her presence seemed to be taken for granted. In some of the couples who were striving to achieve equal sharing of parenthood tasks, the woman nonetheless functioned as the backup. This meant that her partner was able to forgo doing a task related to the children because he knew that she would be there to pick up the slack.

Not surprisingly, the couples who shared housework equally gave the most gender-neutral accounts of the practical tasks of caring for children. Moreover, they voiced a conscious desire to share responsibility for their children equally. For some of them, this desire coincided with an equally strong investment in family life by both partners. For other couples, it was the woman's strong investment in paid work that determined their decision to share parenting tasks.

Internal limits and boundaries in modern heterosexual couples

In allocating paid work, leisure, child-care, and housework between men and women in heterosexual couples, women's time and labor seem to be much more flexible and negotiable than men's. It is usually the woman who adjusts her working life to the demands of "the family." Also, it is usually the woman who assumes responsibility for home life as a whole (Statistics Sweden, 2010). These arrangements are connected to the organization of boundaries and limits within a couple and therefore to women's and men's identities. Examining couples' talk closely enables us to see some ways in which men's and women's boundaries are sustained. A way to think about such gendered boundaries is to draw a distinction between limits and boundaries in a relationship. *Limits* demarcate the extent of an individual's (physical and psychological) space and freedom of movement, while *boundaries* refers to an individual's ability to defend that space against others' attempts to infringe on it. Traditionally, men have had wider limits, that is, a wider space and freedom of movement, than women. Moreover, it has been easier and more acceptable to infringe on women's space than on men's space. In other words, it has been easier to transgress women's boundaries than men's (Kaschak, 1992).

Let us first examine the couples who shared family responsibilities most unequally. In the interviews, nearly all men in such couples stated what work and how much of it they were willing to do in the household – a strong declaration of their boundaries. The women in these couples did not make such overt declarations. The men also referred to boundaries indirectly (for example, by such phrases as "doing things as usual"). Sometimes, men made their boundaries explicit in the interview. A common form of such boundary demarcation consisted of emphatic statements of their characteristics and interests. For example, when the conversation revealed that the men did not perform certain tasks or failed to take responsibility for certain aspects of family labor, they might respond, "That's because I am like that" or "That's just what I'm like" or "She knows she can't make me do that" (Magnusson, 2006, p. 191). Such statements met no opposition from the men's partners during the interviews. These statements were accompanied by markedly larger freedom of movement for the men than for their partners (for instance, more leisure time or more time for recreation outside the home). No such self-delineating assertions were spoken by the men in the equally sharing couples. Nor were such assertions ever offered by women.

Another indication of men's boundaries were instances when men seemed to have the privilege of not performing a task even when they had agreed to it. It seemed far more common and more acceptable for the man in a couple to disregard his responsibility for a chore or an area of responsibility or to renege on an agreement. This occurred in a few couples in all three groups. The couples explained such occurrences not as an indication of male privilege but by saying that the man was "liable to forget" to do things. The men used words such as "she covers for me" or "she has the overall control."

In daily life, if one partner chronically underperforms (for example, by habitually forgetting tasks), then the other must overperform (that is, not "forget") if life is to flow smoothly. A woman may have to relinquish her boundaries (for example, boundaries that protect her leisure time) in order to make sure that her partner "remembers" his responsibility and to "cover" for him if he does not. This gendered pattern of "forgetting" and "covering" is reinforced by the social environment. A woman will usually receive more social opprobrium than a man if she "forgets" or neglects her responsibilities for children and home.

Culturally based patterns of boundaries and limits in people's daily lives become psychological patterns. That is, they become parts of people's personal identity. Among the couples who did not share house-work and child-care equally, asymmetrical boundaries and limits were regarded as normal or natural (if not perfectly fair) and therefore part of their identities. Put another way, power differences between these men and women were often built into practices that they saw as ordinary, natural, and self-evident. This is power of the kind we have earlier called "disciplinary power" or "productive power." In the case of these couples, we could also term it "the power of the ordinary." It is worth noting that references to naturalness were absent in the accounts by the equal couples.

The different meanings of gender

The men and women often ascribed psychological and practical mean-ings to their own and their partner's sex category. Sometimes these meanings were explicit; they consisted of claims that "men are like this and women are like that" (with "this" and "that" being opposite or mutually exclusive). More commonly, speakers ascribed meaning by using certain interpretative repertoires – that is, terms and phrases that depict familiar and "well-worn," culturally shared images that are often taken as natural or self-evident. (See Chapter 7 for a discussion of interpretative repertoires.) For instance, a member of a couple might invoke a repertoire of gendered parenthood by a statement implying that a "good mother" is required to be more present in her child's daily life than a "good father." Another example is a man's statement that "She can't make me do that" or "I'm just not like that." Such statements invoke a repertoire that grants to men wide freedom of movement and impregnable boundaries. The unavoidable counterpart of this repertoire is another one that grants women less freedom of movement and weaker barriers against others' demands. Couples hardly ever voiced this repertoire overtly, possibly because it violated the gender equality ideologies espoused by the governments of the Nordic countries. Nonetheless, several women told of feeling guilty when they deviated from the unexpressed repertoire of women as responsible and adaptable.

The couples who did not share household work and child-care equally provided a number of different explanations for their practices, all of which focused on male–female differences. For example, some described themselves as adjusting to "sex roles" or "the old sex role pattern" – that is, to something external that they could not alter. Or they said that because of "practical reality," it was best for one partner (invariably the man) to spend most of his time in paid work and the other (the woman) to spend most of her time in taking care of the household and the children. Others justified their unequal sharing on the basis of ideas of intrinsic sex differences. For example, some participants brought forward ideas about genetic differences between women and men. Others brought up differences in their upbringing: The men had not been taught to cook or take care of children and therefore the asymmetric distribution of family work was inevitable. Among the most unequally sharing couples, the rhetoric of "difference" seemed to draw attention away from intimations of power differences in the relationship. Invoking these supposed male–female differences made it easy to explain their own gendered patterns of positions and tasks as resulting from difference, not from inequality or domination.

The couples who shared equally stood in contrast to the others. Some of them stated explicitly that they wanted sex categories to have neutral meanings in their relationship. They stated, for instance, that they were equal as caregivers for their children, workers in the household, and workers outside the home. These couples, however, also told of being marked as deviant in the eyes of others in their surroundings. In other words, these couples wanted to give neutral meanings to the sex categories, but their everyday experiences reminded them that the sex categories are not *culturally* neutral.

Taking stock: what can interpretative research tell us about identity and power in heterosexual couples?

We conclude by pointing to some methodological and theoretical strengths of the research strategies used in this study. The research asked people to relate detailed stories about their everyday experiences. The interviews thus generated material that was directly relevant to their lives. Whereas in laboratory experiments the researcher often must extrapolate about how a set of results might shed light on real-life behaviors, in this study there was no need for such "translation" or extrapolation. In the course of the interviews, the couples spontaneously confirmed that they struggled daily with many of the issues that they discussed in the interviews. They often provided rich and specific narratives about events and experiences. Now and then, heated arguments erupted between a woman and a man, especially when they heard each other give different accounts of a practical matter, such as how often each of them picked up the children from day care. This leads to the next point, which has to do with the value of studying language usage.

The men and women who participated in the study were couples in their everyday lives and they were also interviewed as couples. When the couples were answering questions and giving accounts of their daily life, they were also engaged in being a couple. This made it possible to observe their modes of interaction and negotiation. And it enabled Eva to carry out analyses that focused on *how* the participants talked as well as *what* they said (Cameron, 2001). Additional analyses are described in the book *She, he, and their home: gender in the daily life of Nordic families with children* (Magnusson, 2006).

In most circumstances, narrators strive to tell stories that are as credible as possible. That is, they actively manage accountability (Horton-Salway, 2001; see also Chapter 7). This point was crucial for the analyses of how couples "did couple" in the interviews. Eva examined how couples managed accountability by focusing on their rhetoric. Specifically, she examined the range of interpretative repertoires that couples drew on to talk about sharing (or not sharing) family labor. Let us examine one such rhetorical analysis: The couples who did not share housework and child-care often invoked conventional cultural repertoires about what women and men can and should do in the family. They invoked these repertoires in order to justify their own practices. Often these repertoires were invoked in the course of offering a derogatory evaluation of couples who shared housework and child-care equally. Why did couples justify their traditional choices by derogating other couples who made nontraditional choices? As we noted in Chapter 7, people use justificatory strategies when they confront the need to defend something. Did these couples have a need to defend themselves that the other couples did not have? Perhaps. These couples gave accounts of unequal distributions of housework and child-care even though they lived in societies in which the official ideology promoted equal distribution of such tasks. However, all the unequally sharing couples declared that the distribution of chores between man and woman had "happened naturally" or "just happened."

Thus, by implication, it was not something that needed to be discussed or that was "ideological." Seen against the background of the official state ideology, however, couples who did not share housework had not assumed a "default" position but had indeed made an ideologically charged choice.

The next point concerns the theoretical possibilities of interpretative research. In this chapter, we have briefly pointed to personal identity as culturally shaped and maintained. This analysis of personal identity can be further developed. One way would be to use the analytical tools of mastery and appropriation that we presented in Chapter 4 and Chapter 8. Another way would be using the concept of personal order that we presented in Chapter 7.

Yet another point is that the theoretical constructs boundaries and limits offer a lens for analyzing power in a couple's interactions. Consider this brief illustration. Women in many societies are often expected to accede more easily than men to others' needs and demands. (Indeed, sometimes, this is prescribed to women under the guise of "flexibility" or "cooperativeness" or "responsiveness to others.") This means that their personal boundaries are more easily breached. The limits placed on women's freedom of movement have diminished over the previous century in many parts of the world: Women are allowed to do far more things today than a hundred years ago. However, women's boundaries against infringement have not changed to the same extent. It still seems unusual (and perhaps morally objectionable) for a woman to set boundaries that are as impenetrable as the boundaries that men have traditionally set. This socially anchored boundary-setting remains a key to present-day versions of femininity and masculinity. When a man in a heterosexual couple enacts this version of masculinity (autonomous, impervious to others), his partner must maintain a certain version of femininity (adaptable, flexible, responsive to others). If she did not, this version of masculinity would make it impossible to sustain family life.

Such boundary maintenance and identity production are embedded in the wider cultural surround. If gendered boundaries are pervasive and self-evident in a couple's surroundings, these boundaries may appear to be the natural consequences of sex differences in men's and women's personalities. When asymmetries are taken to be natural, people may not think to ask whether or not they are fair. The asymmetries may even appear to be fair. Interpretative researchers have the tools to question what is taken to be natural by examining how boundaries and limits are gendered in the broader culture. Researchers can do this by taking into account the cultural gendering of boundaries and limits, for instance. They also have the tools for serious examination of whether some observed differences between individual men and women are based not on intrinsic differences but culturally based ones.

This discussion of the everyday lives of heterosexual couples with children is only one of many studies of such couples in several parts of the world (Björnberg, 2004; Deutsch, 1999; Dixon and Wetherell, 2004; Dryden, 1999; Nordenmark and Nyman, 2003; Roman, 2004). Because of their desire for social change, feminist interpretative researchers are especially interested in time periods, political settings, and couple relationships in which gender asymmetries are questioned or in flux. In such settings, diverse interpretative repertoires are available. There is a sense that nothing can be taken for granted. In such circumstances, change is possible.

10 Coercion, violence, and consent in heterosexual encounters

In the course of their lives, many women and girls face sexual coercion and physical or sexual violence. Across the world, such gender-linked violence has been a major focus of feminist movements, beginning in "speak-outs" and anti-rape demonstrations in the 1970s (Gavey, 2009). Until then, it was believed that rape and other forms of sexual assault were rare; rapists were assumed to be violent criminals attacking unknown female victims. Feminists have shown that both these surmises are wrong (Gavey, 2009). Sexual coercion and violence by men against women are not rare. The typical perpetrator of violence and sexual coercion is not a stranger, but someone known to the woman (Swedish National Council for Crime Prevention, 2002).

Feminist researchers view sexual violence as a broad continuum of acts, with rape as the extreme. Thinking in terms of a continuum of sexual violence opens the way to new conceptions of both sexual violence and heterosexual intimacy. For example, many of women's experiences that were previously seen simply as sex might be reconceived as sexual victimization. Furthermore, normative heterosexual practices – both normal male sexuality and normal female sexuality – need to be rethought and re-evaluated (Gavey, 1999). In this chapter we present the work of Nicola Gavey, one of the feminist researchers who have led the way toward such rethinking and reconceptualization. Gavey's way of thinking about and researching issues of heterosexual coercion and violence draws on discursive psychology and post-structuralist theory as well as feminist thought.

From technologies of heterosexual coercion to the cultural scaffolding of rape

Nicola Gavey, who is a New Zealand-based psychologist, has studied women's experiences of rape and sexual coercion. Her research has focused on how women who have experienced rape or other forms of unwanted sexual encounters come to understand those experiences, and how their understandings bear the traces of cultural discourses about male heterosexuality, heterosexual relations, and good femininity. It is often difficult for women to apprehend that a coercive sexual encounter with a man actually is coercive and non-consensual. Powerful cultural (and therefore personal) obstacles hinder such an interpretation. These obstacles are packaged within what Gavey called "social technologies of heterosexual coercion" hinder such an interpretation (Gavey, 1992).

Gavey studied how women's interpretations of their experiences of rape and sexual coercion vary. She used critical discursive methods to examine cultural ideas of men's heterosexual sexuality, looking in particular at how these ideas constitute what she called the "cultural scaffolding" of rape. In her book *Just sex? The cultural scaffolding of rape*, Gavey described the background of her research in this way: "The problem . . . lies in the way that normative heterosex is patterned or scripted in ways that permit far too much ambiguity over distinctions between what is rape and what is *just sex*" (2005, p. 2). Gavey studied how this ambiguity diminishes women's agency or choice in sexual encounters with men. Here, we discuss some of Gavey's empirical work in detail.

Studying technologies of heterosexual coercion and their psychological effects

Gavey (1992) interviewed a small number of New Zealand women about their experiences of unwanted or coerced sex within heterosexual relationships. All the women were white, well educated, and middle class; all identified themselves as heterosexual. They were aged from 28 to 52. They were not chosen at random, but were included because they were interested in participating in the research. Some initiated the participation themselves and some accepted invitations to participate from Gavey or one of her colleagues. Gavey pointed out that they were not chosen to participate because they claimed to have had particular kinds of sexual experiences; rather, several of them pointed out before the interview that their experiences of sex with men were very ordinary. Gavey noted that anonymity and confidentiality are particularly important to participants in research on sexuality and coercion; she therefore took great care to protect the anonymity of the women she interviewed.

The interviews covered a number of topics chosen to shed light on the research questions. The interview guide was loosely structured, so that Gavey did not adhere to a rigid set of questions or a rigid order. At the beginning of the interview, Gavey asked each participant to describe what she saw as the ideal sexual relationship between a woman and a man.

Gavey then went on to ask the participant how typical she thought this ideal was for her own relationships and for the relationships of most women. Using her participant's answers to these questions as the starting point, Gavey then moved on to gather accounts of experiences of unwanted or coerced sex with men and to facilitate reflections on these experiences. The most productive way to do this was usually to focus on a particular experience or relationship and trace it in some detail.

All interviews were audio-recorded and transcribed verbatim. After all interviews were completed and Gavey had written a draft of her report, she consulted her participants about how their accounts were presented. All found the accounts accurate. Gavey analyzed these accounts with an eye to locating the patterns of explanation and description that were shared among the different narratives. Such shared themes provide clues about the cultural discourses that ground accounts of heterosexual encounters. In what follows, we describe four of the themes that Gavey described in her analyses.

The tyranny of "normal" heterosexuality

The first theme concerned what is "normal" heterosexuality. In their narratives, the participants expressed a strong concern about being normal and having a normal sex life, coupled with uncertainty about exactly what constituted "normalcy." This concern colored the women's choices in their relationships with men. For instance, some participants pondered what the "normal" frequency of sexual encounters was. They used their notions of a normal frequency to decide how long it was acceptable to delay having sex when they did not desire it. Also, all the participants assumed that "real" (that is, "normal") sex is penetrative vaginal intercourse. Physical intimacy with a man, regardless of how it had begun, was always expected to end in intercourse, because inter-course was seen as normal sex and was expected by the man. If a woman flirted with a man, she expected to "pay her dues" for flirting by engaging in intercourse, whether or not she wanted it. The women talked about engaging in sexual intercourse in such situations because it did not occur to them to question it. Often they had intercourse because this was the "normal" way, even if they were not particularly interested. In other instances, they did not want sex at all, but felt obligated to engage in it.

Is it possible to say no?

Most of the women told of situations in which they had acquiesced in sexual encounters that they did not want. Their acquiescence in effect made the encounter consensual. Many had acquiesced because they believed that if they said no, it would have had no effect. Further, if they had said no without any effect, then, to quote one of the women, "You'd be raped ... and then it would be terrible" (Gavey, 1992, p. 334). This woman, as well as some of the other participants, drew a sharp distinction between agreeing to sex that they did not want and overtly trying to avoid sex without succeeding. In the latter case, a woman would have to admit to herself that she was a victim of rape.

The women also talked about not having a way to say no. That is, they had no words that could convey forcefully enough that they did not want sex. As the participants looked back on their experiences of acquiescing in unwanted sex, they reflected on how not signaling clearly their non-consent rendered them "unrapeable." Their choices in heterosexual encounters were so limited by their own expectations about heterosexuality and by their partners' expectations and demands that there was no discursive space in which it would have been possible to do other than consent to having sex. Whether or not they wanted to have sex, there was no way to define unwanted intercourse as rape.

Saying no to a man with whom a woman had already had sexual intercourse was seen as nearly impossible. One woman expressed what she saw as the man's point of view: "If you've been to bed with them once, then there's no reason why, that you shouldn't go to bed with them again, in their heads." For this woman, the expressed male view was experienced as forceful and even normative; the woman goes on to comment, "And of course – I mean – you can see that point of view" (Gavey, 1992, p. 335). The woman recounted instances in which she did not want to have sex with a man. In such instances he would draw on their earlier sexual encounters to argue that she should. This had made it impossible for her to say no. Because she had once said yes, he expected her to agree to sex at any time in the future. In the interview, she made it clear that his viewpoint was the only one available to her at that time of the relationship. In effect, for her and for other participants, the male partner defined what constituted sex and what the conditions for sex were; the female partner acquiesced in those definitions. In these examples, the social technology of heterosexual coercion consisted of discourses that marginalized or silenced the female partner's experiences and agency.

What happens if the woman refuses?

Women who said no to sex found themselves accused of being sexually "abnormal," Gavey's participants told her. Accusations of being sexually abnormal were often used by men to make the women agree to sex. Being sexually unwilling or sexually unresponsive also led to being labeled in derogatory ways – by a male partner in a relationship, by a rapist, or even sometimes by women themselves. Such labels placed women in a "troubled" position. The interpersonal dynamics surrounding such a troubled position are different from those we described in the previous section. The women now had clearly indicated on a particular occasion that they did not want sex; that is, they had shown that they did not see the situation as the male partner did. However, these women realized that there would be a price to pay later if they did not behave in the expected way. A woman who had once refused sex could count on being labeled sexually uptight, or called "Miss Prissy" or "a fucking bitch." One of the women said that in the long run such labels were more unpleasant than acquiescing in sex she did not want. Another woman reflected on how accusations of being uptight and abnormal had influenced her for several years. She had had the feeling that if she did not want sex, it was a sign that something was wrong with *her*, not with the situation or with her partner. The label "uptight" had invaded her identity such that if there were things she did not want to do in a sexual encounter, she attributed her reluctance to her "abnormality" and forced herself to acquiesce. Gavey notes that such labeling of women who assert their right to refuse a sexual encounter creates enduring negative positionings, often ladened with guilt and shame. The labelings influence women's identity, emotions, and actions. They are a powerful technology of coercion.

Men as "needing" sex and women as nurturant – or pragmatic?

Another discourse emerged in the narratives of some of Gavey's participants. In these narratives, the imperative to have sex that they did not want was connected to the ideal of women as nurturant. If a man needed sex so badly, these women reasoned, they ought not to refuse. Therefore, even when they did not want sex, they "let sex happen" rather than resist. Some of the women couched this in terms of "giving" sex to the man, an act that was not necessarily unpleasant. However, as one of them noted, "Sometimes there is giving of your own accord, and sometimes there is giving because you feel you have to … giving spontaneously and giving begrudgingly" (Gavey, 1992, p. 343). This technology of coercion draws heavily on notions of a good woman as nurturant and giving. Think of the expression, "She gave herself to him." If women are responsible for serving men's needs, then no explicit coercion is necessary, because "giving" a man sex becomes an imperative.

For some participants, giving sex turned into what Gavey called "sex for pragmatic reasons." These women talked about engaging in sex as part of a mundane ritual. In the words of one participant, "[I]t was just ordinary, it is just like having a cup of tea" (Gavey, 1992, p. 345). Having sex was something that she had to do at the beginning of every day. This technology of coercion downplays the consensual element of sex and turns it into something that "might as well happen." No overt threats, force, or violence are needed.

Discourses of male (hetero)sexuality and the cultural scaffolding of rape

A starting assumption of studies such as Gavey's is the assertion that sexual desires, practices, and identities are constituted by normative discourses and practices. This means that sexual desires and practices cannot be taken to be natural (Diamond and Butterworth, 2008; Gavey, 2005; Holland et al., 2004; Phillips, 2000; Tiefer, 2004; Tolman, 2002). Cultural discourses and practices position women and men differently in relation to sexuality; power relations between women and men are therefore part and parcel of men's and women's sexuality.

Feminist theories about coercion in heterosexual encounters have drawn upon Michel Foucault's (1980) concept of "power/knowledge." "Power" (in French, pouvoir) in this expression has the dual meaning of might or control (for instance, power over somebody) and of the ability to do something. "Knowledge" (in French, savoir) refers to understanding in the broad sense of the term. Coupling power and knowledge serves to indicate that the ways in which one is able to make sense of something both enable and constrain what one is able to do. The construct "power/knowledge" thus points to the material and practical effects ("doing") of discourses ("knowledge"). A dominant discourse, that is, the culturally accepted way of making sense of things, therefore both enables and constrains what people are able to do. A dominant discourse also influences how people perceive themselves when they are acting in a certain way. People's decisions and choices – and ultimately their identities and personalities – are "scaffolded" by the surrounding culture. The term scaffold here refers to the network of dominant discourses that give legitimacy and often a sense of naturalness to certain practices. Some ways of thinking and being are scaffolded as the preferred ones. Other ways of thinking are dis-preferred – sometimes they are so dis-preferred that members of a culture cannot think of them at all. What appear to be an individual's choices, then, always must be understood within the limits put in place by the cultural scaffolding.

The scaffolding determines which options are available to a person in a particular position. It also regulates the costs and benefits connected to different options.

Gavey's work concerns the cultural scaffolding of rape. The accounts that she has collected about women's experiences of unwanted sex provide a window for observing discourses about heterosexuality. As Gavey showed, these discourses enable certain ways for women to see themselves and act in a sexual encounter and disable other ways. Gavey also showed the power/knowledge of such discourses. For instance, she pointed out that the women she interviewed had sometimes taken their male sexual partner's ideas about "normal" heterosexuality as truths and disregarded their own wishes.

From cultural scaffolding to individual psychology

Feminist researchers such as Nicola Gavey and the British sociologist Janet Holland (Holland et al., 2004) have argued that a central part of the cultural scaffolding of heterosexuality consists of discourses about the nature of male heterosexuality and about sexuality as virtually always heterosexual intercourse. This can be seen in popular culture, such as film, television, humor shows, and advice books, which consisently portray male sexuality as a strong and almost irresistible urge to have intercourse. These two cultural discourses about male heterosexuality, that is, that men must have sex and that sex is intercourse, are central meanings of heterosexuality that also enter into people's identities and relationships in western, industrialized countries. For instance, in the 1980s, the British psychologist Wendy Hollway studied women's and men's narratives about their heterosexual experiences (Hollway, 1984, 1989). Among the men and women she interviewed, the image of men's sexuality was heavily influenced by what she termed the "male sexual drive" discourse. Healthy, normal men, according to this discourse, have a natural and almost unstoppable drive or need to have sex – that is, heterosexual penetrative intercourse. They are, according to the same discourse, prepared to go to great lengths to satisfy that need. The male sexual drive discourse holds that men's sexual needs take priority over women's needs or desires and that heterosexuality must be organized around satisfying men's needs. The narratives that Hollway's partici-pants provided also referred to discourses about women's sexuality. In these discourses, women's sexuality was not defined in its own right, but rather as subordinate and ancillary to men's sexuality. One discourse of female sexuality that Hollway identified was one that she termed the "have/hold" discourse (Hollway, 1989). The expression "have/hold" is taken from a phrase in many Christian wedding vows. In Hollway's usage, it alludes to the notion that women are not interested in sex for its own sake, but agree to sex as a means to get a man to agree to marriage or a lasting relationship, or to have children.

Hollway thus points out two complementary discourses. In the sexual drive discourse, men are sexual predators who only want sex, not lasting relationships or emotional engagement. In the have/hold discourse, women agree to sex mainly as a means to secure a long-term relationship. Following the logic of these discourses, one would expect men to make sexual advances and women either to receive or reject these advances. This, of course, creates a distinct asymmetry between a man and a woman in a heterosexual couple. It is the man's prerogative to initiate sex; the woman may either satisfy the man's demands or deny them. She is not expected to act to provide for her own sexual pleasure. Even today, it is still culturally acceptable to tell narratives of heterosexual encounters without making reference to the woman's desire or pleasure. As Nicola Gavey observed, "the absence of a woman's desire and pleasure is not only permissible, but almost unremarkable" (2005, p. 142).

The discourse of men's unconquerable sexual drive does not necessarily benefit all men. Far from all men today recognize themselves in its imagery. Moreover, in addition to being used by men to pressure women, the discourse can be used by both men and women to pressure men to take part in sexual encounters that they do not want.

The sexual revolution and modern women's heterosexuality

Research and observations such as those above offer a stark contrast to the ideals and images of women's sexuality in the "post-sexual-revolution" era. These images portray women as both active and agentic, and not fettered by old ideals of chastity, passivity, and subordination. Does this mean that for young people today, Hollway's and Gavey's ideas no longer hold? Perhaps not. At least not according to the results of a study of young people's narratives about their sexual experiences carried out by the British researcher Janet Holland and her colleagues (Holland et al., 2004). That study pointed to the persistence of such asymmetrical patterns in heterosexual relations between young adults. The researchers concluded that for young people in Great Britain in the 1990s, "Heterosexuality is not, as it appears to be, masculinity-and-femininity in opposition: it is masculinity. Within this masculine heterosexuality, women's desires and the possibility of female resistance are potentially unruly forces to be disciplined and controlled, if necessary by force" (p. 10).

Holland and her colleagues argued that contemporary masculine heterosexuality among young people enables men to use force to overcome a woman's resistance. Using force, then, is not seen as something outside the normal and expected. In this way, discourses of male heterosexuality, such as the male sexual drive discourse, can serve to scaffold rape and sexual coercion as an unremarkable ingredient of what many people see as "just sex."

Analyses such as those we have presented here open windows on the discursive and practical connections between the common view of male sexuality and the persistence of laissez-faire societal attitudes toward men who sexually assault and coerce women (see Gavey, 1999, 2009). They also point to wider connections between heterosexuality, femininity, and masculinity.

From complementary heterosexuality to complementary femininity and masculinity

Research about how discourses such as the male sexual drive discourse function to scaffold rape and sexual coercion necessarily raises questions about masculinity and femininity more generally. It is hardly reasonable to expect discourses of male sexuality to be divorced from discourses of masculinity, or discourses of female sexuality to be unrelated to discourses of femininity. On the contrary, researchers such as Gavey, Holland *et al.*, and Hollway argue that normative images and ideals of feminine and masculine demeanor and behavior are closely aligned to discourses about normal male and female heterosexuality. They also argue that idealized images of femininity and masculinity often compromise the possibility of women's agency in heterosexual encounters. Consequently, those who want to learn more about modern women's and men's heterosexuality have every reason to be versed in critical psychological studies of femininity and masculinity. And those who want to understand femininity and masculinity need to be versed in critical feminist studies of heterosexuality.

Conclusions from interpretative research about heterosexual coercion

What is it possible to learn from the type of research we have described here? The research is based on a small number of interviews with well-educated women in one particular locale. How do these limitations influence the credibility and utility of the research? These are, of course, pivotal issues for any researcher: Researchers want to be able to claim that the results of their research apply to something outside the lives of the actual people they have studied.

In her reports Gavey points out that her aim is not to make universal statements about "women." Nor is she interested in making statistical generalizations about a particular population. She has other kinds of generalizing ambitions. Her ambitions are based in the connections she sees between the experiences of the women she has studied and the culture in which they live, especially the culturally anchored discourses about heterosexuality. Gavey had selected research participants whose sexual experiences were not unusual or odd. This made it possible to interpret their stories as drawing upon a limited number of culturally shared interpretative repertoires relating to heterosexual sexuality and relationships. At the same time, Gavey points out that she studied a moment in time; she does not claim that her results will be applicable forever. She also notes that, because of the limitations of her sample, she can give only a partial account of the possible extent of women's experiences of unwanted heterosexual encounters.

11 Women's eating problems and the cultural meanings of body size

In many parts of the world and for most of human history, fatness has been positively regarded, especially for women (Gremillion, 2005). However, in the high-income, industrialized societies of Europe and North America, present-day medical standards of health and fitness, as well as present-day beauty standards, prescribe thin, fat-free bodies, particularly for women. In these societies, chronic discontent about weight and body size, as well as body shame, has been normative for women and girls for more than forty years (Rodin *et al.*, 1984). Many women and girls in these societies have problematic relationships with food and many engage in extreme practices (such as fasting, vomiting, laxative abuse, and surgery) to manage their body weight, shape, and size.

Preoccupation with the size and shape of one's body and extreme practices of weight management are identified and treated as psychiatric disorders (e.g., anorexia nervosa, bulimia nervosa, and binge eating disorder) in contemporary European and North American societies. Identifying these practices as illnesses serves to privatize them; that is, it suggests that they are personal problems that are caused by pathological factors within the individual that can be fixed by person-level remedies. In contrast, feminist scholars have emphasized that women's preoccupation with the size and shape of their bodies and women's disturbed eating practices must be understood in the context of cultural expectations regarding women, ideals of femininity, and bodily appetites. Therefore, feminist scholars have explored gendered meanings of body size and gendered meanings of eating practices, appetite, self-discipline, and self-restraint.

We begin with some general background about eating problems and then describe three feminist research projects that explore cultural and personal meanings given to eating and body size by women from diverse backgrounds.

Eating problems: setting the stage

The core features of anorexia and bulimia include disturbances in body image (such as the overvaluation of thinness, an intense fear of gaining weight, and a preoccupation with body weight and shape); drastic over-control or undercontrol of food intake (for example, prolonged fasting or binge-eating); and extreme regimens to control one's weight (such as fasting, excessive exercise, self-induced vomiting, and laxative or diuretic use).

The incidence of eating problems and body dissatisfaction among women and girls spiraled upward in North America and Europe in the latter decades of the twentieth century. Bulimia nervosa, for example, was not described in the mental health literature until 1976, but, today, it is the most commonly diagnosed eating disorder in many countries. Moreover, there is evidence that younger and younger girls are expressing excessive concern about their weight and shape, as well as engaging in extreme restriction of food intake and other dieting practices in an effort to lose weight.

From the beginning, those suffering from these problems were mainly girls and women. According to one recent US study, roughly 95 percent of patients diagnosed with eating difficulties are female (Matlin, 2004). In western, high-income countries, most of those who receive diagnoses of anorexia nervosa (hereinafter "anorexia") or bulimia nervosa (herein-after "bulimia") have been white, middle class, young, and female, although nonwhite, non-middle-class, and older women, and some men and boys, may experience these difficulties. There is also evidence that eating disorders and preoccupations with body weight are increasing among women and girls in countries outside the west in response to the flow of western images and ideals of beauty into those countries (Becker et al., 2002; Watters, 2010).

Eating problems pose significant risks to physical and mental health. Over the long term, the weight management practices associated with anorexia and bulimia can have severe physical health consequences. These include cardiovascular and neurological complications, impaired physical development, and other medical morbidities, such as esophageal problems related to chronic vomiting (Chavez and Insel, 2007). Indeed, anorexia nervosa is reported to have the highest mortality rates of any psychiatric condition. Anorexia, bulimia, and other eating disorders have a number of negative psychological and psychosocial consequences as well. These include depression, suicide risk, disrupted relationships, shame, secretiveness, and temporary impairments in concentration brought on by starvation.

In the USA, the lifetime prevalence estimates for women have been roughly 0.1 percent for anorexia and 1.5 percent for bulimia (Striegel-Moore and Bulik, 2007). Similar estimates have been made for western European countries (e.g., Swedish National Board of Health and

Welfare, 2009). It should be noted that there are many additional women who engage in severe food restriction, binge-eating, and purging or who struggle with body dissatisfaction and shame, but do not fully meet the formal diagnostic criteria. In the USA, such individuals now account for the majority of those who are receiving treatment for eating problems. No doubt there are many more individuals who meet diagnostic criteria for an eating disorder, but who are not in treatment. If there were a way to count all these individuals, the prevalence estimates would be much higher. In the UK, for example, one study found that between 5 percent and 15 percent of adolescent girls sometimes resorted to self-induced vomiting or laxative and diuretic use in order to control their weight (Bryant-Waugh, 2006).

A number of therapeutic approaches have been developed for eating difficulties, including inpatient hospitalization; residential treatment programs; nutritional counseling; several forms of individual, group, and family therapies; and pharmacological treatments. However, although treatment is successful in some cases, eating problems remain difficult to treat. Consider anorexia. Although various psychotherapies are far superior to nutritional counseling and pharmacotherapy, only about 50 percent of individuals with anorexia make a full recovery (Råstam et al., 2003; Swedish National Institute of Public Health, 2004; Wilson et al., 2007). Even then, relapses or recurrences may occur in response to crises or during stressful times. Treatment for anorexia is most likely to succeed for patients who are young and whose condition is not long-standing (Chavez and Insel, 2007). Of individuals with bulimia, roughly 50 percent fully recover with therapy and many others make substantial improvement; however, recurrences are common. Moreover, it is common for individuals to shift among different disordered eating practices. In particular, individuals who have recovered from anorexia not infrequently develop problems of binge-eating and purging.

Feminist approaches to women's eating problems

Susan Bordo, an American feminist philosopher who has applied feminist theory to eating problems (Bordo, 1993), described anorexia as the "crystallization of our culture." For Bordo and other feminist scholars, women's preoccupation with their weight and body size, as well as the eating problems that follow from this preoccupation, must be seen as connected to culture. These problems are closely linked to a specific time in history, to particular countries, and to specific sociocultural groups within those countries. Therefore, feminist scholars have examined societal and cultural factors rather than factors "inside" the individual, such as putative genetic factors, personality traits, and faulty cognitions, which are the usual targets of psychiatric research.

Feminist researchers have been concerned not only to locate body dissatisfaction and eating difficulties in the cultural, social, and historical context, but also to build theories of how such problems are gendered. Some researchers have documented the "thin ideal" of feminine beauty that is promoted by the mass media. For example, they have noted that such feminine icons as Barbie dolls, fashion models, and film stars are extraordinarily slender; indeed, quite a few models and movie stars have received diagnoses of eating disorders. Researchers have argued that the prevalence of such images encourages women and girls to mimic unattainable body shapes. However, casting blame exclusively on the mass media or popular culture provides limited avenues for change or activism: Who or what creates "popular culture" and how could an individual hope to change it? In addition, some feminist theorists have raised concerns about viewing the "culture of thinness" as the explanation for women's eating problems because such a view implies that women and girls are dupes who are readily taken in by the mass media and incapable of critical reflection.

Without denying that contemporary popular culture places an extreme value on thinness and beauty for women and girls, many feminist scholars see the overvaluation of thin female bodies as only one piece of a more complex picture. Bordo (1993), for instance, noted that dieting and thinness are imbued with moral significance that traces back to the Cartesian mind–body dualism and even to Judeo-Christian ideals about renouncing bodily pleasures. The thin body is the "good" body insofar as it marks the triumph of mind and reason over body, emotionality, and sensual indulgence (Malson, 1997). Moreover, contemporary western discourses place a high value on individual self-improvement, self-control, and self-discipline, as well as feminine self-abnegation (Gremillion, 2001). These cultural presuppositions fuel the body management practices associated with eating disorders. They also produce covert (and sometimes overt) admiration for the "self-control" of women who suffer from anorexia, as well as disdain and contempt for women suffering from bulimia (Burns, 2004). These cultural presuppositions are so powerful and so engrained that even professionals who specialize in the treatment of eating disorders may unwittingly subscribe to them (Burns, 2004; Gremillion, 2001).

Feminist scholars also worry that framing eating disorders solely in terms of distorted body images and false ideas about weight management is not sufficient to encompass the diversity of women's experiences. As you shall see below, when women and girls offer their own accounts of their struggles with food, eating, and body size, they bring forward many different accounts of the origins, functions, and meanings of disturbed eating and desired and dreaded body sizes. As one might expect, these differences are related both to cultural patterns of meaning and to specific experiences associated with women's social locations. The feminist researchers whose work is described below focus their attention on the diversity of experiences associated with body size, food, and eating. At the same time, the researchers turn attention to the meanings that women themselves give to their bodies, food, and struggles with eating. Like other researchers whose work we have been considering, they view people as engaged in intentional activities and as continually reflecting on themselves and their experiences. They view women's eating practices and bodily preoccupations not merely as symptoms of a mental disease, but as practices that are undertaken to achieve a valued and self-affirming purpose and that are situated in a complex social and cultural matrix.

Interpretative research on eating problems: some examples

In what follows, we explore some feminist interpretative research projects that have explored women's eating problems. Two assumptions that frame this book also guide the researchers: that human beings actively make meanings about their experiences, circumstances, and relationships; and that humans are agents who make choices and engage in activities based on those meanings.

We begin by discussing work by Leeat Granek and by Becky Thompson, both of whom interviewed women who had recovered from serious eating problems. Both used intensive life-history interviews in order to situate the eating problems in the context of women's lives. Next, we turn to a project carried out by Lisa Rubin, Mako Fitts, and Anne Becker, which was aimed at uncovering cultural differences regarding body management, appearance and self-presentation, and eating. The project concerned US women of African heritage and of Latina heritage. All the projects move beyond the view of eating disorders as discrete, disease-like entities. The results of the studies also cast doubt on universalized theories of causation and on universalized symptom criteria.

Probing the relational context of white women's eating problems

Leeat Granek, a psychologist working in Canada, interviewed five middle-class, white Canadian women aged 25–30 years who had suffered from serious eating difficulties and received a diagnosis of anorexia (Granek, 2007). All of them had ended treatment at least one year prior to the interview; none of them were experiencing clinically significant distress about eating and body weight at the time of the interview. Granek used semi-structured interviews with open-ended questions that enabled her participants to construct their accounts as they chose. Her interview questions included what she called a time-span chronology, with questions about the time before the participant became anorexic, her experience during the time she was anorexic, and the time after she recovered.

Granek analyzed the interviews by an approach similar to that developed by grounded theorists (e.g., Glaser and Strauss, 1967). That is, she first identified meaning units in the interviews. By systematically comparing these meaning units to one another, she was able to derive a set of categories that captured the commonalities in the interviews. The main categories were then broken down into more fine-grained categories. In parallel, Granek also composed extensive memos detailing her ideas, impressions, and tentative interpretations as she worked with the interview material. These reflections provided a record of her hunches and "gut feelings." Equally important, the memos enabled her to check and counter the biases, assumptions, and projections she may have brought to the data analysis.

Granek found that a recurring theme in the interviews was the social facilitation of disturbed eating practices. That is, participants talked at length about women friends who initiated, encouraged, maintained, and nurtured many aspects of their anorexia. These friends were engaged in similar struggles with body dissatisfaction and in similar disturbed eating practices. According to the participants, disturbed eating and acute dissatisfaction with body weight and shape were pervasive among their female friends. The participants reported intense peer group pressures to engage in extreme dieting and excessive exercising. The peer group also pressured participants to pay intense and continual attention to physical appearance. Participants described many social rewards for becoming thin and many social penalties (such as teasing and shaming) for being fat.

A second theme in the interviews was that being thin and losing weight were regarded as valued accomplishments. This was closely related to the social embeddedness of eating problems. If they could achieve a thin enough body, participants believed, they would be valued more by others (such as parents, boyfriends, and female friends) and they would be able to feel like a worthy person. In the participants' accounts, the men in their lives (fathers and boyfriends) exacerbated their feelings of low self-worth by criticizing their body size. When a man accepted a woman regardless of her weight, such acceptance gave her a heightened sense of self-worth. Thus, in the narratives that the participants told about their lives, others – especially men – were part of the reason for their eating difficulties, but those same people also could make important contributions to their recovery.

A third theme concerned the duration of the participants' eating difficulties. As the participants recounted their life histories, they traced their eating difficulties to a time well before their teenage years. For some, the problems had begun as long as twenty years earlier. These self-reports contradict the standard view that eating problems begin in adolescence. Over the duration, the eating difficulties had waxed and waned in intensity and sometimes changed their form. For example, a woman might have some periods during which she engaged in severe food restriction and other periods in which she practiced binge-eating and purging. This fluidity, which other researchers have noted as well, raises questions about the customary diagnostic practice that considers anorexia and bulimia to be distinct conditions. It also raises doubts about the value of revising the diagnostic system to include more and more discrete categories of eating disorders in the hope of discovering a specific cause and a specific treatment for each one.

A final theme that Granek found concerned the participants' experiences of recovery. As the participants saw it, their recovery was not accomplished through professional therapies designed to induce them to gain weight by eating more and exercising less. Rather, the participants attributed their recovery to developing or deepening personal relationships that provided alternate sources of self-worth. They saw their anorexia as a quest to achieve a body that would enable them to feel worthy, valued, and loved. Recovery, for them, entailed a change in their conception of what makes a person worthy. It was through relationships with others that they were able to make this conceptual shift.

In sum, for Granek's participants – white, middle-class, young Canadian women – anorexia involved a desire for self-worth that was mediated through control of eating and weight. The mass media and its relentless glorification of thinness for women, Granek suggests, served only as a background factor. It was day-to-day relationships – with female friends, fathers, mothers, and male partners – that played the key role both in producing and maintaining disturbed eating practices and in enabling the women to relinquish them.

Looking beyond white, middle-class women

Like Leeat Granek, Becky Wangsgaard Thompson (1994, 1996) took issue with the prevailing notion that eating disorders reflect the "relentless pursuit of thinness," which is set in motion by unattainable cultural ideals of femininity. Thompson, an American sociologist and gender scholar, noted that although feminist scholars had tied the origins of women's eating problems to cultural and social imperatives, few of them had analyzed how such social structural factors as women's race/ethnicity, social class, and sexuality shaped their relationships to their bodies and their struggles over eating. Indeed, many feminist analyses had accepted the widespread belief that eating problems were solely the province of young, white, middle-class, heterosexual women, perhaps because these were the women who presented for professional help. This was an assumption that Becky Thompson wanted to challenge.

Thompson investigated eating difficulties among women who did not fit the stereotype of an eating-disorder patient. Given the private and sensitive nature of the topic, Thompson chose to rely on personal contacts to recruit participants. Moreover, Thompson, a white, middle-class woman, intended to interview women of color and women who were poor. In such cross-race and cross-class interviewing, Thompson needed to have personal introductions in order to gain participants' trust. The group of women that Thompson interviewed included African-American women and Latinas, as well as white women. Some of them lived as lesbians; most lived as heterosexuals. Some had immigrated to the USA as children. Many were poor. All in all, Thompson interviewed eighteen women.

As Granek had found, most of the women whom Thompson interviewed had experienced a number of different eating problems, including binge-eating, bingeing and purging, and highly restricted eating. Many had experienced large fluctuations in their weight; these fluctuations averaged 74 pounds (33.5 kg). Like the women in Granek's study, many traced the onset of their eating problems to a time prior to adolescence; the average age when their problems began was 11.

Thompson's interviews focused on gathering life history data from the participants. Her interpretative method involved locating themes and conceptual categories in the data, using the procedures of grounded theory (Glaser and Strauss, 1967). The women she interviewed drew connections between their eating problems and painful and oppressive situations they had endured. These situations included childhood sexual abuse, heterosexist and homophobic bullying, sexual harassment, and acute poverty. For example, one woman traced her use of food to relieve distress to a period during her childhood when she and her sister were frequently molested by their father. They used nighttime snacks to comfort themselves and assuage their fears. Another woman said that she began to binge during adolescence; her weight gain served to shield her body from unwanted groping and sexual advances by men and boys. For another woman, excessive eating was a way to blot out the daily strains associated with extreme poverty. Another woman began a course of extreme dieting at the insistence of her parents, who wanted a daughter thin enough to conform to the beauty standards of their newly achieved middle-class status. In short, Thompson's participants understood their eating practices as responses to distressing circumstances.

Thompson's work suggests that there are many different pathways to eating problems. It suggests that the "thin ideal" is not the explanation for all the eating problems that women experience, though it may have validity for some women. By speaking to women who were not white, not middle class, and not heterosexual, Thompson uncovered accounts of eating problems in which body dissatisfaction and low self-worth appeared to play little or no role. Rather, racism, poverty, class prejudice, childhood sexual abuse, and sexual harassment played significant roles.

"Body aesthetics" or "body ethics"?

A project aimed at understanding the experiences of women from ethnic minority groups in the southern USA provided further evidence that the meanings of body size and eating, as well as the nature of concerns about weight, differ for different groups of women. Lisa Rubin, Mako Fitts, and Anne Becker (2003) noted that attempts to ascertain the incidence of eating disorders among women from ethnic minority backgrounds in the USA have produced contradictory findings. Moreover, empirical studies attempting to relate women's eating disturbances to their acceptance of the "thin ideal" have yielded inconsistent findings. This led Rubin and her coworkers to examine the meanings that African-American women and Latinas give to body size, food, and eating practices.

The researchers' approach was closely akin to what we have called an interpretative stance. Their goal was to observe the meanings that women of color give to body size, self-representations, and eating practices. In the USA, women of color must negotiate two such sets of meanings: the meanings from the dominant white culture and the meanings from their own culture. A crucial element of the dominant white culture is a beauty standard that denigrates what is non-white (Collins, 2000). The denigrated features include body size and shape, as well as skin color, hair, and facial features.

Rubin and her coworkers recruited women who had taken university courses on gender or ethnicity or who had participated in multicultural campus organizations. Through this purposive selection process, they aimed to gather a group of women who had studied gender, ethnicity, and cultural difference and who had engaged in critical thinking or activism about these issues. Most of the women were young adults, with a mean age of 25. The researchers gathered the women into small groups for discussion. Five such group discussions were held, with a total of eighteen women taking part. Each group was homogeneous with respect to ethnicity.

Rubin and her coworkers had intended for the discussion groups to explore body ideals and preferences. However, the women's talk brought forward a rich set of discourses about bodies, self-representation, body ethics, and cultural politics that the researchers had not anticipated. Neither the Latinas nor the African-American women held a specific body size or shape as their standard of beauty, even though they were well aware of the ideal body size and shape for white women. Instead the participants elaborated a body ideal that was based on style, self-care, and spirituality. The researchers named this "body ethics." Style referred to a self-presentation that embodied self-respect, care for one's appearance, careful grooming, and hygiene. Several participants drew on religion and spirituality as the rationale for accepting their bodies as they were and for refusing to engage in the extreme body-management and body-modification practices demanded by contemporary beauty standards. For example, one woman said, "God gave me whatever he gave me." In other words, her body and her appearance were God-given, not of her own making, and therefore not to be tampered with.

Other prominent themes in the focus groups reflected the women's efforts to resist and combat the devaluation of ethnic minority groups by the white majority culture and to refute negative stereotypes about ethnic minority women. The women spoke about carefully managing aspects of their self-presentation, such as their appearance, grooming, and public comportment. In the focus groups of both Latinas and African-American women, the participants engaged in a substantial critique of mass-media representations of ethnic minority women. For example, they were critical of many African-American and Latina celebrities because they saw them as little more than tokens who allowed themselves to be used to create a false appearance of inclusion. Furthermore, they noted that the celebrities' body size and shape, as well as their hair, features, and pale skin, conformed to the "white" ideal.

In sum, by listening to Latina and African-American women, Rubin and her coworkers were able to identify forms of body talk that departed substantially (if not entirely) from the body talk that many researchers have reported for white women and girls (e.g., Nichter, 2000).

There was, for example, little evidence of dissatisfaction with weight, appearance anxiety, or the power of the "Barbie" image. For these women of color, the focus was not on the aesthetics of the body, but on the ethics of the body and on the race-related politics of appearance. This does not mean that women of color in the USA (or elsewhere) are automatically protected from eating difficulties. Nor does it mean that all women of color are protected from a desire to change their bodies. However, as Becky Thompson's work has also shown, such practices and wishes can be embedded in and reflective of a variety of culturally based meanings.

Stepping back: what can interpretative research uncover about women's body projects?

The three projects we have described give only a small taste of the interpretative work on body size and eating problems that feminist psychologists, sociologists, and anthropologists have pursued. Researchers have addressed topics such as covert gender assumptions in treatment regimens (Burns, 2004; Gremillion, 2003); men's body projects (Gill et al., 2005); mother–daughter conversations about dieting, body shape, and weight; and the thematic content of "pro-ana" (pro-anorexia) and "pro-mia" (pro-bulimia) internet sites (Archives of Resistance, n.d.; Day and Keys, 2009; Dias, 2003), as well as novel interventions using the methods of participatory action research (Burns and Tyrer, 2009; Piran, 2001).

Apart from the specific findings, the three projects illustrate several general points. One is that when researchers allow women to talk freely about their bodies and eating practices, the women bring forward stories and meanings that are not evident when researchers rely on preconceived questionnaires. For example, by listening to African-American women and Latinas, Lisa Rubin and her colleagues heard discourses of body ethics that were distinctly different from the discourse of body aesthetics characteristic of white women. These discourses have not been noted in the clinical literature on eating problems.

A second point concerns the importance of considering intersecting identities and cultural specificity when studying women's bodily ideals and eating difficulties. It is nearly impossible for any woman in high-income, western countries to remain unaware of the cultural idealization of thinness. Nonetheless, body weight, size, and shape do not have one single meaning for all women. The meanings are shaped by women's ethnic identification, experiences of class oppression, and sexual orientation. For example, Lisa Rubin and her colleagues found that African-American women were positioned to develop a critical consciousness of mainstream beauty ideals; this critical consciousness enabled them to withstand pressures to conform to the mainstream ideals. Becky Thompson's work also focused attention on the impact of social location and structural oppression. In sum, when researchers attend to the intersection of gender with other social categories, their work uncovers striking differences in eating difficulties, body satisfaction, and self-representations.

A third point is that interpretative studies like the ones we have described challenge the medicalized model of eating disorders that dominates psychological and psychiatric research. This model locates the women's eating problems inside the person by pointing to such factors as personality problems (e.g., perfectionism, low self-esteem, or a girl's difficulties individuating from her mother) and genetic predispositions as possible causes. But women's narratives about their eating difficulties and body dissatisfaction have much to say about the social, cultural, and societal context of their struggles – their family, peer, or romantic relationships and larger societal structures. Both Granek and Thompson, for example, found ample evidence of interpersonal pressures on girls and young women to be thin. Both also noted that several research participants tied their problematic eating to experiences of bodily violations, such as childhood sexual abuse.

Finally, interpretative studies can enlarge our understanding of eating disorders by tying these problems to the contemporary cultural politics of body size. They open the way to viewing eating problems and body dissatisfaction not as outward "symptoms" of an inner disease, but rather as the end of a continuum of culturally approved practices of dieting, fitness regimens, self-denial, and self-surveillance. They also open the way to theorizing how body dissatisfaction, continual bodily scrutiny, and cycles of self-deprecation and self-improvement are part and parcel of normative femininity.

12   Psychological suffering in social and cultural context

One of the key themes of this book is that human action cannot be understood outside the matrix of social relations and cultural frameworks of which people are a part. Context matters deeply. Further, what people know about themselves and their world is shaped by the systems of language and meaning available to them. In this chapter, we argue that this is true for mental health practitioners and their clients, as well as for researchers who study matters of mental health and illness. This chapter, which addresses psychological suffering – what is ordinarily called mental illness – turns its attention to ways in which such suffering is embedded in culture, social context, and language. In earlier chapters, we introduced several ideas about language and linguistic practices that are relevant here. One general point is that social categorizations seldom "carve Nature at its joints," as we pointed out in Chapter 2. Such categorizations are best understood as products of ongoing collective efforts to order and make sense of the world. Social categorizations create and convey meanings; they also conceal meanings. Psychiatric diagnoses are potent social categorizations.

We discuss the history and function of psychiatric diagnosis in the first part of the chapter. Building upon that discussion, we then examine how psychological suffering, deviance, and dysfunction are intimately bound up with cultural contexts, as well as with the inequitable distribution of social and material power and resources across social groups, including gender and ethnic groupings. Stepping back to examine the categorizations and language systems in use in psychiatry and psychology does not mean that psychological suffering is no more than a language game. Nor does such an examination imply that people who receive psychiatric categorizations do not suffer. However, judgments about suffering, dysfunction, and deviance are necessarily made through the lens of culture. Moreover, such judgments often serve to shore up the prevailing social structure and norms. In modern societies, the mental health professions have become a prime regulatory force, offering judgments of what is normal versus abnormal, as well as pronouncements about what makes people healthy, happy, and fulfilled. As feminist critics have pointed out, these judgments often encode gender imperatives, as well as class, cultural, and ethnic biases.

Psychiatric diagnosis

A psychiatric diagnosis is an especially potent kind of social categorization. It is also a preeminent example of an interactive category. That is, receiving a psychiatric diagnosis may cause people to alter their actions and feelings and to think of themselves in new ways. When people seek help from the mental health system, their encounters often begin with their receiving a diagnosis (or several diagnoses) that is used to organize the treatment they receive. The power of diagnoses extends far beyond individual treatment decisions, however. Diagnoses also influence "judicial deliberations, third-party [insurance] payments, budgetary allocations by private and governmental bodies, and many other key institutional functions" (Rogler, 1997, p. 9; see also Brante, 2006). Psychiatric diagnoses are the *lingua franca* of the mental health system and, as such, they define a wide and growing swath of social reality and personal life. This expansion is one reason why feminists and other critical theorists have long been concerned with psychiatric diagnoses (Caplan and Cosgrove, 2004; Cosgrove, 2005; Marecek, 1993, 2001). Moreover, the epidemiology of diagnoses shows sharp gendered, class-based, and ethnic patterns, raising questions about the power politics of diagnosis. Can it be that deviance is in the eye of the beholder? How much do judgments of behavior as "mad" reflect androcentric, middle-class, or Euro-American standpoints of mental health professionals? Feminist psychologists have raised such questions about many diagnostic categories historically associated with women, such as borderline personality disorder, hysteria, nymphomania, passive-dependent personality disorder, and depression (Becker, 1997; Chesler, 1972; Groneman, 1994). They also have raised broader questions about the diagnostic category system itself: What is the framework of meaning that underlies the diagnosing system? What implicit assumptions lace through the system? What alternate meanings of suffering does this framework conceal? (Hare-Mustin and Marecek, 1997; Marecek, 2001; Marecek and Hare-Mustin, 2009).

If we look across history and across cultures, many models and metaphors for psychological suffering come into view (Drinka, 1984; Kakar, 1991; Kleinman, 1988; Siegler and Osmond, 1974). In nineteenth-century Europe and North America, mental illness was mainly synonymous with severe disability and psychosis. These conditions were presumed to result from diseases of the brain or the nervous system, although few specific causes, apart from syphilitic paresis, were known. The psychodynamic theories that rose to prominence during the early twentieth century offered an alternative point of view. By mid-century, this point of view had superseded the biomedical view in many settings. Psychodynamic theories focused on mental processes and the interior psychological self. Experiences of distress and dysfunction were presumed to be symbolic manifestations of underlying conflicts that could be traced back to childhood experiences and relationships. Talking therapy was the remedy. During the era when psychodynamic theories were dominant, the purview of the mental health professions expanded greatly. Many mental health professionals moved from hospital settings into outpatient offices where they treated individuals, couples, and families with milder forms of distress and dysfunction. They helped people to manage a broad and ever-expanding variety of problems in living. These included marital, relationship, and family difficulties; diffuse life dissatisfaction; bad habits, such as smoking, drinking, overeating, shopping, and gambling; and developmental problems. In short, mental health professionals came to offer care not only for the severely disabled, but also for the "worried well."

Beginning in the 1970s, the psychiatric establishments in many western countries repudiated psychodynamic theory in favor of a return to a biomedical point of view (Kärfve, 2006; Wilson, 1993). This re-medicalization was not a result of new scientific discoveries. Rather, it was the result of dramatic changes in the external economic, political, and social environment of medicine (Horwitz, 2002). In the USA, for example, an increasingly corporatized and bureaucratic medical system made it imperative for psychiatry to appear to treat precisely defined, symptom-based disease entities. Similar patterns of re-medicalization have also been noted in European countries with different systems of mental health-care (Hallerstedt, 2006; Johannisson, 2006). The future of psychiatry demanded that it reinvent itself to resemble biomedicine. However, as this reinvention took place, psychiatry did not revert to hospital-based treatment of severely disabled individuals. Instead, its purview remained the expansive and amorphous collection of personal difficulties and dissatisfactions, troubling experiences, and conflicted relationships that had been brought under psychiatrists' care in the heyday of psychodynamic theories and therapies. This collection of experiences became recharacter-ized as diseases. It therefore became necessary to devise specific concrete indicators that would enable a practitioner to diagnose them.

Today, the language of biomedicine comes easily to the lips of mental health professionals and those whom they treat. Consider, for example, terms like mental *"health,"* mental *"illness,"* disease, patient, symptom, diagnosis, prognosis, relapse, and remission. The language of the mental health professions is so saturated with biomedical terms that professionals would be hard pressed to communicate without using such language. Nonetheless, this biomedical language is usually metaphoric, not literal; most of the problems for which people seek mental healthcare are not biomedical diseases. Moreover, the language of biomedicine is commonplace in everyday talk about psychological life as well. This is part of a broader social process that has been termed *medicalization* (Conrad and Schneider, 1980). That is, certain events or characteristics of everyday life and certain social and behavioral conditions become medical issues, and thus come within the purview of health professionals to study and treat. Medicalization typically involves changes not only in terminology but also in social attitudes (Conrad, 2007).

Diagnostic category systems

There are two main systems of psychiatric classification in use today. One is part of the *International Statistical Classification of Diseases and Related Health Problems*, published by the World Health Organization. The other is the *Diagnostic and Statistical Manual of Mental Disorders* (hereinafter DSM), formulated in the USA and published by the American Psychiatric Association. Both of these systems, which are quite similar to each other, are frequently revised and updated. A major effort is now underway to bring the two systems into closer alignment.

We focus here on the DSM. First published in 1952, the DSM is now undergoing its fifth major revision, which is scheduled for completion in 2013. The process of compiling and revising the DSM has been the subject of much critical scrutiny by both those inside the mental health field and those outside. A striking feature of these revisions is that the number of categories has grown in successive editions – from 106 in 1952 to 340 in 1994. Another striking feature is the sweeping reworking of the categorization scheme that took place in the third revision, the DSM-III, in parallel to the re-medicalization of psychiatry that we described earlier.

DSM-III (American Psychiatric Association, 1980) involved a thorough reconception of diagnosis, one that mimicked the disease categories of biomedicine. Among other things, the revised manual defined psychiatric conditions in terms of checklists of symptoms. The symptom criteria were intended to be objective; in particular, the writers of the manual were careful to eliminate all psychodynamic assumptions about etiology. Some of these new symptom criteria were drawn from the research literature;

others reflected the consensus of committees of practicing psychiatrists. In addition, roughly eighty new disorders were included.

The format introduced in 1980 has remained in use through successive revisions, despite objections from many quarters (e.g., Alliance of Psychoanalytic Organizations, 2006; Kirk and Kutchins, 1992; Widiger and Trull, 2007; Wylie, 1995). Feminists and other critical theorists have criticized some fundamental assumptions of this format. One is the assumption that psychological suffering can be carved up into a set of discrete, non-overlapping syndromes or categories. Another assumption is that such syndromes pre-exist and are independent of the language used to describe them. (In other words, they are assumed to be natural kinds, a term we introduced in Chapter 2.) A third assumption is that psychological suffering is equivalent to physical disease and can be understood within the same epistemological framework. A fourth assumption, put forward by some prominent psychiatrists, goes even further to assert that all or most of the conditions that psychiatrists treat stem from brain pathologies or other biophysical abnormalities, implying that psychological suffering is reducible to biophysical pathologies (e.g., Chavez and Insel, 2007).

Many sociologists, medical anthropologists, philosophers, and psychologists take exception to conceiving of psychological suffering as if it were akin to a biomedical disease. These social scientists do not deny or discredit people's suffering, nor do they claim that such suffering is not real. They insist, however, that suffering – like all forms of human behavior – cannot be understood apart from its sociocultural surround (Chapter 4 in Hacking, 1999). Even when distress and dysfunction have biological correlates or substrates, people express their suffering in accordance with cultural and social dictates. Such dictates vary among social groups, locations, and time periods; thus, the form that suffering takes varies from social group to social group, place to place, and time to time. For example, the expressions of depression in Euro-American societies and the moral judgments made about those exhibiting depressive symptoms reflect a shifting array of religious and cultural ideas stretching back to medieval times (Jadhav, 1996). Outside Euro-American societies, people experience and express demoralization in different ways, notably through bodily symptoms (Kleinman and Good, 1984; Obeyesekere, 1984). A further example is post-traumatic stress disorder (PTSD), which Allan Young, a medical anthropologist in Canada, studied from a sociocultural perspective (see also Becker, 2004; Summerfield, 2001). As Young observed, "The disorder is not timeless, nor does it possess an intrinsic unity. Rather, it is glued together by the practices, technologies, and narratives with which it is diagnosed, studied, treated, and represented and by the various interests, institutions, and moral arguments that mobilized these efforts and resources" (1995, p. 5). This could be said for many disorders.

The use of "disease" as a metaphor for understanding people's suffering implies that such suffering is an outward manifestation of an underlying internal illness or pathology. There is then little need to take into account external conditions, such as culture and social context. Neither the broad sociopolitical and cultural context nor the person's immediate interpersonal context is considered relevant to the diagnostic assessment or the subsequent treatment. This approach works well for many physical conditions: An orthopedic surgeon need not know whether a patient broke her arm while skiing or by slipping in the bathtub because fractured bones can be adequately diagnosed from a radiographic image. However, in the case of psychological suffering, the social context not only plays a crucial part in creating and prolonging suffering, but it also determines the form suffering takes and gives suffering its meaning. Psychiatric diagnoses, therefore, cannot be culture and context independent.

In biomedicine, diseases and treatments are usually defined on the basis of pathogens (such as bacteria or viruses) or disordered bodily processes or structures (such as arthritic joints or cancerous cells). By and large, biomedical practitioners diagnose and treat such causes, not symptoms. For example, fever is a presenting symptom of many biomedical conditions. Physicians therefore do not primarily aim to treat fever; they identify and treat the specific causes of fever. By contrast, most psychiatric diagnoses consist of lists of presenting symptoms (for example, low mood, suicidal ideation, a sense of hopelessness). In some cases, an underlying disease may not exist; in many cases, an underlying disease has not been identified. A further contrast with biomedicine is that the treatments offered by mental health professionals (whether pharmaceutical, behavioral, or psychotherapeutic) nearly always address symptoms; they rarely address the causes.

Two other problematic assumptions are that psychiatric diagnoses are conditions that are discrete from one another and also discontinuous with normal behavior. That is, the logic of the DSM holds that each diagnostic category is a distinct disease and that each is clearly differentiated from normality. However, many experiences, such as depressed mood, anxiety, agitation, and difficulties in concentrating, sleeping, or eating, are symptom criteria for many diagnoses. Moreover, in everyday life, people customarily talk about and experience these difficulties on a continuum. For example, people use the word *anxiety* to speak about feelings ranging from worry to mild apprehension to full-scale panic.

Similarly, people use the word *depression* to cover a wide range of emotions from momentary "blues" to unrelenting and incapacitating demoralization.

Ordinarily, diagnoses of biomedical diseases can be made without reference to the social and cultural background of the patient. The disease model of psychological disorders similarly presupposes that judgments of normality and abnormality are akin to judgments of health and illness and therefore can be made without reference to social or cultural context. However, this presupposition is not valid: Psychiatric diagnoses necessarily depend on cultural and societal values, morals, and ideologies regarding acceptable and unacceptable behavior, as well as ideals about the good life. Consider, for instance, the various psychiatric diagnoses pertaining to sexuality. One example is the psychiatric diagnosis of nymphomania, which was applied during the late nineteenth and early twentieth centuries to women and girls who were viewed as having "excessive" sexual desire (Groneman, 1994; Hamreby, 2004). If cases were regarded as intractable, clitoridectomy might be recommended. The category of nymphomania dropped out of use when cultural views about female sexuality changed. Today, in what we might call the Viagra era, psychiatric diagnoses of sexual dysfunction have proliferated; however, what is labeled as abnormal is no longer "excessive" desire, but rather "inhibited" or "insufficient" sexual arousal and desire (Tiefer, 2006). Another example concerns the classification of homosexuality as a mental illness in modern, western psychiatry. Its official status in American psychiatry was changed by a referendum of the members of the American Psychiatric Association in the early 1970s; it was then removed from the next edition of the DSM in 1980. As with nymphomania and other kinds of sexual dysfunction, the "de-pathologizing" of homosexuality reflected a change in cultural and social values, not new scientific findings (Brante, 2006; Metcalfe and Caplan, 2004). The malleability of psychiatric diagnoses in response to cultural change is not unique to diagnoses concerning sexuality. It can be traced in many diagnostic categories, including autism, psychopathy, bipolar disorder, borderline personality disorder, attention deficit disorder, depression, multiple personality disorder, and eating disorders.

The power of social context and cultural meaning is even more apparent when we compare different cultures. For instance, the anthropologist Gananath Obeyesekere (1984) has noted that many of the cognitions, affects, and outlooks that western mental health professionals regard as symptoms of depression are understood among Theravada Buddhists in Sri Lanka as the recognition of existential truths about human existence. These experiences are embraced and sometimes deliberately cultivated through meditation practices. We look closer into other examples of cultural differences in the meanings ascribed to painful affects and problematic behaviors in the next section of this chapter.

To sum up, the idea that psychological disorders can be "packaged" as diseases and specified by lists of symptoms belies the fact that human actions and experiences are always embedded in social and cultural contexts. The norms and values of the cultural surround inevitably influence the psychiatric diagnoses developed in a particular setting. To hark back to the discussion of categories in Chapter 2, psychiatric diagnoses are *contingent* categories – that is, categories that emerge from ongoing collective efforts at meaning-making. When professionals view suffering as individual pathology, they draw attention away from the powerful effects of societal inequalities, and political and interpersonal oppression, as well as situational stresses.

The power of social and cultural contexts

Contextual influences are of particular interest to psychologists who are concerned with the relation of social injustice to psychic suffering. Such contextual influences include institutional arrangements, cultural norms and expectations, and interpersonal power relations. Around the world, for example, feminists have called attention to the extent of women's victimization in the form of gender-linked violence and (hetero)sexual violations. They have also called attention to the psychological harm that such victimization may cause, such as depression, anxiety, sexual and relationship difficulties, substance abuse, and severe dissociative reactions. Rape, stalking, harassment, and intimate violence persist unchecked more often than not. Women who have been victimized in these ways may be forced to make drastic life changes, such as leaving jobs, quitting school, moving to another locale, or "going underground" (Weinehall *et al.*, 2007). Further, victims' experiences in the criminal justice and medical systems set up to help them often constitute what has been called a "second victimization" (Campbell, 2008). Although no woman is completely protected from these abuses of power and masculine privilege, there are dramatic disparities in women's vulnerability. For example, women and girls living in impoverished urban communities are at particularly high risk (Miller, 2008), as are women living in chaotic conditions of war or displacement (Hyndman, 2008).

Culture plays a further role in shaping the meanings and attributions associated with gender-linked violence and abuse; such meanings in turn shape the psychological and social consequences (Haaken, 1998; Helliwell, 2000). All too often, women are blamed and shamed for their victimization. For example, in some cultural settings, a girl who has been sexually molested or a young woman who has been raped is deemed unmarriageable (Marecek and Appuhamilage, 2011). In some cultural settings, rape victims may be put to death in order to expunge the dishonor that their victimization has brought to the family. Also, as you read in Chapter 11, "bad" victims – those whose appearance, actions, or social background do not fit the ideal image of an innocent victim – risk being discredited or ill treated when they attempt to bring the offender to justice (Lamb, 1999). Indeed, such women may be more likely than others to hold themselves responsible and to excuse perpetrators (Phillips, 2000).

People experience and express psychological distress (i.e., their "symptoms") in ways that are patterned by their culture. Cultural researchers use such terms as *idioms of distress* or *symptom vocabularies* to capture this idea. For example, the configuration of feelings, thoughts, and bodily states that we call depression is specific to western, high-income countries (Jadhav, 1996; Kleinman, 1988). It is not common in many other countries and thus rates of depression in those countries are low (Marsella, 1978). In many cultural groups, people express or experience demoralization not through depressive thoughts and feelings, but through bodily experiences, such as pain, headache, fatigue, burning sensations, and cold sensations.

Another example of cultural patterning can be seen by considering schizophrenia. Schizophrenia is a condition that is widely regarded as having a substantial inherited component and associated brain pathologies. Nonetheless, culture seems to play a role in patterning the expression of schizophrenia, including the recognition of the disorder, the symptoms an individual presents, the course of the disorder, and family and community responses (Jenkins and Barrett, 2004). Comparisons of high-income, industrialized countries and unindustrialized "Third World" countries have shown that, at least in some "Third World" settings, people who have been diagnosed with schizophrenia have shorter periods of acute illness and a greater likelihood of substantial or complete remission over the course of several years than comparable individuals in Europe or the USA (Hopper *et al.*, 2007; World Health Organization, 1979). Although the risk of schizophrenia appears to be similar for men and women in Europe and North America, this is not true everywhere. In Ethiopia, for example, schizophrenia is diagnosed five times as often in men as in women (Alem *et al.*, 2009). Moreover, in Europe and North America, women tend to have a more favorable prognosis than men (Canuso and Padina, 2007); however, in some countries outside the west, it is men who have a more favorable prognosis (Alem *et al.*, 2009).

Cultural ideologies and local practices related to gender and ethnic identity also shape expressions of distress. For example, in western, high-income countries, troubled boys typically express more "externalizing" behaviors (such as aggression, disruptive behavior, conduct problems, and attention deficits) while troubled girls typically express more "internalizing" behaviors (such as anxiety or depression) (Swedish National Board of Health and Welfare, 2008, 2009). Rather than assuming that this is an expression of an innate sex difference, one might view the children as living up to the gender imperatives of their culture. In other words, they are engaging in the normal way to be abnormal (Eskner Skoger *et al.*, 2011). Another example is the high incidence of eating difficulties among some groups of girls and young women in western, high-income countries. As we noted in Chapter 11, there are racial, ethnic, and class-based differences in cultural meanings of the body, food, and eating in these countries. In middle-class, white European and North American culture, the overvaluation of thin female bodies, the high social utility placed on women's bodily appearance, and the moral value placed on bodily control and self-discipline all play a role.

Culture and social context also influence the judgments of normality and abnormality that mental health professionals make. Psychiatric diagnoses, as we pointed out earlier, are imbued with cultural norms regarding the appropriateness, meaning, and morality of behavior. For example, when does caution cross over the line between "normal" prudence and "abnormal" phobic avoidance? When does shyness become the clinical disorder social phobia? The role of cultural meanings is particularly apparent when mental health professionals work across cultural divides. For example, mental health practitioners in the USA are taught that normal bereavement should last no longer than 2 months. In contrast, the proper period of mourning prescribed for widows in some countries (for example, India, Nepal, and Greece) is a year. Also, in many cultures, it is normative (and highly functional) to worry continually about secret enemies and the possibility of sabotage by close associates and neighbors (Adams, 2005). Worries like this might be regarded as paranoia in some other cultures. In some cultures, it is expected that recently deceased relatives will speak to their loved ones as they slowly make their way to another world; according to western diagnostic systems, "hearing voices" of this sort is a paradigmatic symptom of psychosis.

If mental health professionals judge behavior through the lens of culture, then gendered meanings and gender-specific norms, as well as the class and ethnic backgrounds of professionals, will influence clinical judgments. Such diagnostic criteria as "inappropriate" anger, "excessive" crying, and "intense fear" of gaining weight, for example, are unlikely to be free of cultural ideologies of gender or of cultural values specific to class and social background. In addition, mental health professionals may overlook the constraints imposed by social class, racial discrimination, and gender norms and thus hold people responsible for situations outside their control or mistake adaptive responses to adversity for clinical symptoms. For example, Lorraine Radtke, a feminist psychologist in Canada (2009), observed that researchers and clinicians underestimated the dangers faced by women with violent partners and, consequently, tended to judge the strategies that these women used to protect their children as "bad parenting." Another example is drawn from an account given by Michelle Fine (1989) of counseling a rape victim in the emergency room of an urban hospital in the USA. Fine, a feminist psychologist, described "Altamese," a young African-American woman who had been gang-raped by neighborhood men. Altamese refused to inform the police; she declined counseling and did not want referrals to social service agencies. She wanted only to go home and put the experience out of her mind. Many diagnostic labels might be placed on Altamese, such as "learned helplessness" or "passive personality." Fine argued, however, that Altamese's choices were not a reflection of inner psychopathology but of her external circumstances. As a young, poor, Black unmarried mother, living in a chaotic and violent urban neighborhood, Altamese was unlikely to receive fair treatment from the criminal justice system. Moreover, if Altamese sought help from the police, she would put herself, her children, her mother, and her brothers in jeopardy. To hark back to the discussions of reasons and causes in Chapters 3 and 5, paying attention to Altamese's reasons sheds more light on her actions and choices than searching for causes that attribute her actions to psychopathology or personality. Moreover, taking seriously Altamese's reasons exposed the deeply oppressive conditions under which Altamese lived – conditions that many poor women in many parts of the world share.

Taking the long view

What are the implications of these discussions? First, we have argued that diagnostic categories are not stable, disease-like entities, but rather cultural products that are influenced by a variety of social and political forces. If this is so, then research aimed at documenting sex differences in the incidence and prevalence of various disorders is of limited value. (We take up the subject of sex-difference research in Chapter 14.) In addition, researchers need to be wary of comparing the incidence of disorders across time, cultural groups, ethnic categories, or regions of the world. Such comparisons likely involve a categorical fallacy – that is, lifting a diagnostic category from one cultural setting and projecting it onto people in a quite different one (Kleinman, 1988).

As we noted earlier, the number of psychiatric diagnoses in the diagnostic manuals has increased, at the same time as the criteria for many diagnoses have loosened. Therefore, more and more individuals meet the criteria for more and more diagnoses, and more and more individuals become candidates for treatment (Kärfve, 2006). In some cases, this expansion is the result of active claims-making and marketing by interested parties (Hacking, 1995). For example, for the past several years, there have been aggressive efforts in the USA to promote the new diagnosis childhood bipolar disorder, funded heavily by a pharmaceutical company that manufactures a relevant medication. In roughly fifteen years, the number of children who have received this diagnosis has increased fourteen-fold. Another example, also from the USA, concerns autism. Until recently, autism was thought to affect three children in 10,000; today, advocates for the disorder claim that autism affects one in every 110 children. If this were true, it would represent an increase of 660 percent since the mid-1990s (Grinker, 2007): a true epidemic. There is no way to find out the "actual" prevalence of autism. Its definition and the diagnostic criteria are in flux. Moreover, the criteria are applied in different ways in different locales (Kärfve, 2006). There have been similar (though less dramatic) shifts in criteria for diagnosing ADD/ADHD, PTSD, depression, and eating disorders. Some people applaud the expanding reach of the mental health professions as a beneficent effort to relieve suffering, but others are wary of overdiagnosing and overmedicating (Brante, 2006; Summerfield, 2006; Tannenbaum and Rochon Ford, 2006). For instance, feminists have criticized the practice of prescribing psychotropic medication or psychotherapy to women, while leaving unexamined the material and sociopolitical difficulties they face (Hare-Mustin, 1983; Ussher, 2010).

In the eyes of feminists and other critical psychologists, psychiatric diagnoses – no matter whether they serve a useful purpose – are a potent form of social regulation. The increased number of diagnostic categories serves to bring more and more aspects of daily life under the gaze of the mental health professions. Psychiatric diagnoses are prime examples of interactive categories (which we have discussed in Chapter 2). Diagnoses do not merely label behavior; they shape the way people understand and experience themselves. Diagnoses also govern the social meanings of that behavior. A diagnosis influences moral judgments made about an individual, as well as his or her social standing and social relationships. What follows, for instance, when eccentricities or mild forms of social deviance are relabeled as psychiatric diagnostic categories? And what follows when behaviors that were matters for the criminal justice system (e.g., shoplifting, gambling, drunkenness, and sexual assault) are similarly relabeled? (Cushman, 2002; Hacking, 1998; Horwitz, 2002; Kirk and Kutchins, 1992).

Questions about the truth status of diagnoses, and of their power of social regulation, become even more acute if we take a global perspective. During the era of European colonial imperialism, psychiatrists posted to colonized countries frequently rendered judgments about the psychological maturity of their colonial subjects. Noting the low incidence of depression among native populations in such areas as colonial Africa, Malaysia, and Java, psychiatrists deemed the people of those regions to be irresponsible and unthinking and characterized by a primitive psychological organization and psychic underdevelopment (Fernando, 2003). Pronouncements like these, of course, served to reaffirm the colonial rulers' assertions that their native subjects were incapable of governing themselves and required foreign rule (Hook, 2004a). In this way, mental health professionals served as agents of social and political control; their ministrations, masked as care, served to justify colonial rule (Duncan *et al.*, 2004).

It is ironic that feminists and other critics have taken issue with many aspects of psychiatric categorization at the same time as the language of psychiatric diagnosis and disease has swept into popular usage in several western societies. For many, the intrusion of this and other forms of "psy talk" into everyday life is alarming. Some have charged the mental health professions (and pharmaceutical companies) with "disease-mongering" (Moynihan *et al.*, 2002). The term refers to such practices as widening the boundaries of diagnostic categories, inventing new categories of disorder (such as "internet addiction," "money disorders," "atypical theft offender disorder," and "cellphone dependence"). Other critics object to lavish advertising campaigns, school-based prevention programs, celebrity testimonials, and infomercials that are ostensibly intended to inform the public. Too often these endeavors are designed and paid for by pharmaceutical companies seeking to expand the market for their products.

Conclusion

The use of the disease metaphor of psychological suffering focuses attention "beneath the skin and between the ears," to use the sociologist Hugh Mehan's (1993) evocative phrase. This chapter criticized diagnostic practices that attribute psychological suffering primarily to hypothetical, disease-like entities "inside" the person. These practices conceal or negate the potent role of the sociopolitical, material, and cultural context. Ignoring such sources of distress deflects attention from difficult, value-laden questions about what is wrong with the social order. When people's responses to the chaotic conditions of urban poverty, or to prolonged thwarting of ambition and economic advancement, or to persistent intimate violence, or to armed warfare, are viewed and managed primarily as mental health problems, one may lose sight of the fact that they are also social problems requiring social change.

Many feminist theorists and researchers have challenged and criticized the diagnostic systems, the disease model of mental illness, and specific diagnoses. They have also produced an alternative body of knowledge about the social and cultural origins of women's experiences of distress and dysfunction. Activists and advocates have pressed for societal changes, such as changes in the law and public policies, as well as increased public support and community-based resources for sufferers. Many have engaged in developing forms of psychotherapy and counseling that build on feminist ideals and practices. The next chapter turns to these psychotherapeutic practices and their historical development.

13   Feminism and gender in psychotherapy

In little over a hundred years, psychotherapy has expanded from a tiny, marginal, quasi-medical profession to a multi-billion-dollar healthcare industry. As we said before, in the nineteenth century, the forerunners of modern-day psychiatrists limited themselves to managing "mad" people confined in lunatic asylums (as mental hospitals were then called). There were no clinical psychologists, counselors, family therapists, psychiatric social workers, or life coaches in those days. It was only in the latter half of the twentieth century that the reach of the mental health professions began to expand into everyday life as professionals shifted their sights toward making the general population more satisfied, better adjusted, and more productive (Horwitz, 2002). This expansion began in North America, where it has been especially pronounced, but similar patterns of growth have occurred in several other western, high-income countries.

People in many western, high-income countries today turn to therapeutic experts for authoritative advice about who they are, who they could be, and who they should be. Consultations with psychotherapists are no longer restricted to mental hospitals or even to therapy offices. Instead, therapeutic experts dispense advice via TV talk shows, the internet, self-help books, radio call-in programs, and self-improvement videotapes and seminars. Therapeutic experts render judgments and advice in courtrooms, in educational settings, in general medical practices, in election campaigns, and in government departments of defense, security, and intelligence. And therapeutic experts rush to give assistance at sites of manmade and natural disasters, as well as criminal investigations. Therapeutic practitioners are called on to offer expert evaluation, advice, relief, and reassurance for nearly every aspect of people's lives from infancy to death.

As mental health practitioners moved beyond treating the "mad" in institutions and into the everyday world, women became the prime users of their services, whether on their own behalf or to get care for their children and families. Therapeutic culture thus created a space and a

145

language for women's discontents; however, that language did not go uncontested. Even before the turn of the nineteenth century, the American feminist thinker Charlotte Perkins Gilman raised objections to a diagnosis and treatment regimen often prescribed for women (Gilman, 1892/1980). Closer to the mid-twentieth century, feminist psychoanalysts, notably Karen Horney (1967) and Clara Thompson (1964/1971), offered trenchant critiques of central elements of Freud's theory of female development and of psychoanalytic models of femininity. The critical scrutiny intensified as women's movements took hold in the 1970s. Feminists of that era challenged the mental health professions' ways of diagnosing and conceptualizing women's difficulties (Chesler, 1972; Greenspan, 1983; Hare-Mustin, 1983; Lerman, 1986). They also put forward new theories of femininity (Eichenbaum and Orbach, 1985; Miller, 1976) and offered new models for therapy (Axelsen, 1984; Burstow, 1992; Frithiof, 1984).

We begin with a discussion of the protests that feminists lodged against the mental health professions and of the broad legacy of critique and challenges to diagnostic and therapeutic orthodoxy. Then we describe some elements central to feminist therapies; these elements reflect efforts to translate feminist principles into practical action. We next describe the efforts of some feminist practitioners to stand aside from the coercive and ideological power that mental health institutions wield, and to challenge that power. Last, we discuss the development of narrative approaches in feminist therapy, which make use of narrative therapy strategies to help clients to observe and challenge the effects of ideological power in their lives.

Feminist protests against psychotherapy and psychiatry

In 1963, Betty Friedan published *The feminine mystique*, a scathing critique of middle-class American family life of the 1950s. Friedan, who had studied psychology at university, argued that the ready acceptance of Freudian ideas about femininity and about women's mental health in the post-war USA had "dehumanized" and "infantilized" women. The Freudian view, she said, encouraged women to suppress their ambitions and interests in order to achieve fulfillment through marriage, domesticity, and motherhood. Even though middle-class housewives were regarded as (and regarded themselves as) having attained the American dream, she argued that many of them were plagued by diffuse feelings of depression and a persistent sense of emptiness and meaninglessness. Friedan labeled these experiences "the problem with no name," and she accused experts such as psychotherapists, child psychologists, and theorists of human development of having set a trap for women. *The feminine mystique*, described by one commentator as the book that "pulled the trigger on history," struck a chord in middle-class readers. The book, which sold three million copies and was translated into several languages, served as an important impetus to the nascent women's movement.

By the beginning of the 1970s, the new women's movement had gathered steam in many western countries. The movement engaged a broad swath of women in self-reflection and social critique, often in a small-group format known as "consciousness-raising." Feminist activists also vigorously protested against many forms of institutionalized and interpersonal discrimination and oppression. The protests soon turned on the mental health professions and the ideas about normal female development and femininity they propounded. Feminist thinkers in academic psychology and in the mental health professions challenged psychological theories that denigrated and pathologized women who stepped outside the norms of the time (for example, lesbians, career-oriented women, single women, women who chose not to have children, and feminists). These feminist critiques of the mental health professions resonated with those of many other social critics of the time who had voiced concern about the power of psychiatric authorities to define normality and deviance.

Feminists as theorists and practitioners of psychotherapy

Feminists in the mental health professions soon moved from critique to the project of developing new approaches to therapy. The 1970s was a time of heady conversations about an overarching ethical framework for psychotherapy and counseling based on feminist ideals of equality and social justice. The 1970s was also a time when feminist practitioners experimented with therapy techniques (such as consciousness-raising and other forms of group work) that embodied feminist ideals. In subsequent decades, feminist practitioners developed therapeutic approaches for diverse populations of women and for specific problems that were common among women. These included eating problems, adult difficulties stemming from childhood sexual abuse, sexual victimization, and agoraphobia.

The takeup of feminist ideas has varied considerably across different schools of psychotherapy. Feminist thinking had its greatest impact among family therapists, narrative therapists, and counseling psychologists.

Today, however, there are few, if any, approaches to psychotherapy and counseling in which feminist practitioners and theorists have had no impact. Even psychoanalysis, originally the target of feminist ire, now boasts a large cadre of feminist theoreticians and practitioners and a body of sophisticated feminist theory (e.g., Dimen and Goldner, 2002; Goldner, 1999). Carolyn Zerbe Enns (1993/2010) has provided good overviews of the range of principles and practices promoted by feminist therapists. Several feminist principles concerning ethical practice, power relations, and integrity in the conduct of therapy have been integrated into the general standards of good practice in psychotherapy. Feminist practitioners have also devised models for clinical assessment that shifted the diagnostician's focus from a narrow concern with symptoms to a broad assessment of the relational and cultural context of a client's life, her or his strengths, and the resources and constraints afforded by a client's material and sociocultural circumstances (Worell and Remer, 1992/2002). Members of the Feminist Therapy Institute (FTI) developed a code of ethics for feminist therapists (Brown, 1991; Lerman and Porter, 1990). Perhaps one of the most striking aspects of the FTI code is that it holds that feminist therapists should be active in social change beyond therapy (for example, via public education, professional advocacy, and lobbying for legislative actions).

Feminist practitioners brought the analysis of gender into psychotherapeutic theory and practice. The initial focus was mainly on women, but this focus expanded during the 1980s, as the gendered nature of men's lives became a popular concern and as some male therapists became interested in questions of masculinity. Feminists' central premise was that people's experiences – and their emotional difficulties, personal distress, and relationship problems – were inextricably tied to the larger societal context, to their place in the social structure, and to cultural discourses. To repeat a well-worn slogan of the women's liberation movement, "the personal is political." For feminist therapists, a therapy client's private experiences are not solely her own; they are part of a matrix of interpersonal relations and also part of a broader pattern of relations of power in society. The issues to be addressed in therapy thus must be understood in the context of a client's interpersonal relationships and her location within structures of power and privilege, as well as the cultural meaning systems that shape her worldview.

The field of marital and family therapy (now often referred to as couples therapy) was an especially fertile field for the development of feminist thinking. Feminists in the field put forward analyses of gender relations in heterosexual couples and in gay and lesbian couples. They argued that relations between members of a heterosexual couple were inevitably shaped by gendered asymmetries in the larger society (such as women's lesser earning power) and by cultural norms and practices regarding marriage and families. Feminists in family therapy also called attention to gender-linked physical violence in couples and to the sexual abuse of female children in families. Some key contributors to feminist family therapy in the USA were Virginia Goldner (1985, 1999), Rachel Hare-Mustin (1987), and the Women's Project in Family Therapy, which was codirected by Betty Carter, Peggy Papp, Olga Silverstein, and Marianne Walters. Feminists also developed new ways of theorizing masculinity and of working with men in therapy. Examples include the work of Louise Silverstein (2001), as well as collections of essays by Christopher MacLean, Maggie Carey, and Cheryl White (1996) and by Michele Bograd (1990).

A different approach to therapy with women was put forward by the Stone Center, a group of therapists associated with Wellesley College in the USA and led by the psychiatrist Jean Baker Miller. The theories developed by this group focused on what they saw as women's special needs for connection and relationships and what they saw as the special capacities of female therapists for empathy (Jordan et al., 1991; Miller and Stiver, 1997). Many therapists and counselors have found such ideas of natural feminine empathy, capacity for connection, and need for relationships appealing. Other feminist psychologists, however, criticized the assumption of an essential female nature and the focus on differences between men and women (Becker, 2005; Hare-Mustin and Marecek, 1990).

In recent years feminist therapists – like feminist scholars and researchers – have increasingly endeavored to understand and address the psychological harm connected to racial and ethnic inequality, class injustices and poverty, and immigration, as well as to homophobia and heteronormativity. They have also endeavored to understand the life experiences, personal strengths, and community resilience of people from racial and ethnic minority backgrounds, as well as individuals who do not identify as heterosexual. Feminist therapists have also scrutinized their own clinical theories and practices for implicit racism, ethnocentrism, class bias, homophobia, and heteronormativity (Bryant-Davis et al., 2009; Comas-Diaz and Greene, 1994; Lyness, 2006; Root and Brown, 1990; Szymanski et al., 2008).

Gender, power, and ethics in psychotherapeutic relations

The remainder of the chapter takes up the intertwined issues of power and ethics in therapy relationships. These issues have been of central concern to feminists in the mental health professions, regardless of their specific theoretical orientation or the specialty areas of their work. The first section below discusses what we call "power on the inside" – that is, relations of power in client–therapist relationships. We describe some new practices that feminists developed in order to redistribute the balance of power more equally between therapist and client. In the second section, we turn to "power on the outside" – the institutional structures in which therapy is embedded and the ways in which these structures shape therapeutic practices and therapists' identities. We describe feminist psychotherapists' efforts to make the institutional context of therapy relationships visible and to challenge institutional practices that reaffirm and sustain oppressive relations in society. In the third section, we consider cultural ideology – what we have called the "power of the ordinary" – in therapy. We use the metaphor of "discourses in a mirrored room" to capture the idea that dominant discourses, such as those concerning gender, often predetermine the content of therapy conversations. These dominant discourses circulate between therapist and client, akin to mirrored images bouncing back and forth. We discuss the work done by feminist narrative therapists to heighten therapists' reflective awareness of these discourses.

Power on the inside

The first practitioners who identified themselves as feminist therapists were part of the women's liberation movement of the 1970s (Mander and Rush, 1974; Marecek and Hare-Mustin, 1991; Viestad, 1977). As part of the women's movement, they held equality between men and women as a central goal and they opposed the large-scale subordination of women in private relations and in public life. They also challenged the treatment of women in therapy relationships, arguing that, both in process and in content, psychotherapy perpetuated the pattern of male dominance and female subordination that permeated the society at the time. With regard to therapy relationships, the American psychotherapist Phyllis Chesler (1972), for example, argued that because most therapists at that time were men and most clients were women, therapy dyads often resembled a patriarchal marriage. In Chesler's eyes, such dyads involved female clients in relations of dependency and submission to the authority of male therapists. With regard to the content of therapy, feminists argued that therapy often served to adjust women to patriarchal norms of society, rather than challenging or questioning those norms.

Feminist therapists looked for ways to undo the dominant position of therapists and the subordinate role of their clients in their own practice.

Some feminist practitioners experimented with ways of investing power in their clients. One example was the use of therapy contracts. By negotiating contracts as the therapy began, clients and therapists jointly decided such aspects of therapy as the problems to be addressed, the responsibilities and contributions of therapist and client, and how they would jointly evaluate progress (Hare-Mustin *et al.*, 1979). Another example was the use of group therapy for women, with the therapist limiting her role to that of a facilitator (Johnson, 1976). This group model was intended to confer control and responsibility on the group members, to foster their autonomy and self-sufficiency, and to highlight for the women in the group the value of their everyday knowledge and expertise.

Feminist practitioners also put forward models of psychological assessment that went beyond symptom-focused diagnostic interviews to explore a client's life experiences and to place them in the context of her personal relationships, and the social and cultural setting in which she lived. In addition, some feminist therapists adopted the practice of making explicit inquiries about experiences of intimate violence or sexual abuse in a client's life, knowing that women might be reluctant to mention these problems without receiving a signal that it was acceptable to do so. As we discussed in Chapter 12, formal diagnoses typically signal that the client's problem is "inside" her and that it is she who needs to change. Feminist assessments reframed clients' difficulties by connecting them to their life situations. Abstracted symptoms might be reframed as responses to difficult relational contexts or as strategies (albeit not necessarily the best ones) for coping with distressing life circumstances. Moreover, feminists were concerned that what is regarded as normal reflects the experiences and perceptions of dominant groups. Such norms confer a privileged status on members of dominant groups and place a positive value on their experiences. Feminist therapists pointed out that conventional ideals of mental health and personal maturity reflected masculine ways of being and behaving, and also ways of being and behaving associated with white, middle-class individuals, both male and female, and with heterosexual individuals. Another aspect of feminist models of assessment was careful attention to clients' strengths, to their resources and networks of support, and to the efforts they had made to alter their situations prior to seeking professional help (Worell and Remer, 2002).

Shifting the role of the therapist

Not only did feminist therapists devise practices intended to increase clients' power in therapy, but they also devised practices intended to minimize their own power vis-à-vis clients. For example, many advocated that therapists assume a less formal and more interactive stance, and more "real" presence, in comparison to the distanced, silent, and "abstinent" role that had originated in orthodox forms of psychoanalysis but had become more widespread. Furthermore, among the many asymmetries built into the therapist–client relationship, feminists noted especially the asymmetry in personal disclosure. In most forms of therapy, clients were required to disclose intimate details about their lives and to share their private thoughts. In classic psychoanalytic psychotherapy, for example, clients were enjoined to "say whatever comes to mind," no matter how embarrassing or seemingly irrelevant. Therapists, in contrast, not only remained largely silent, but also could refuse to answer direct questions asked by a client. Many feminist practitioners challenged this practice. They advocated that therapists share (albeit in a cautious and deliberate way) some information about themselves, their personal histories, and their emotions and experiences during the therapy sessions. Such disclosures, they argued, could serve to demystify the therapy process and the person of the therapist, and, in that way, diminish the therapist's power.

Experiments with more open therapist–client relationships and more sharing of experiences have spurred many reflective conversations and deliberations among feminist practitioners. What, for example, are the necessary conditions for such disclosures? What kinds of personal content should therapists disclose? What therapeutic purposes could be achieved by such disclosures? Under what conditions are such disclosures harmful? What are the ethical constraints on such disclosures? Over time, feminists' conversations opened out to incorporate broader issues of boundaries and boundary violations in therapy. As readers might surmise, feminists with different therapeutic orientations brought different visions of the therapeutic process and, therefore, different concerns and interests to these discussions.

Feminist therapists' concerns about gendered power hierarchies in the larger society sensitized them to power inside therapy relationships and to the risk of inadvertently exploiting clients' vulnerabilities. They insisted that therapists need to understand the subtle power dynamics inherent in therapy and interrogate the role of power in their work as therapists and as trainers and clinical supervisors. The discussions, which were framed in terms of ethical practice, opened the way to wider discussions of boundary violations, dual relationships, conflicts of interest, and frank abuses of power in therapeutic encounters. The latter included sexual relations with clients in the course of therapy. These explorations of power and inequality in therapy opened the way to revisions in the guidelines for therapy practice promulgated in some professional associations. In some countries, feminist activism forced changes in the ethical standards of the mental health professions and the inclusion of explicit and stringent standards regarding sexual contact between therapist and client.

There are, of course, paradoxical elements in the innovative practices that feminists tried. For example, "handing over" power to clients in therapy was intended to foster their empowerment – that is, autonomy, independence, self-determination, and self-confidence. This way of think-ing about power sees it as a trait or quality that is lodged inside an individual. It does not take note of the extent to which gendered power is a feature of the societal structure, not a characteristic of single individ-uals. Moreover, from a systems perspective, the idea that a therapist has the capacity to "hand over" power to a client (or not) implies that the therapist has power over power. In other words, he or she possesses a kind of meta-power. Yet another set of concerns is raised by the idea of "empowering" clients. Some feminist therapists looked askance at the assumption that autonomy and self-determination should be taken uncrit-ically as goals of psychotherapy (or criteria of mental health). The ideal of autonomy, with its close connection to liberal individualism, is not equally valued across all cultures. Even within western, high-income countries, it is inconsistent with the values, assumptions, and practices of many social groups (Hare-Mustin and Marecek, 1986). Moreover, even if autonomy is highly valued, it may not be equally accessible to all members of the group. Another paradox that some feminist therapists encountered was that their clients were not all that eager to share power. For example, some clients were reluctant to engage in making contracts with their therapist because the notion of a contract signified binding obligations, chicanery, and hidden fees. In other cases, clients had sought therapeutic help with the aim of receiving expert advice; they were disap-pointed and confused when their therapists vacated the role of expert and instead offered to help them find their own solutions.

No therapist can remove power from therapy relationships by personal effort, no matter how diligent. A therapy relationship is not just a private relationship between a therapist and a client. It is inevitably embedded in the institutional framework of the mental health professions and in society at large.

The outside of therapy: an ethics of resistance

In the 1970s when feminist therapy was gaining in prominence, a substantial proportion of therapists was engaged in the independent practice of psychotherapy. In the ensuing years, such independent practice of psychotherapy has all but died out in many countries. One way or another, few therapists now work independently as solo practitioners; most work within institutional settings. Therefore, we must ask about therapists' power relations *outside* therapy as well as *inside* therapy. In doing so, we turn our sights to the institutional and corporate settings in which therapy is now situated. These include publicly funded clinics; state-supported, employer-supported, and privately funded payment schemes; state psychiatric hospitals; school-based counseling services; and so on. When therapists work within such frameworks, how are they implicated in larger systems of institutional power?

To address this question, we turn to the writings of a group of feminist practitioners who reflected at length on their work in various mental health settings in Canada (Rossiter *et al.*, 1998). As these practitioners noted, the ideas, discourses, and practices of such institutions flow freely into therapeutic work with clients. Despite the privacy and confidentiality accorded to therapeutic relationships, the boundary separating such relationships from their institutional settings is far from impermeable. The Canadian practitioners reported, among other things, that clients received differential treatment according to their gender, class, race, ethnicity, and sexuality. Such differences were often so deeply embedded and routine that they were nearly unnoticeable.

Situating therapy and mental healthcare in the institutional setting where it takes place brings a number of critical ethical questions to the fore. For example, how do therapy and other forms of mental healthcare operate as social control in modern societies? How do the discourses of mental health institutions, along with specific therapeutic practices, foster practices of self-discipline and self-surveillance? (Rose, 1996; see also Chapters 11 and 12). As we discussed in Chapter 12, mental health professionals who work in institutional settings routinely must classify people as "healthy" or "sick" and classify people's actions and thoughts as "normal" or "abnormal." In what ways does such classifying promote conformity (willing or not) to societal dictates? As we have said, the use of medical metaphors like abnormal and sick conceals the social regulation involved in these judgments (Edelman, 1982).

Rossiter and her colleagues examined their own professional experiences and work conditions for evidence of the ways that mental health practitioners are subjected to the disciplinary power of the state, of corporate medicine, and of institutions of care such as hospitals, clinics, and other mental health services. They noted that practitioners were continually obligated to comply with numerous regulations imposed by these settings. Moreover, therapists' identities and worldviews were inevitably reshaped by the institutional structures within which they worked and by their roles in those institutions. One example was the institutionalized hierarchy between the professionals and the patients. To sustain this hierarchy, therapists were continually required to engage in elaborate role enactments involving demeanor, dress, language, and self-presentation (Rossiter *et al.*, 1998). Another way that the hierarchy between professionals and patients was secured was through the use of assessments and diagnoses that often rendered patients' meanings and explanations of their difficulties as irrelevant or misguided, or as symptoms that served to confirm their diagnosis (for example, labeling patients' ways of understanding their experiences as "faulty cognitions," "depressogenic" thinking, or "projective identification"). In a study of Swedish psychotherapists who identified as feminists, Anna Indra Windh (2005) uncovered a similar pattern of institutional forces. Windh reported that these psychotherapists felt that the individualist thinking and biomedical approaches that were institutionalized in their work settings deprived them of space to act in accord with their principles and ethical ideals or to make use of their contextualized understanding of their patients' difficulties.

As a counter-strategy for feminists working in mental health institutions, Rossiter and her coworkers (1998) proposed what they called an *ethics of resistance* – that is, a stance of continual vigilance and active resistance to the disciplinary power of those institutions. Such an ethics of resistance does not replace the ethics of power-sharing that we discussed above, but rather complements it. An ethics of resistance calls for therapists and other mental health practitioners to scrutinize the ways in which their everyday routines and therapeutic practices may become caught up in societal structures of power and even complicit with those structures (see Guilfoyle, 2008, for a similar discussion that pertains specifically to cognitive behavior therapy). A fundamental aspect of an ethics of resistance is rigorous self-scrutiny that entails learning to discern the normalizing discourses that can lead therapists to choose to embrace the regimes of power to which they are subjected.

Discourses in the mirrored room: productive power in therapy

Rachel Hare-Mustin, a psychologist whose ideas have profoundly influenced the development of feminist family therapy, used the metaphor of a "mirrored room" to represent the idea that conversations in the therapy room cannot go beyond reflecting back the discourses that a therapist and a client bring into the room (Hare-Mustin, 1994).

Both the content of the therapeutic conversations and the solutions to the clients' difficulties are often predetermined by dominant societal discourses, because these discourses are likely the ones that both client and therapist embrace. Dominant discourses reflect prevailing cultural ideologies, including ideologies about gender relations, masculinity, femininity, family life, and sexuality. Alternate discourses that challenge these ideologies usually remain subordinated or marginalized. If the therapist and the client are unaware of these subordinated discourses, then the "mirrors" of the therapy room can only reflect back the prevailing ideologies and meanings.

Narrative therapy is a therapeutic approach that builds upon ideas about the power of dominant discourses and synthesizes them with Foucauldian ideas about productive and disciplinary power, such as those we discussed in Chapter 4 (White, 2007). Narrative therapists endeavor to develop reflective awareness of the operation of dominant discourses in clients' lives and to work with clients to bring forward subordinated discourses. Many feminist practitioners have been drawn to narrative therapy because it undertakes the task of disrupting productive (that is, ideological) power. Moreover, narrative therapy shares with feminist practice a commitment to genuine collaboration with clients, to respecting clients as authorities on their own life experiences, to avoiding language practices that pathologize clients, and to interrogating and challenging structural inequalities. In what follows, we briefly explore some of the practices of feminist narrative therapists, focusing especially on those that have the aim of subverting ideological power.

Like feminist therapists, narrative therapists hold that a reliance on formal diagnostic categories is not only insufficient but also harmful to clients. Narrative practitioners instead focus on stories: They work with clients to develop experience-near, "thick" accounts of their difficulties and of the problems that these difficulties have created in their lives. As part of the focus on storying experience, practitioners help their clients to explore in minute detail the effects of telling a particular, "problem-saturated" story about their lives, of telling the story to a particular audience, and of selecting only a narrow subset of many possible elements of their experiences to make into a story. This paves the way for retellings of lived experiences and for expanded life stories. These new stories may reshape the client's views of his or her earlier experiences and relationships, thereby reshaping identity or sense of self as well (Russell and Carey, 2003).

Narrative practitioners often say, "The person is not the problem; the problem is the problem." Reframing the individual's problems as "external" to the person is a core therapeutic strategy of narrative therapy. "Externalizing conversations" involve identifying and describing the client's problem as something that is separate from the person, examining the history of the problem, and tracing the trouble that the problem has made in the client's life. This strategy of assessment is distinctly different from traditional diagnostic assessment. But it is not only "technique": Michael White, the co-founder of narrative practice, has argued that suspending the use of conventional diagnostic categories is not simply a therapeutic technique. It reflects an epistemological commitment, as well as a political stance. According to White, it is a "counter-practice" that serves to objectify the problem, as opposed to what he calls "the cultural practices of objectification of people" (White, 2007, p. 26).

Narrative therapists rely on questions to invite clients to move away from mono-thematic "problem-saturated" stories to richer stories that include aspects of their experiences that were previously "unstoried" or dismissed. In narrative practice, one way to disrupt dominant and unhelpful stories that people tell about their lives is to expose and then question taken-for-granted discourses that support these stories. Feminist narrative practitioners, for instance, might invite clients to reflect on the ways that gendered relations of power in the broader society have influenced their lives. Narrative therapists also may pose questions that invite clients to reflect on dominant discourses that undergird the "problem-saturated" life stories they tell. With regard to gender relations, such dominant discourses may include those that naturalize men's violence and sexual domination; those that take as natural views of women as nurturant, self-sacrificing, and ever-forgiving; and those that render heterosexuality and heteronormativity as mandatory. Conversations in narrative therapy may also reflect on the cultural and interpersonal tactics that are responsible for promoting certain ideas and discourses and marginalizing others.

For narrative practitioners, psychotherapy is inevitably political. Therapy involves addressing problems that often have been created and sustained by relations of power, both at the interpersonal level and at the societal level. The practices of narrative therapy – such as externalizing conversations, generating experience-near accounts of problems, restorying subjugated aspects of personal history and identity, and reflecting on dominant discourses – aim to bring such power into awareness (Brown and Augusta-Scott, 2008).

Conclusion

Since the early 1970s, feminist psychotherapists and mental health professionals have developed a wide range of critical perspectives, theories, and therapeutic practices. We have focused on only a few of them. One is a commitment to create collaborative therapist–patient relationships that accord dignity to clients and that respect their ways of seeing the world. Another is feminists' sensitivity to relations of power in therapy, in the institutions of mental healthcare, and in society at large. A third is exposing and interrupting the workings of ideological power. As must be apparent, no single chapter (or even a whole book) could cover the multitude of ideas, critiques, practice-oriented knowledge, and ethical and moral debates that feminist practitioners across several countries have engaged in.

14   Comparing women and men: a retrospective on sex-difference research

Conversations about gender and psychology, casual conversations as well as scholarly debates, often begin with the question "What are the *real* differences between women and men?" We believe this question begs many questions that are more fundamental. Research on differences between men and women, or girls and boys, has been a part of psychology since the early days of the discipline. Such research has always been a site of contention, in part because researchers have conceived of both sex and gender in many ways. Research on male–female differences has long been criticized for oversimplified conceptions of sex and gender, as well as for methodological shortcomings that cannot be remedied. Yet, research comparing men and women has not abated. A search of PsycInfo, the major electronic database of psychological research, for articles on human sex differences and gender differences (terms the field has come to use interchangeably) yielded 4,011 hits for 2009.

We begin by reviewing the history of psychology's engagement with questions about the differences between men and women. We then discuss how this history has shaped the most common research approaches to these questions. We then proceed to a summary of contemporary research about psychological differences and similarities between women and men and between boys and girls. Then we examine the critiques that have been brought to bear on such research. These critiques have addressed not only methodological difficulties but also broader conceptual limitations and epistemological concerns. Finally, we discuss the strengths and weaknesses of the reductionist explanations that are often used in studies comparing men and women.

"Differences" in the history of gender in psychology

The question of differences between women and men, and boys and girls, has been a perennial focus of psychological research. "Difference" as the meaning of sex categories has dominated much of psychology's interest in sex and gender. The final decades of the nineteenth century and the first decades of the twentieth century were a time when fledgling psychologists were striving to establish psychology as a scientific discipline separate from philosophy. Two developments during that period were of particular importance for psychologists' study of sex and gender. One was the development of evolutionary theory and the other was the emergence of a feminist movement and women's demands for legal rights and suffrage.

Early evolutionary theory

The evolutionary theories that were developed in the latter half of the nineteenth century were important in shaping the young discipline of psychology (Richards, 2010). Early evolutionary theories portrayed the western white man as the most highly developed and intelligent organism, placing white women lower on the evolutionary scale, and non-white men and women lower still. White women and girls and all non-white people were posited as having less mature brains and bodies than white men. Most scientists believed that women's and men's different positions in the evolutionary hierarchy would manifest themselves in numerous mental traits. Women were expected to be inferior to men in intelligence as well as other psychological attributes, such as emotions. Taking men's superiority as self-evident, scientists looked for bodily sites of this superiority. For a long time, men's larger brains were seen as the site of, and explanation for, their intellectual superiority. However, this explanation did not survive the realization that there are several "lower" mammals that have larger brains than humans. Some researchers argued that one rightly ought to calculate brain size relative to body weight in order to gauge superiority; however, such calculations revealed that female brains were generally larger in proportion to body weight than male brains (Gould, 1981; Hamberg, 2005; Jordan-Young, 2010; Shields, 1975). Evolutionists who were convinced of men's superiority over women then proposed other bodily locations of this superiority, such as the size or shape of certain parts of the brain, or the size of certain other parts of the body (Rowold, 1996; Taylor and Shuttleworth, 1998). The unshakeable conviction of men's intellectual superiority was not to last, however. An important force that undermined this conviction was the women's movement.

The early women's movement

Around the end of the nineteenth century, a feminist movement took shape, giving voice to women's demands for civil rights and citizenship. Women in western countries gained many such rights during the first three decades of the twentieth century. The changes occurred against a backdrop of fierce political, civic, and scientific debates about whether women were fit to take part in public life on the same conditions and with the same responsibilities as men. In these debates, evolutionary ideas clashed with political activism informed by new social theories, including those put forward by feminists. Early psychologists were active on both sides of these debates, along with physicians, psychiatrists, and biologists (Bohan, 1992; Rosenberg, 1982; Scarborough and Furumoto, 1987; Taylor and Shuttleworth, 1998).

Nearly all the arguments against women's demands for political rights were couched in terms of women's putative differences from men. The arguments were usually framed in terms of medical, biological, evolutionary, or psychological evidence. The fields of education and medicine (especially gynecology), and parts of the budding fields of psychology and psychiatry were among the arenas where battles were fought about "the woman question," as it was often called. Some of those battles, such as those over the issue of whether higher education would shrink women's wombs and breasts, or make them infertile or mentally ill, may seem outlandish and bizarre these days, but such issues were hotly contested in those days (Russett, 1989; Showalter, 1987; Taylor and Shuttleworth, 1998).

The received truth of those days about "the Sex" (as women were often called) was that being female meant being naturally destined to a domestic life of childbearing and caring for family members. Women were thought to risk serious bodily and psychological damage if they pursued higher education or ventured into the public arena. Many social commentators of the day argued further that women were constitutionally unable to attain the intellectual and moral stature of men; therefore, educating women was simply a waste of resources. Feminists – both political activists and scientists – engaged in fierce public and scientific debates about such views.

Early psychology and difference thinking

It is not surprising that the cultural and scientific assumption of men's superiority – and the focus on how women differed from men – would be a central feature in early psychology. A number of psychologists during this early period searched for differences between women and men. For many of them, the impetus was a wish to show that there were many evolution-based psychological differences and that educators should bar girls from higher education (Hall, 1907). A few psychologists, such as the feminist Helen Thompson Woolley, had the opposite aim: to study men's and women's performances in order to show that there were very few differences (e.g., Woolley, 1910, 1914). This first phase of psychological research on sex differences roughly coincided with the period in which psychology established itself as an academic discipline. Thus, thinking about women and men in terms of "differences" was built into the discipline's ways of studying and thinking about sex and gender from its very beginnings. As the following discussion of meta-analyses of sex-difference research shows, difference thinking remains a prominent strain of thought within the discipline. Moreover, this strain of thinking is still characterized by two opposing goals: either to demonstrate that intrinsic differences exist or to demonstrate that there are hardly any differences at all.

The discipline's tendency to frame questions about gender in terms of male–female differences may also reflect the prominence of difference-oriented thinking, especially group comparisons, in psychological research overall. Historians of psychology have pointed out that this tendency was built into the discipline's research methods. That is, early in the history of the discipline, priority was given to experimental and statistical techniques that favored the investigation of differences rather than commonalities (Danziger, 1985; Gigerenzer *et al.*, 1989; Robinson, 2000). Common statistical tests, for example, were based on theoretical assumptions that allowed the tests to show whether groups were different, but not whether they were identical. This historically shaped inclination to search for differences may well contribute to the inclination on the part of researchers and theorists to focus on "sex differences."

Could it be, then, that a difference focus in general and a "sex-difference" focus in particular during the early period of disciplinary consolidation left psychology with a legacy of assumptions and methods that leads many psychologists to think in terms of "difference" whenever sex categories or gender are in focus? Could this in turn explain the limited impact that critiques have had on this difference perspective? Could it perhaps also explain some of the difficulties that arise when one tries to "integrate gender perspectives" into conventional academic psychology? We return to these questions after the next section, which discusses research on women and men as it is typically carried out in conventional psychology.

Contemporary psychological research on differences between women and men

This section focuses on present-day research on psychological differences between women and men.[1] The question of "sex differences" is

---

[1] We emphasize that the research we write about in this chapter concerns intrinsic similarities or differences in individual abilities and traits. It is not about differential treatment or unequal conditions of women and men. We point this out, because expressions like "gender differences" and "differences between women and men" are sometimes used to refer to such unequal treatment of women and men or the different conditions under which they live.

a common starting point for discussions of gender and psychology. For instance, in the mass media, in popular psychology books about women and men, and in advice books, the focus is on putative ways that women and men differ. Sometimes it is claimed that these differences reflect innate and supposedly immutable traits based on evolution. In some cases, it is argued that the differences explain (and perhaps excuse) the social subordination of women. Are the claims of large psychological differences between women and men justified? Or might they be rhetoric that justifies the maintenance of gendered hierarchies and injustices? These are some of the many controversies that have surrounded research that compares women and men.

The research that we discuss here makes use of the methodological paradigms that have been dominant in much psychological research. That is, it relies on quantitative measurements and it is couched in a realist or empiricist epistemology (Slife and Williams, 1995). This research also stays within the bounds of the conventional two-sex model. That is, it assumes that there are two, and only two, sexes and that no more are possible. As we discussed earlier (in particular, in Chapters 2, 3, and 4), these paradigms are not the best ones for building an adequate psychology of gender.

Within psychology, research comparing women and men was originally called sex-difference research. Over the last few decades, however, it has become common to use the expression *gender-difference research* instead. Some writers wish to use the term *gender differences* to refer to characteristics that are supposedly more influenced by social processes and to use the term *sex differences* to refer to those that are closely connected to the bodily aspects of women and men. However, gender studies scholars have pointed out that this is a dubious distinction (e.g., Butler, 1990; Fausto-Sterling, 2000a). Moreover, researchers in psychology do not use these terms consistently. Regardless of which term is used, this kind of research compares the behavior or characteristics of women to the behavior or characteristics of men in order to draw conclusions about intrinsic differences or similarities between them. Throughout the chapter, we use the more neutral expression "psychological differences between women and men" whenever possible.

Are there psychological differences between women and men, and boys and girls?

The first answer to this question is likely to be "Of course there are psychological differences between men and women! Just look around and you will see how different women and men are." We agree: Men often engage in different activities than women, they are located in different places, and their physical appearance and demeanor often differ greatly from women's. Therefore, many of people's everyday experiences provide evidence of differences between the sexes. A few examples will suffice. Many men exercise in order to increase their body size, whereas many women exercise in order to decrease their body size. Many men have never had responsibility for the daily care of an infant, but many women have. Male and female students usually cluster in different disciplines when studying at the university level. More of those who commit violent crimes are men than women. Many more women than men are raped. And so on.

Although people may agree that such differences exist, they often disagree about the origin of the differences and, consequently, about what the differences ultimately mean. Some would say that women and men (and boys and girls) do different things because the sexes are different from each other in fundamental ways. This position is sometimes labeled "essentialist." Others would say that although women and men in a particular setting do different things, this does not reflect fundamental differences between the sexes, but rather socialization patterns and social pressures (see Bohan, 1993, for a review). Psychologists who base their thinking in one or the other of these two stances have studied possible differences and similarities between men and women for many years.

Results of research on psychological differences between women and men

Researchers have searched for differences between women and men in virtually every area of human behavior. The topics include aspects of children's psychological development such as cognitive, social, and moral development; several kinds of cognitive abilities in adults; personality traits; academic achievement; self-esteem; communication abilities and styles; leadership abilities; sexual behavior; aggressive behavior; health-related behaviors and attitudes; attitudes about gender equality; and frequency of various psychological disorders.

We first discuss compilations of the studies of differences between men and women or boys and girls. These compilations make use of a statistical technique called meta-analysis that was developed in the late 1970s to synthesize the results of many studies – sometimes more than a hundred. In the case of studies comparing women and men, the purpose of meta-analysis is to assess the stability and replicability of a difference (or similarity) across many studies. To make the studies reasonably comparable to one another, a statistic called "effect size" (d) is used. An effect size is computed for each study included in the meta-analysis. It adjusts the observed difference in mean values between women and men for the variation in the values for the group of women and the group of men who took part in the study (Hyde and McKinley, 1997). By using effect-size calculations, a researcher can say something about whether a difference obtained in a study is large enough to be of practical importance or so small that it is negligible. This is not possible by looking only at conventional statistical significance (that is, p levels). Significance tests show only whether there is a small or large risk that a particular difference has been obtained by chance. They say nothing about how large or meaningful an observed difference is. The effect-size calculation is an attempt to add that crucial piece of information. Generally, effect sizes below $d = 0.10$ are considered to be negligible (Hyde, 2005; Hyde and McKinley, 1997). Although researchers are not in full agreement about larger effect sizes, values of d from 0.11 to 0.35 are commonly considered to be small, those from 0.36 to 0.65 are considered moderate, and values of 0.66 and above are considered large.

Here we review reports of meta-analyses published after 1990. Readers interested in earlier work might consult the review by Janet Shibley Hyde (2005). The meta-analyses that show the largest differences between women and men (or in some studies girls and boys) are those that compile studies of motor behavior, such as throwing velocity (12 studies) and throwing distance (47 studies). Not surprisingly, these meta-analyses show that men and boys consistently outperform women and girls. Effect sizes for these differences are generally very large with ds in the range of 2.0 (Hyde, 2005; Spelke, 2005). Other meta-analyses that show substantial differences concern measures of sexual behaviors and sexual attitudes. For example, in a meta-analysis of ten studies, men had more favorable attitudes toward casual sex than women: ds about 0.8 (Oliver and Hyde, 1993). In a meta-analysis of ten studies of tender-mindedness (a personality trait involving compassion, as measured by paper-and-pencil inventories), women showed more tender-mindedness, with ds around 0.91 (Feingold, 1994).

Meta-analyses that show moderate effect sizes include those of studies measuring different kinds of aggressive behavior (75 studies of aggression in real-world settings; men show moderately more aggressive behavior; ds between 0.30 and 0.60 (Archer, 2004)). Meta-analyses find larger differences for physical aggression (41 studies) than for verbal aggression (22 studies) (Knight et al., 2002). Other meta-analyses report moderate effect sizes for frequency of smiling (418 studies), with women smiling more often than men (LaFrance *et al.*, 2003); assertiveness (10 studies with men showing more assertiveness (Feingold, 1994)); and spatial perception (92 studies) and mental rotation[2] (78 studies), with men having higher scores in both cases (Voyer and Bryden, 1995).

Meta-analyses that show small effect sizes concern, for instance, moral reasoning (women slightly higher on "care orientation" in 160 studies; men slightly higher on "justice orientation" in 95 studies; *d*s around 0.20 (Jaffee and Hyde, 2000)); perceptual speed (adolescent girls slightly faster than adolescent boys); and mathematical and science abilities (adolescent boys slightly higher on both) as measured in national surveys in the USA over a 30-year period (Hedges and Nowell, 1995).

Age differences
Some of the effect sizes reported in sex-difference research vary depending on the ages studied. Self-esteem is a case in point. Boys tend to score increasingly higher than girls from the age of 7 through secondary school, although the difference is never more than a moderate one. However, for adult women and men, a meta-analysis of 216 studies from several western countries found negligible effect sizes (*d*s around 0.10 (Kling *et al.*, 1999)).

Social context
Several meta-analyses show variations in effect sizes due to contextual factors. Studies of whether men or women interrupt more in conversation, for instance, show that men interrupt very slightly more than women (53 studies). The effect size varied, however, depending on the number of people present: In dyads, there was no male–female difference, but in larger groups, men interrupted more often than women (Anderson and Leaper, 1998). Other patterns of variation due to contextual factors were found. For example, when LaFrance *et al.* (2003) compiled 418 studies of smiling, they found that in studies in which the participants were aware of being observed, there were moderate differences in smiling frequency (girls and women smiling more than men and boys). However, in studies in which the participants were not aware of being observed, there were only small differences.

---

[2] Mental rotation is a type of spatial ability often included in intelligence tests. It is usually defined as the ability to mentally rotate an image of a three-dimensional object in order to picture how it looks from sides other than the one that is shown.

Cognitive sex differences or similarities:
the case of science and mathematics

In recent years, questions about the existence and size of differences between women and men in cognitive abilities have been driven by public concern about the low proportion of women studying science and mathematics at the university level and working in natural science professions. Although the number of women studying at universities has increased such that women students are now in a slight majority overall in many countries, the proportion of students in science, mathematics, engineering, and technology who are women remains low. Several explanations for this discrepancy have been suggested by policymakers and researchers. Some argue that women and men are by nature fit for different kinds of cognitive tasks, whereas others argue that the low number of women in science and mathematics is due to differential treatment of boys and girls, coupled with gendered cultural expectations.

When studies of the cognitive abilities of men and women are summarized today, the general verdict is that although there are some differences between girls and boys and between women and men, the differences are small and in many cases negligible (Halpern *et al.*, 2007; Hyde, 2005). A group of American researchers who recently reviewed the field cautioned that "[t]he similarities between males and females are so numerous and obvious that we tend to overlook them and take them for granted. We need to heed the caveats that the overemphasis on studies of differences can distort the countless findings of 'no significant differences' that routinely are ignored or unreported" (Halpern *et al.*, 2007, p. 4).

A recent study of the mathematics performance of seven million US schoolchildren between 7 and 17 years old (Hyde *et al.*, 2008) found practically no differences between girls and boys, regardless of their age. In no age group was the effect size larger than 0.06. The pattern was the same for children in all the ethnic groups they studied. Similar results have been found for other western countries, such as Sweden (Swedish National Agency for Education, 2007). One further feature reported by Hyde and her colleagues was that there was no discernible tendency for girls to have lower scores as the children reached adolescence. This finding is particularly interesting in the light of earlier findings of such tendencies and earlier assertions that their cause was the hormonal changes in girls that accompany puberty (Halpern *et al.*, 2007). If boys and girls nowadays do not perform differently in mathematics at puberty, it is hardly likely that earlier findings of differences at puberty were due to "hormones." Parallel findings, drawn from cross-national databases, were reported by Guiso *et al.* (2008) and by Else-Quest *et al.* (2010).

In discussing their findings of no sex differences in mathematics performance, Hyde *et al.* (2008) noted that exposure to mathematics courses in school has changed over time for children in the USA. Earlier, girls generally took less difficult mathematics courses as soon as mathematics courses became optional. For some time now, however, girls and boys in the USA have tended to take similar mathematics courses. This, the researchers argue, explains the current similarity in their mathematics performance.

Students who go on to higher studies of mathematics and science are those who have received grades at the top end of the distributions of grades in those subjects. Traditionally, boys have heavily outnumbered girls among the highest performers, but this pattern has changed. Whereas in the USA in the beginning of the 1980s there were as many as 13 boys for every girl who scored in the top range on mathematics tests, by 2005 this ratio had dropped to 2.8 boys per high-scoring girl (Halpern *et al.*, 2007).

In many western, high-income countries today, girls and boys perform equally well on nearly all measures of school performance or girls have an advantage. For instance, in Sweden, girls on average have higher grades than boys in practically all school subjects throughout secondary school (Swedish National Agency for Education, 2006, 2007). The advantage for girls is smallest, however, for mathematics and science, and in some cases, boys and girls perform equally. However, at the university level, men in western, high-income countries tend to outperform women in science and mathematics; this tendency becomes more pronounced at higher academic levels (Halpern *et al.*, 2007).[3] In an attempt to understand this pattern, a group of US experts looked into a range of possible explanations that might account for the low numbers of women who pursue academic science and mathematics careers (Halpern *et al.*, 2007). Below are some of their thoughts.

Could it be that girls, at critical points in their education, are less encouraged than boys to go on studying mathematics? Through such differential encouragement, are girls also encouraged to use different strategies of approaching mathematical problems and could this make a difference? Studies by Gallagher and DeLisi (1994) and Gallagher *et al.* (2002) hint at such a possibility. They found that on advanced

---

[3] In Sweden, for example, women in 2008 accounted for 33 percent of students studying mathematics at the university level. Women accounted for 24 percent of PhDs awarded in mathematics that year. The proportion of women among full professors of mathematics in Sweden was 7 percent. Similar disparities appear in many academic disciplines, although they are not so extreme.

mathematics tests at the university level (such as the GRE in the USA), the difference in scores favoring men can be either maximized or abolished by varying how the mathematical problems are presented. For instance, when instructions emphasized that optimal performance demands cognitive processes traditionally associated with men, differences between men and women were maximized.

Apart from the effects of such gendered expectations, the experts (Halpern *et al.*, 2007) also opined that the discriminatory treatment experienced by many women who engage in mathematics or science at university level likely influences their decisions to steer clear of these fields. Several researchers have documented such discrimination (Steele *et al.*, 2002; Stratton *et al.*, 2005; Wennerås and Wold, 1997).

Evolutionary theories are sometimes brought forward to explain the low participation of women in science and mathematics. Halpern *et al.* (2007) summarized such arguments. Advanced mathematics and science were not part of the evolutionary past, so evolutionary psychologists cannot claim that contemporary differences in men's and women's careers could have evolved directly. Rather, evolutionists might argue that the mathematics and science differences are indirectly related to other evolved differences in interests and abilities and in brain and cognitive systems related to those interests. Halpern and her colleagues, however, caution against this kind of argument: "A detailed consideration of potential indirect evolutionary influences on sex differences in math and science ... may not be possible given our current state of knowledge in these areas" (p. 20; see also Jordan-Young, 2010).

Critical opinions of sex-difference research

Gender scholars in psychology, especially those interested in social justice issues such as gender equality, have debated whether the study of psychological sex/gender differences is a worthwhile pursuit for psychology researchers (cf. Kitzinger, 1994). Some psychologists have argued forcefully in favor of sex-difference research. These psychologists do not all agree on the conclusions of the research so far. Some have claimed that research has shown few psychological differences between women and men (cf. Hyde, 2005). Others claim that the research shows large differences. Nonetheless, these psychologists argue for continuing such research. Some have even recommended that researchers always report research results for women and men separately, regardless of the original purpose of a study (Eagly, 1987). The reasons that these psychologists give are as follows. First, by reporting all sex comparisons, whether or not they show a difference, lingering, mistaken notions about male–female differences would be put to rest. Second, these psychologists argue, it is important to pinpoint the differences that exist in order to take them into account in social planning. These arguments imply that the researchers see women and men as social groupings that are homogeneous enough that it is possible to generalize about them. The arguments also rest on a faith that psychological research can uncover universal truths.

Other feminist psychologists are critical of the methods and conclusions of much sex-difference research. They argue that gender-biased practices of socialization and education have such foundational impacts on children that it is impossible to measure anything other than the effects of variations in such practices. One could never know the "true" psychological differences, if any. These scholars see observed differences between men and women as a kind of "icing on the cake" produced by socialization. The "cake" is the unknown original psychological differences, if any (Unger, 1979). According to these researchers, sex-difference research actually measures the effects of differential socialization practices and unequal treatment of women and men.

Yet other feminist psychologists argue that it makes little sense for psychologists to consider "women" and "men" as homogeneous categories that can be meaningfully compared in order to find out universal truths about their differences or similarities. These scholars argue that researchers need to specify *which* women and *which* men they are studying. Following from this, they also argue that researchers should not propose psychological theories about women and men as two homogeneous unitary categories. These scholars also point out that difference explanations risk reaffirming stereotypes about women and men and the mistaken image of women and men as homogeneous groups. By continuing to search for differences between women and men, these psychologists say, researchers will reinforce existing cultural ideas of the importance of "differences," even when they find no differences (Hare-Mustin and Marecek, 1994; Shields, 2008). Therefore, these feminist psychologists argue, psychology researchers should stop studying sex differences.

Against this general background, we now examine in some detail the most prominent critiques that feminist psychologists have made about psychological sex-difference research.

Falsely inflated claims of difference incur serious costs to both individuals and society

Janet Shibley Hyde (2005), in a much-cited article, summarized several decades of meta-analyses of psychological sex differences. She concluded that most studies found little difference: Therefore, it was more accurate to talk about studies of "gender similarities" rather than "sex differences." A research focus on "differences," she argued, invites researchers, policymakers, and others to make claims that go far beyond what the data justify. Hyde pointed to the costs of such exaggerations, especially those that reaffirm established stereotypes. She offered the example of long-standing ideas that boys are better than girls at mathematics. She argued that these ideas had been shown to be false. If the stereotype of girls' lesser mathematical abilities persisted, then there was a risk that mathematically talented girls would not be encouraged (or their talents even noticed) by parents and teachers.

Hyde also pointed to research in the USA showing that parents had lower expectations of their daughters' mathematics performance than their sons'. Frome and Eccles (1998), for instance, reported that although sixth-grade girls earned better grades in mathematics than boys, the children's parents rated girls' and boys' ability similarly. Either parents of girls underestimated their daughters' mathematics abilities or parents of boys overestimated their sons' abilities. Girls also received higher grades than boys in language arts. In contrast to mathematics, for language arts parents of girls attributed greater ability to their daughters than parents of boys attributed to their sons. Frome and Eccles concluded that cultural stereotypes of mathematics as "masculine" keeps parents from acknowledging their daughters' actual performance and grades in mathematics. The study also found significant correlations between parents' expectations of their children's performance and the children's confidence in their mathematics ability. Frome and Eccles suggest that such expectations are one way in which cultural stereotypes come to stand in the way of girls' choice to study mathematics.

Cultural images of women as universally caring and nurturant provide another example of inflated claims of difference. Such notions about differences gained popularity in the early 1980s when some American scholars claimed that women possess a uniquely care-oriented way of reasoning about moral issues (Belenky et al., 1986; Gilligan, 1982). Their studies were subjected to severe criticism from many quarters for both methodological and theoretical shortcomings. Furthermore, the claims of large differences in moral reasoning proved difficult or impossible to substantiate (cf. Jaffee and Hyde, 2000). However, as Hyde and several other critics have pointed out, this did not stop the claims of the original studies from being taken up widely among policymakers, researchers, and perhaps especially journalists and popular writers. The cultural images of women as naturally nurturant and men as unable to nurture, even though not supported by research, were given a pseudoscientific aura. These images, Hyde claimed, did damage to both men and women. Hyde pointed out the possible costs for women in the workplace: If they lived up to the stereotype of being nurturant and nice, they would not be seen as good material for promotion; if they did not, they would also be penalized. Hyde also pointed to the costs for families if men and women were to imagine that men are unable to care for small children.

Critiques of falsely inflated differences are formulated within the differences paradigm, by scholars who argue that there are very few psychological sex differences. These scholars think it is worthwhile to do research that compares women and men, but they worry about the uses to which much of that research is put.

Other difference-producing mechanisms
are confounded with sex category

Other critics have noted that observed differences between women and men are often interpreted as reflections of biological differences even if they might be produced by the environment. Because much sex-difference research foregrounds sex category, often with "biological difference" implied, such research shifts all other possible contributing contextual dimensions to the background (Crawford and Chaffin, 1997). In this way, a number of questions remain unstudied and unanswered because researchers are preoccupied with intrinsic differences between men and women.

The studies of mathematical abilities provide an example of this phenomenon. Mathematics tests measure mathematical achievement. However, the results of such tests are very often taken to reflect mathematical ability – that is, intrinsic potential. This distinction is important when considering earlier studies done when girls and boys studied different amounts of mathematics in school. In spite of this difference in exposure, differences between boys and girls on tests of mathematical achievement were typically interpreted as reflecting differences in intrinsic ability. Claims about male "math genes" quickly followed.

Spatial ability, especially "mental rotation," is a field where differences favoring boys and men have been seen as reliable, even if the size of the differences has diminished over time. Recent experiments by Austrian psychologists have found that "priming" male and female participants to imagine themselves in different traditional gendered roles can make differences on tests of mental rotation either vanish or increase (Ortner and Sieverding, 2008). It is interesting that performances on spatial ability tests could be easily influenced by such minor contextual manipulations.

The methodological point to be made here is one that also has political implications. If conditions other than sex category make large contributions to the results of sex-difference research, then why not study those conditions directly, instead of via the detour of sex category? (Baumeister, 1988). If researchers are not prepared to do this, could it be that they want to keep the spotlight on "sex differences" in order to obscure the role of contextual factors? Directing attention away from contextual dimensions has another consequence that may be difficult to discern while thinking within the sex-differences paradigm – because of what the paradigm directs researchers to look for and not look for. We focus on this in the next section.

Focusing on individual differences draws attention away from group inequalities

A preoccupation with possible differences between the sexes in internal qualities diverts attention away from differences in their *external* conditions. By concentrating on the study of individual traits and abilities, sex-difference research encourages explanations that rest on assumed inner psychological or biological differences. Inevitably, this comes at the expense of attention to external context, including social inequalities. In this way, the search for male–female differences reaffirms the cultural tendency to locate the causes of social inequality within individuals. As the feminist critics Mary Crawford and Roger Chaffin (1997) argued, such research in fact studies the effects of the unequal gender order. It may also come to function as an integral part of it.

Critics also question whether the divisions and hierarchies that are upheld in the name of sex differences actually *follow from* differences between women and men. Might it be that the process of upholding categories and hierarchies not only creates ideas about differences between women and men but also produces the differences themselves? These differences are then conveniently invoked as the rationale for differential treatment. It is not surprising that such socially produced and socially supported differences also produce subjective experiences of difference, thus effectively constructing gender *as difference*.

These criticisms do not presume that there are no "true" psychological differences between women and men. What is at issue is not the presence or absence of male–female differences. The point is that culture and society continually impose distinctions by sex category in both private life and public life. Therefore, it is not possible to tease out the contributions of "sex category" from experience, hierarchy, or other contextual factors in a specific social setting (Crawford and Chaffin, 1997).

*A finding of a male–female difference has no meaning
in and of itself*

In and of itself, a research finding of a male–female difference has no explanatory value. In technical terms, when researchers seek cause–effect relations, they must be able to manipulate the variable they want to study (i.e., the independent variable). This enables them to observe whether different values or levels of the independent variable reliably produce differences in another variable (i.e., the dependent variable). But researchers cannot manipulate the sex category of individuals. "Sex category" is not an independent variable, but a subject variable (Grills and Prus, 2008). It is not possible for a researcher to expose the same individual to different values of the "variable" sex category (or to randomly assign subjects to "sex category"), and then study the effects of this manipulation. Sex category is something other than a variable. Indeed, it is a constant. This means that no conclusions about cause–effect relationships can be drawn from sex-difference research (Jordan-Young, 2010). Such research can only point to correlations.

Research results that point to male–female differences have served "as raw material for constructing a variety of contested interpretations, cultural meanings, and political agendas" (Hare-Mustin and Marecek, 1994, p. 532). The meaning affixed to any empirically observed male–female difference is always the product of social negotiation. Such negotiations take place "in the context of a pre-existing system of meanings in which sex difference is both polarized and hierarchically ordered" (Crawford and Chaffin, 1997, p. 82). Research findings of male–female differences might best be seen as indexing how the local gender order is expressed in individual women's and men's ways of experiencing themselves and one another. Researchers who do not take these politically charged dimensions into account may – directly or indirectly – contribute to maintaining inequalities.

*The risk of disregarding variations among women
and variations among men*

Women are not a homogeneous group; neither are men. Women and men can be found in all sectors of society, including all social classes, ethnic groups, and racial groups; women and men are of different sexual orientations, ages, and levels of ability and health. It is not surprising that variations in experiences, traits, abilities, and achievements among the members of each sex category are usually much larger than the average differences between the sex categories.

Feminist critics, especially those who study people who are not white, of European descent, or middle class, have long pointed out the risks associated with researchers' use of the blanket categories "women" and "men." In fact, these critics point out, there are seldom grounds to consider "women" and "men" as homogeneous categories. These caveats receive further support from research that challenges the two-sex model (Fausto-Sterling, 2000a; Fine, 2010; Jordan-Young, 2010). The intricate interactions between the different categories that braid together over an individual's lifetime require richer and more complex models of explanation than those offered by sex-difference research (Cole, 2009). Focusing only on "sex differences" compels researchers to close their eyes to the daily play of inequalities, similarities, and differences in any human activity and squeeze that activity into an image of static opposites (Thorne, 1993).

Biological explanations and scientific reductionism

We end this chapter with a discussion of reductionism, which is used in explanations common in sex-difference research. Few would dispute that the human brain is involved in all psychological phenomena. This is so self-evident that it seems trivial. However, disagreements abound when theorists try to specify the nature of this brain involvement. Should we take the brain's involvement in everything that is "psycho-logical" to mean that all psychological functions and phenomena can ultimately be understood as exclusively a matter of brain structure and physiology? Or are there meaningful explanations at the psychological level that cannot be dispensed with? Some psychologists connect psychological life very closely with the physical-biological substrate of the brain and nervous system; indeed, they sometimes portray these as virtually identical (Kalat, 2009).

Critics of biologically oriented explanations of sex differences point out that the brain is certainly central to human psychological functioning; nonetheless, humans do not exist in isolation from one another. Many – perhaps most – psychological phenomena involve humans in interaction with other humans (Rogoff, 2003; Smith, 2007; Wertsch, 1997). Psychological phenomena are not localized exclusively in isolated brains; they exist socially, that is, among interacting individuals, in which cultural meanings are always active.

Those who are critical of biological explanations of male–female differences argue that such explanations often portray culturally and socially produced similarities and differences between people as purely biologic-ally determined (Fine, 2010; Jordan-Young, 2010). The critics point out that biological explanations mainly do this by the use of a strategy called scientific reduction. We therefore briefly discuss what scientific reduction entails. Scientific reduction is an explanatory tool that has long been used in the natural sciences. It presumes that processes on one conceptual level (e.g., the movements of atoms) can be fully explained in terms of more basic processes or structures (such as the behavior of elementary particles). Both biological psychologists and evolutionary psychologists frequently use reduction as an explanatory strategy. They invoke processes or structures on a biological microlevel or on an evolutionary macrolevel in order to explain phenomena on the psychological level. In so doing, they assume that psychological phenomena can be reduced to these other levels. For instance, a theorist might claim that a certain psychological experience (e.g., pain) can be wholly understood in terms of nervous system activity. In principle, reductionist explanation is a neutral tool. But not all ways of using reductionist explanations are either meaningful or successful (Richards, 2010; Robinson, 1995; Yanchar and Hill, 2003).

Epistemologists and evolutionary biologists have criticized the ways that some biologically oriented psychologists and some evolutionary psychologists use reductions in their explanations of psychological phenomena (Fausto-Sterling, 2000b; Gould, 2000; Gowaty, 2001; Richardson, 2010). The critics point out that the consequences of using reductionist explanations depend on the conceptual levels at which the explanations are situated. The concepts and language that are used in reductionist explanations – above all, the words used to denote that which is to be explained – are crucial for the ultimate scientific meaningfulness of an explanation. If we were to seek reductionist explanations for experiences that people express with words such as "humane," "a dreadful thing," "self-assertive," "feminine," or "masculine," the terminology of biological psychology or neuroscience is unlikely to be useful. Put more strongly: Such experiences cannot be expressed, *as experiences*, in biological or neurological terms. Psychologically and experientially descriptive words and biologically descriptive words refer to two different conceptual levels that cannot be converted into each other; the psychological and physiological levels of meaning simply do not "talk" about the same things.

When are reductionist explanations of psychological phenomena in terms of biological processes possible? First, the psychological experience must be amenable to specification in the language used to describe the specific biological process. In other words, the psychological experience must be expressed on the conditions of the biological process. This requires that the words used to describe the psychological experience be independent of person, culture, and history, because person, culture, and history cannot be given meaning in the language of physiology. Physiological and brain-anatomical terms do not reach beyond bodily processes and structures. Critics doubt that any experiences, or other types of culturally localized psychological phenomena, can be meaningfully described in physiological terms. Might there be spheres of psychological life and experiential reality for which knowledge about brain structures and brain functions does not increase psychological knowledge? (Magnusson, 2003; Richards, 2010; Yanchar and Hill, 2003). Further, even when neuroscientific research shows patterns of activity in certain areas of the human brain when certain activities are taking place, it is not the brain that thinks and feels. The brain exists in a person, and it is the person – who is always in a social and historical setting – who thinks and feels (Smith, 2007).

Reductionist explanations of psychological phenomena are not necessarily wrong. Far from it. But they are not always psychologically interesting. Moreover, they may blind researchers and other people to the complexity and cultural specificity of the phenomena under study (Robinson, 1995).

15　Psychology's place in society, and society's place in psychology

It is difficult to imagine daily life in western, industrialized countries today without psychology – the academic discipline, the professions that use and promulgate psychological knowledge, and the burgeoning self-help industry. Psychology has undoubtedly played an influential role in modern societies. Over the last hundred years or so, psychologists' ways of explaining individual lives have become increasingly central to many people's self-understandings (Rose, 1989, 1996). In addition, psychological ways of helping people and addressing social issues have become commonplace and are increasingly advocated. If psychology did not exist, many of people's daily experiences would be understood in quite different ways than those now in vogue. If psychology creates particular ways of making sense of daily life, then, without psychology, people today would perhaps even have different kinds of experiences than they do.

While psychology has influenced the cultures of modern societies, those cultures also have influenced and molded psychology, such that one could talk about cultures of psychology. Could psychology in its current guise in modern, western, industrialized societies have developed elsewhere? Hardly. The social mores, traditions, and zeitgeists in European and North American societies were decisive in specifying and identifying the most pressing social problems for psychologists to investigate and solve. Psychologists, eager to promote their discipline, were keen to respond to such societal needs; psychology's aims and trajectory were thus shaped in line with social trends. As social needs and problems changed historically, so has psychology changed, both in its research foci and its societal roles and functions. For much of its history, the discipline was peopled almost exclusively by white, middle-class men; this, too, shaped the form and direction of psychologists' endeavors. This too has now changed. Change continues. Such continual change is to be expected of a field that is so firmly wedded to the social. It is also to be expected that the cultures of psychology will be different across regional and national boundaries.

Psychology's main object of study is human beings and thus psychology is beset by recursivity. Humans (as opposed to, say, atoms, star systems, or DNA molecules) are able to reflect upon and act in light of the theories that are proposed about them. This ability stands out in bold relief when a particular psychological theory takes hold: People change their ways of talking about themselves, adopting the terminology of the new theory. (Consider, for example, talk of "the unconscious" in Freud's day or talk of "chemical imbalances" in our own times.) In this way, psychological theory can change people's ways of describing and understanding themselves and eventually their ways of being and behaving (Richards, 2010). Over time, these changes will manifest themselves in psychological theorizing, completing the recursive cycle.

What about the truth claims of psychological theories? What has happened when psychologists develop new theories? Have they discovered new things about reality and new facts about existing things? Or might the new meanings of concepts and research findings be created by researchers? To us, the latter seems quite likely. We note that researchers with varying theoretical, cultural, and political investments often draw different interpretations from the same data and propose different theories. Many feminist scholars and other critical scholars point out that researchers in particular gendered, classed, or geopolitical positions have favored particular research questions and particular ways of addressing these questions, to the exclusion of other questions and approaches.

Against this background, we believe that psychologists who want to study gender and culture need to familiar with the historical and political situatedness of psychology. They also need to be aware of the historical flux, the cultural variations, and the inevitable recursivity of the discipline. They must also engage with critiques that have been brought to bear on psychology. Taken together, these requirements constitute what we call disciplinary reflexivity.

Disciplinary reflexivity

Sue Wilkinson, a British feminist psychologist, has argued that every academic discipline has the responsibility to engage in disciplinary reflexivity – that is, to explain its forms and its influence in society. In her call for disciplinary reflexivity, Wilkinson (1988) urges psychologists – researchers and practitioners – to analyze critically their parts of the discipline, with the dual aim of learning more about its nature and history as well as about how the discipline has influenced the larger society. Such scrutiny of the psychology discipline has usually been carried out by scholars outside psychology – in fields such as history of science, sociology of science, philosophy of science, feminist studies, or critical race studies (Richards, 1997, 2010; Rigné, 2002; Rose, 1989, 1996). Some critical psychologists have also engaged in disciplinary reflexivity (Bohan, 1992; Koch, 1981; Mednick, 1989; Robinson, 1995, 2000; Sherif, 1979; Slife and Williams, 1995; Stam, 2006). Often, such critiques are given little place in the discipline. They are usually published in sources outside psychology that are read by few psychologists (Hegarty, 2007). For psychologists, it has always been risky to engage in such critical work. It has seldom counted as "scientific" psychology and has not been deemed valuable within the discipline. We are among those psychologists who believe that such disciplinary reflexive work is crucial for keeping the discipline vital and an important means to improve its quality. Reflexive analyses belong squarely inside the discipline.

In Chapter 6, we described reflexivity in scientific endeavors in terms of several different activities. We argued that personal and methodological reflexivity are powerful tools for researchers, tools that ought to be acquired during one's training as a researcher. Here we argue that disciplinary reflexivity should be part of courses in the history of psychology and courses about psychology's methodologies and epistemologies. Disciplinary reflexivity issues also deserve to be the subject of internal debates in the discipline (Fox and Prilleltensky, 1997; Robinson, 2000; Slife et al., 2005).

Scrutinizing one's own discipline

One type of disciplinary reflexivity by psychologists involves analyses of the social relations within academic psychology in order to learn more about how processes of legitimation and exclusion operate. Using such knowledge, the discipline might be able to devise strategies for interrupting internal social processes that prevent certain groups from advancing. An historical example of such a process is worth recounting: Prior to the 1970s, few women had gained prestigous positions in academic psychology in the USA. Some feminist psychologists studied how essays and articles alleged to have been written by men or by women were assessed. They found that an article that appeared to be written by a woman received less favorable reviews than the same article when it appeared to be written by a man (Friend et al., 1979; Goldberg, 1968; Paludi and Bauer, 1983).[1] Such disparities in reviewers' judgments led feminist

---

[1] For a more recent example, in another field, see the study of the Medical Research Council in Sweden in the 1990s, which found that female grant applicants were less favorably treated by reviewers than male applicants, when merits were identical (Wennerås and Wold, 1997). This study was widely discussed and led to some changes in the handling of research applications to research foundations in Sweden.

psychologists to lobby for policies mandating blind reviews of journal articles (that is, reviews in which the reviewers did not know the names of the authors) (APA, 1972; Weller, 2001).

Although such efforts to end explicit discrimination have had positive effects, certain categories of individuals are still underrepresented in high positions in academe. Let us illustrate with psychology in one country: At the time of this writing, there continues to be a striking disparity between the proportion of students studying to become licensed psychologists who are women (between 70 and 80 percent, a proportion that has remained stable for a couple of decades) and the proportion of full professors of psychology in Swedish universities who are women (marginally above 20 percent).[2]

A second type of disciplinary reflexivity concerns the informal ranking of different kinds of knowledge and different kinds of research methods in psychology. Critical historians of psychology have scrutinized the processes through which certain fields, certain topics, certain forms of knowledge, and certain research methods have come to be regarded as central to the discipline, while others have been shunted to the margins (Danziger, 1990; Hornstein, 1988; Morawski, 1988). Not surprisingly, there are regional and national variations in these processes; there is no globally agreed prestige rating. Remarkably often, however, topics that concern women, gender, race, social class, sexualities, and cultural differences have been considered as marginal issues or as specialties of limited interest with no import for the discipline in general. Above all, such topics have not been seen as areas of basic research, which is the type of research that is generally awarded the highest status in the discipline (Bohan, 1992; Rabinowitz and Weseen, 2001; Woolgar, 1996).

Research approaches other than experiments or questionnaire studies using standardized quantitative scales have often been labeled as "anecdotal," "unscientific," or even "not psychological." Students have been dissuaded from using such approaches. Research that employs such methods has often been deemed unsuitable for publication in prestigious psychology journals. Similarly, alternate ways of thinking about psychological knowledge – ones that do not take their starting point in empiricism and/or positivism – often have been seen either as

[2] See statistics from the Swedish National Agency for Higher Education: www.hsv.se/statistikomhogskolan (retrieved March 29, 2010). The figure of slightly above 20 percent of professors of psychology is in its turn marginally higher than the proportion of professors across all social science disciplines (18 percent) who are women. Considering that there has for several decades been a particularly high proportion of women among psychology students, one might expect there to be a substantially higher number of female professors in psychology than in other social science disciplines.

outside psychology proper or as undermining its status as a science and threatening its prestige (Camic *et al.*, 2003a; McMullen, 2002; Robinson, 2000; Stoppard, 2002; Yanchar and Hill, 2003).

A third type of disciplinary reflexivity scrutinizes the discipline's knowledge claims and research practices. For example, in terms of knowledge claims, it is common for psychologists, unlike most social scientists, to envision their research as producing universal, enduring, law-like generalizations. Yet, as the American psychologist Jeffrey Arnett (2008, 2009) recently argued, a very high proportion of these generalizations is drawn from studies of US citizens, a group that constitutes only 5 percent of the world's population. Even if one counted all the research produced in the west, the proportion of the world's population represented in the knowledge base of the discipline would remain very small. In some areas of psychology, this tiny slice of the global population is further narrowed: A high proportion of research studies in psychology rely on convenience samples of college students – that is, late adolescents mainly from privileged backgrounds who have chosen to enroll in psychology courses (Henry, 2009; Sears, 1986). Also, studies typically reflect only a narrow slice of time – the immediate present. Relying on such select groups of people and such a narrow time span to develop theory about humans in general surely risks over-generalization. This has nevertheless been freely done throughout the history of academic psychology.

A fourth type of disciplinary reflexivity begins in the observation that knowledge production in the social sciences is embedded in the social, political, economic, and ideological contexts of their time (Hacking, 1995, 1999; Haraway, 1988; Lacey, 2005). How then might the practices of research – framing questions, defining concepts, designing procedures and measurements, and interpreting outcomes – be shaped by these contexts? (Fleck, 1935/1979).

In some cases it is easy to observe how social processes influence research questions and concepts. For example, one need only recall the heated debates that raged among developmental psychologists and mental health experts in the USA and several western European countries in the mid-1970s concerning the possible ill effects of mothers' employment outside the home. Especially in North America, scores of studies in this period searched for damaging effects of nonparental care on children's welfare and development. From today's vantage point, both the controversy and the questions and theoretical concepts used by the researchers appear distinctly time-bound and culture-bound. The mid-1970s saw a dramatic influx of middle-class women into the paid work force. This took place against a background of accepted psychological knowledge about children and mothers, which had been produced when stay-at-home mothers were the norm, at least in the middle class. Furthermore, this research question was also class-bound and place-specific. The experts rarely considered that many mothers in low-income families had always worked outside the home, as had mothers in many countries other than those studied. For centuries, mothers had engaged in income-generating work (e.g., farm labor) during the years that they were caring for young children. Nonetheless, in research on the possible ill effects of mothers' paid work on children, the image of the child was a child in a middle-class family, and the image of the mother was modeled on the stay-at-home, middle-class mother. Today, owing to broad social changes, those debates are largely forgotten. Mothers who work outside the home are no longer considered a social problem; they are the norm.

Many other topics that have been studied by psychologists, many of the discipline's explanatory constructs, and many of its normative judgments have been found to be time-bound, place-specific, and culture-bound. However, psychologists have often declared them to be universal. Psychology has always produced its knowledge, whether it has made universal claims or not, within specific cultural settings. Specific cultural settings provide specific sets of prereflective understandings (that is, points of view that are self-evident and not consciously processed) that influence both researchers and contemporary consumers of their research. The power of such prereflective understandings is notoriously difficult to appreciate: Fish do not know that they swim in water. Prereflective understandings are much easier to see in hindsight or from afar. The next section provides an example of what such hindsight can bring.

Feminist disciplinary reflexivity close-up

The historical studies carried out by Frances Cherry, a social psychologist working in Canada, provide several vignettes illustrating how "classic" studies of American social psychology were embedded in specific societal settings, cultural contexts, and historical moments. Cherry (1995) terms these settings and moments "stubborn particulars." She showed in detail how researchers' choices of concepts and methods, as well as their blind spots, arise from their culturally and historically specific prereflective understandings.

Cherry discusses the influential research program initiated by John Darley and Bibb Latané subsequent to the 1964 news report that a woman in New York had been raped and murdered while a large number of bystanders failed to respond. As Cherry pointed out, Darley and Latané (1968) distilled the general idea of the "unresponsive bystander" from the news reports of the murder. In doing so, the researchers set aside a number of specific aspects of the crime: the gendered, raced, and classed particulars of the crime; its urban locale; and the gender politics of the times. The latter can be illustrated by the fact that although many people either heard the woman call for help or saw her beaten and raped, most failed to call the police. Some even interpreted the assault as a "lovers' quarrel." If the rape and murder had taken place ten or fifteen years later, after feminists had moved the issues of rape and gender-linked violence to the forefront of public concern, Darley and Latané might have distilled a different idea than "unresponsive bystanders." They might have chosen to investigate men's intimate violence against women. If there had been a woman on the research team, perhaps her personal knowledge and experience might have led her to attend to the gendered character of the crime.

Darley and Latané, as well as the stream of social psychologists who carried out research on bystander interventions, shaped their investigations within the dominant traditions and viewpoints of conventional social psychology. They chose mainly to investigate personological factors (e.g., Who helps in a crisis?) and narrowly situational factors (e.g., Are people more or less likely to intervene when others are present?). These factors are ones that are amenable to study within the limited confines of social psychology laboratories. Larger societal, cultural, and environmental factors that might affect bystanders' reactions to a man's assault, rape, and murder of a woman were not studied by these researchers. Not many years later, of course, feminist scholars made questions about the connection between sexual assault and wider societal issues a focal part of their research (Cherry, 1995).

Reflexive analyses by feminist scholars have examined several other lines of research, showing how researchers' prereflective understandings of gender shaped both the nature of the investigations – the definitions of concepts, the choice of participants, and the choice of methods – and the outcomes. A few of the many topics of psychological research that feminists have investigated in this way are assertiveness (Gervasio and Crawford, 1989), "fear of success," premenstrual distress (Parlee, 1992, 1994a, 1994b), field dependence/independence (Haaken, 1988), aggression (Frodi et al., 1977), and attachment (Birns, 1999).

Cherry's evocative phrase "stubborn particulars" should be a reminder that researchers inevitably bring their everyday lived experience and culture-bound ways of seeing to their scholarly work (Freedman, 2010; Lehrer, 2010). It could not be otherwise and we probably should not wish it to be otherwise. This situatedness and culture-boundness is not in itself a problem, and it does not diminish the value of the scholarly work. But researchers and practitioners need to be conscious of the webs of meaning and societal forces that surround them. And readers need to turn a skeptical eye to the research reports and textbooks they read. In brief, disciplinary and personal reflexivity should always be with us.

Being a critical psychologist: psychology and social justice issues

Can psychology contribute to societal change as well as individual change? Should psychologists strive to make societal change? These are issues that have been perennially discussed both within the discipline and on the margins of the discipline. Today psychology generally portrays itself as producing knowledge about individuals and addressing the problems of individuals. Should these be psychology's only tasks? As you will have gathered by now, we take exception to a view of psychology as only about the "individual" separated from his or her social and cultural surroundings. In fact, we argue that "individuals" cannot be conceived apart from their social and cultural surround. It is what makes people human. We argue further that a psychology that restricts its domain to "the individual," or to mechanisms and structures within the individual, provides a distorted and partial (in all meanings of the word) view of what people are and can be.

In this book, you have encountered the work of many psychologists who share our view. Many of them call themselves *critical psychologists*. They constitute a heterogeneous collection of psychologists from many countries, who embrace a number of critical standpoints (Fox and Prilleltensky, 1997; Fox *et al.*, 2009; Hook, 2004b). For instance, some researchers engage with feminist issues and inequality between men and women, some with postcolonial critique and reform, some with social class issues, others with sexuality issues, and yet others with the social oppression and exclusion of those with physical and mental disabilities. Some critical psychologists engage in community psychology and mental health work; others with issues of rape, war trauma, and human rights; others with poverty and class-based oppression. Social justice features as central to the work of many of these psychologists. They appreciate the fundamental impact of "the external" – such as poverty, unemployment, racial and ethnic prejudice, physical illness, and physical or psychological traumas, together with other social asymmetries and prejudice – on the "interiors" of humans. For these critical psychologists, steering away from the larger social and political questions is simply untenable. Worldwide, the critical psychology movement is growing: There are now international conferences, textbooks, scholarly journals, websites, and electronic fora for discussion. We hope that our book makes a contribution to this movement.

The future of gender and culture in psychology

This book has not aimed to cover the whole terrain of interpretative psychological research on gender and other social categorizations. Indeed, this would have been impossible: The fields and topics are too many and too far-ranging. Our goal was different. We set out with three aims: First, we wanted to describe some tools for thinking about and researching gender, culture, human experience, and psychology. These conceptual tools provide the groundwork for several approaches to empirical research and practice. Second, we wished to offer some starting points for conducting interpretative projects in psychology. Specifically, we described the nature of interpretation, the use of rich talk as data, and some ways of working with such data. Third, we provided some snapshots – in the form of research vignettes – of how these interpretative tools and methods have been put into practice and what insights they yielded. We focused especially on the analytical methods developed by discursive psychologists, but psychologists have several other ways of working with words and meanings. Naturally, our choice of research approaches and examples reflects our tastes and interests, not the full scope of issues related to gender and culture in psychology. Many more topics have been studied. Many more remain to be imagined.

We end by reflecting on how the kinds of knowledge that we have presented in this book can be used: What is the knowledge good for? Is it science? For that matter, what is science, really? These questions can best be answered by considering the actual contributions of science, rather than the various actions and methodological steps that scientists perform when they pursue their profession. That is, the focus of scrutiny should not mainly be on procedures, methods, and techniques. Let us clarify by quoting Daniel Robinson, a preeminent American historian and philosopher of psychology:

> The actual contribution authentic science makes is to our understanding of the universe and the part of it that we occupy or of ourselves as its occupants. And this contribution has always been in the form of theoretical integrations, conceptual clarifications, stern and instructive criticisms of what the many have long taken to be protected truths. (2000, p. 46)

Robinson himself practiced such "stern criticism" of the traditions of psychology journals. He urged journal editors to affirm "the centrality of knowledge" as opposed to "mere congeries of disconnected and only arguably interesting facts" (p. 46). In Robinson's estimation, the latter is common practice in psychology journals. He exhorted journal editors to invite researchers to engage in more critical discussion and to abjure from simply amassing "disconnected empirical findings."

Good science, in this view, is not about applying certain accepted methods or engaging in certain disciplinary rituals, but about enlarging people's understanding of themselves and the universe in which they exist. Science is thus not merely about gathering facts and findings according to certain prescribed procedures. Rather, its major contributions throughout history lie in its clarification of, and new ways of integrating, "facts" that may already be known. Often, scientific contributions do not consist of new empirical findings and facts, but of "stern and instructive criticism" of "protected truths" (that is, criticism of established ways of understanding facts).

Whether or not our book has contributed to good science, the work on which we have drawn certainly has. It undertakes precisely what Daniel Robinson claimed to be the most important tasks of science: to offer stern and instructive criticisms of unhelpful practices and theories, to provide conceptual clarifications that challenge "protected truths," and to propose theoretical integration across boundaries that were previously uncrossed.

References

Aarseth, Helene (2008) *Hjemskapingens moderne magi* [*The modern magic of home-creating*]. University of Oslo, Department of Sociology and Cultural Geography: Unipub.

Adams, Glenn (2005) The cultural grounding of personal relationship: enemyship in North American and West African worlds. *Journal of Personality and Social Psychology*, **88**(6): 948–968.

Ader, Deborah N., and Johnson, Suzanne B. (1994) Sample description, reporting and analysis of sex in psychological research: a look at APA and APA division journals in 1990. *American Psychologist*, **49**: 216–218.

Alem, Atalay, Kebede, Derege, Fekadu, Abebaw, Shibre, Teshome, Fekadu, Daniel, Beyero, Teferra, Medhin, Girmay, Negash, Alemayehu, and Kullgren, Gunnar (2009) Clinical course and outcome of schizophrenia in a predominantly treatment-naïve cohort in rural Ethiopia. *Schizophrenia Bulletin*, **35**(3): 646–654.

Al-Krenawi, Alean, and Wiesel-Lev, Rachel (1999) Attitudes toward and perceived psychosocial impact of female circumcision as practiced among the Bedouin-Arabs of the Negev. *Family Process*, **38**(4): 431–443.

Alliance of Psychoanalytic Organizations (2006) *Psychodynamic diagnostic manual*. Silver Springs, MD: Alliance of Psychoanalytic Organizations.

Ålund, Aleksandra (2000) Etnicitetens mångfald och mångfaldens etnicitet: kön, klass, identitet och ras [The diversity of ethnicity and the ethnicity of diversity: gender, class, identity, and race]. In Eric Olsson (ed.) *Etnicitetens gränser och mångfald* [*The boundaries of ethnicity and diversity*]. Bjärnum, Sweden: Carlssons bokförlag, pp. 27–77.

Ambjörnsson, Fanny (2004) *I en klass för sig: genus, klass och sexualitet bland gymnasietjejer* [*In their own class: gender, class, and sexuality among high-school girls*]. Stockholm: Ordfront.

(2006) *Vad är queer?* [*What is queer?*]. Stockholm: Natur & Kultur.

American Psychiatric Association (1980) *Diagnostic and statistical manual of mental disorders* (3rd edn.). Washington, DC: American Psychiatric Association.

Andenæs, Agnes (1996) *Foreldre og barn i forandring* [*Parents and children in transition*]. Oslo: Pedagogisk Forum.

(2000) Generalisering: om ringvirkninger og gjenbruk av resultater fra en kvalitativ undersøkelse [Generalization: about consequences and re-use of results from a qualitative study]. In Hanne Haavind (ed.)

Kön och tolkning: metodiska möjligheter i kvalitativ forskning [*Gender and interpretations: methodological possibilities in qualitative research*]. Stockholm: Natur & Kultur.

Anderson, Kristin J., and Leaper, Campbell (1998) Meta-analyses of gender effects on conversational interruption: who, what, when, where, and how. *Sex Roles*, **39**: 225–252.

Andrews, Molly, Squire, Corinne, and Tamboukou, Maria (eds.) (2008) *Doing narrative research*. London: Sage.

APA (American Psychological Association) (1972) Eight APA journals initiate controversial blind reviewing. *APA Monitor*, 3(June), 1, 5.

(2007) *Task Force on Socioeconomic Status. Report of the APA Task Force on Socioeconomic Status*. Washington, DC: American Psychological Association.

Archer, John (2004) Sex differences in aggression in real-world settings: a meta-analytic review. *Review of General Psychology*, **8**: 291–322.

Archives of Resistance. Anti-Anorexia and Anti-Bulimia League. www.narrativeapproaches.com/antianorexia%20folder/anti_anorexia_index.htm (retrieved August 26, 2011).

Arnett, Jeffrey (2008) The neglected 95%: why American psychology needs to become less American. *American Psychologist*, **63**(7): 602–614.

(2009) The neglected 95%: a challenge to psychology's philosophy of science. *American Psychologist*, **64**(6): 571–574.

Axelsen, Eva (1984) Kvinner i psykoterapi [Women in psychotherapy]. In Trine Anstorp, Eva Axelsen, and Ingebretsen Reidun (eds.) *Kvinne(p)syke. Kvinners psykiske problemer – forandring og utvikling gjennom terapi* [*Women's psychological problems: change and development through therapy*]. Oslo: Scandinavian University Press.

Bakhtin, Mikhail (1981) *The dialogic imagination: four essays by M. M. Bakhtin*, ed. Michael Holquist, trans. Caryl Emerson and Michael Holquist. Austin, TX: University of Texas Press.

Bamberg, Michael (2004) Form and function of 'slut bashing' in male identity constructions in 15-year-olds. *Human Development*, **47**: 331–353.

Baumeister, Roy (1988) Should we stop studying sex differences altogether? *American Psychologist*, **43**(12): 1092–1095.

Becker, Anne E., Burwell, Rebecca A., Herzog, David B., Hamburg, Paul, and Gilman, Stephen E. (2002) Eating behaviours and attitudes following prolonged exposure to television among ethnic Fijian adolescent girls. *British Journal of Psychiatry*, **180**: 509–514.

Becker, Dana (1997) *Through the looking glass: women and borderline personality disorder*. Boulder, CO: Westview Press.

(2004) Post-traumatic stress disorder. In Paula Caplan and Lisa Cosgrove (eds.) *Bias in psychiatric diagnosis*. Lanham, MD: Jason Aronson, pp. 207–212.

(2005) *The myth of empowerment: women and therapeutic culture in America*. New York University Press.

Becker, Howard (1998) *Tricks of the trade: how to think about your research while you're doing it*. University of Chicago Press.

Bekkengen, Lisbeth (2002) *Man får välja – om föräldraskap och föräldraledighet i arbetsliv och familjeliv* [Men get to choose: about parenthood and parental leave in working life and family life]. Malmö, Sweden: Liber Press.

Belenky, Mary Field, Clinchy, Blythe M., Goldberger, Nancy, and Tarule, Jill (1986) *Women's ways of knowing: the development of self, voice and mind.* New York: Basic Books.

Bengtsson, Margot (1985) Identifikation, kön och klass [Identification, gender, and class]. *Kvinnovetenskaplig Tidskrift* [*Swedish Journal of Women's Studies*], 6(1): 35–48.

(2001) *Tid, rum, kön och identitet. Om föräldraidentifikationens omvandlingar 1959–1993* [*Time, space, gender, and identity. About the transitions of parental identification 1959–1993*]. Lund: Studentlitteratur.

Berger, Peter, and Luckmann, Thomas (1966) *The social construction of reality: a treatise in the sociology of knowledge.* Garden City, NY: Doubleday.

Bergman, Bo (1988) Battered wives: why are they beaten and why do they stay? Stockholm: Karolinska Institutet, doctoral dissertation.

Bhatia, Sunil (2007) *American karma. Race, culture, and identity in the Indian diaspora.* New York University Press.

Billig, Michael (1987) *Arguing and thinking: a rhetorical approach to social psychology.* Cambridge University Press.

(1991) *Ideology and opinions: studies in rhetorical psychology.* London: Sage.

(1998) Rhetoric and the unconscious. *Argumentation*, 12: 199–216.

(1999) *Freudian repression: conversation creating the unconscious.* New York: Cambridge University Press.

Billig, Michael, Condor, Susan, Edwards, Derek, Gane, Mike, Middleton, David, and Radley, Alan (1988) *Ideological dilemmas: a social psychology of everyday thinking.* London: Sage.

Birns, Beverly (1999) Attachment theory revisited: challenging conceptual and methodological sacred cows. *Feminism & Psychology*, 9(1): 10–21.

Björnberg, Ulla (2004) Making agreements and managing conflicts: Swedish dual-earner couples in theory and practice. *Current Sociology*, 52(1): 33–52.

Blumer, Herbert (1969) *Symbolic interactionism: perspective and method.* Englewood Cliffs, NJ: Prentice-Hall.

Bograd, Michele (ed.) (1990) *Feminist approaches for men in family therapy.* Binghamton, NY: Harrington Park Press.

Bohan, Janis S. (ed.) (1992) *Seldom seen, rarely heard: women's place in psychology.* Boulder, CO: Westview Press.

(1993) Regarding gender: essentialism, constructionism, and feminist psychology. *Psychology of Women Quarterly*, 17(1): 5–21.

Bohan, Janis, and Russell, Glenda (eds.) (1999) *Conversations about psychology and sexual orientation.* New York University Press.

Bonham, Vence L., Warshauer-Baker, Esther, and Collins, Francis S. (2005) Race and ethnicity in the genome era: the complexity of the constructs. *American Psychologist*, 60(1): 9–15.

Bordo, Susan (1993) *Unbearable weight.* Berkeley, CA: University of California Press.

Brante, Thomas (2006) Den nya psykiatrin: exemplet ADHD [The new psychiatry: the ADHD example]. In Gunilla Hallerstedt (ed.) *Diagnosens makt. Om kunskap, pengar och lidande* [*The power of diagnosis. About knowledge, money, and suffering*]. Göteborg: Daidalos, pp. 73–112.

Braun, Virginia, and Clarke, Victoria (2006) Using thematic analysis in psychology. *Qualitative Research in Psychology*, **3**: 77–101.

Brown, Catrina, and Augusta-Scott, Tod (eds.) (2008) *Narrative therapy: making meaning, making lives.* Thousand Oaks, CA: Sage.

Brown, Laura S. (1991) Ethical issues in feminist therapy: selected topics. *Psychology of Women Quarterly*, **15**(2): 323–336.

Bruner, Jerome (1990) *Acts of meaning.* Cambridge, MA: Harvard University Press.

(1991) The narrative construction of reality. *Critical Inquiry*, **18**(1): 1–21.

(2008) Culture and mind: their fruitful incommensurability. *ETHOS*, **36**(1): 29–45.

Bryant-Davis, Thema, Chung, Heewoon, and Tillman, Shaquita (2009) From the margins to the center: ethnic minority women and the mental health effects of sexual assault. *Trauma, Violence, & Abuse*, **10**(4): 330–357.

Bryant-Waugh, Rachel (2006) Recent developments in anorexia nervosa. *Child and Adolescent Mental Health*, **11**(1): 76–81.

Buitelaar, Marjo (2006) 'I am the ultimate challenge.' Accounts of intersectionality in the life-story of a well-known daughter of Moroccan migrant workers in the Netherlands. *European Journal of Women's Studies*, **13**(3): 259–276.

Burman, Erica (1994/2008a) *Deconstructing developmental psychology.* London: Routledge.

(2008b) *Developments: child, image, nation.* London: Routledge.

Burman, Erica, and Chantler, Khatidja (2005) Domestic violence and minoritisation: legal and policy barriers facing minoritised women leaving violent relationships. *International Journal of Law and Psychiatry*, **28**(1): 59–74.

Burns, Maree (2004) Eating like an ox: femininity and dualistic constructions of bulimia and anorexia. *Feminism & Psychology*, **14**(2): 269–295.

Burns, Maree, Tyrer, Jane, and the Eating Difficulties Education Network (EDEN) (2009) Feminisms in practice: challenges and opportunities for an eating issues community agency. In Helen Malson and Maree Burns (eds.) *Critical feminist approaches to eating dis/orders.* London: Routledge.

Burstow, Bonnie (1992) *Radical feminist therapy: working in the context of violence.* Newbury Park, CA: Sage.

Bussey, Kay, and Bandura, Albert (1999) Social-cognitive theory of gender development and differentiation. *Psychological Review*, **106**: 676–713.

Butler, Judith (1990) *Gender trouble: feminism and the subversion of identity.* London: Routledge.

Buttny, Richard (1993) *Social accountability in conversation.* London: Sage.

Cameron, Deborah (2001) *Working with spoken discourse.* London: Sage.

Camic, Paul, Rhodes, Jean, and Yardley, Lucy (eds.) (2003a) *Qualitative research in psychology: expanding perspectives in methodology and design.* Washington, DC: American Psychological Association.

(2003b) Naming the stars: integrating qualitative methods into psychological research. In Paul Camic, Jean E. Rhodes, and Lucy Yardley (eds.) *Qualitative research in psychology.* Washington, DC: American Psychological Association, pp. 3–16.

Campbell, Rebecca (2008) The psychological impact of rape victims' experiences with the legal, medical, and mental health systems. *American Psychologist,* **68**(8): 702–717.

Canuso, Carla M., and Padina, Gahan (2007) Gender and schizophrenia. *Psychopharmacology Bulletin,* **40**(4): 178–190.

Caplan, Paula, and Cosgrove, Lisa (eds.) (2004) *Bias in psychiatric diagnosis.* Lanham, MD: Jason Aronson.

Carlsson, Ninni (2009) A time of telling: women working through sexual abuse. University of Göteborg, Department of Social Work, doctoral dissertation. http://hdl.handle.net/2077/19727 (retrieved August 26, 2011).

Charmaz, Kathy (2006) The power of names. *Journal of Contemporary Ethnography,* **35**(4): 396–399.

Chavez, Mark, and Insel, Thomas R. (2007) Eating disorders: National Institute of Mental Health's perspective. *American Psychologist,* **62**(3): 159–166.

Cherry, Frances (1995) *The 'stubborn particulars' of social psychology. Essays on the research process.* London: Routledge.

Chesler, Phyllis (1972) *Women and madness.* New York: Doubleday.

Chodorow, Nancy (1978) *The reproduction of mothering: psychoanalysis and the socialization of gender.* Berkeley, CA: University of California Press.

Clarke, Victoria, Ellis, Sonja J., Peel, Elizabeth, and Riggs, Damian W. (2010) *Lesbian, gay, bisexual, trans and queer psychology: an introduction.* Cambridge University Press.

Cole, Elizabeth R. (2009) Intersectionality and research in psychology. *American Psychologist,* **64**(3): 170–180.

Cole, Elizabeth R., and Stewart, Abigail J. (2001) Invidious comparisons: imagining a psychology of race and gender beyond differences. *Political Psychology,* **22**(2): 293–308.

Cole, Michael (1996) *Cultural psychology: a once and future discipline.* Cambridge, MA: Harvard University Press.

Collins, Patricia Hill (2000) *Black feminist thought: knowledge, consciousness, and the politics of empowerment.* New York: Routledge.

Comas-Diaz, Lillian, and Greene, Beverly (eds.) (1994) *Women of color: integrating ethnic and gender identities in psychotherapy.* New York: Guilford.

Connell, Robert W. (1995) *Masculinities.* Cambridge: Polity Press.
(2002) *Gender.* Cambridge: Polity Press.

Conrad, Peter (2007) *The medicalization of society.* Baltimore, MD: Johns Hopkins University Press.

Conrad, Peter, and Schneider, Joseph W. (1980) *Deviance and medicalization: from badness to sickness.* St. Louis, MO: C. V. Mosby.

Cosgrove, Lisa (2005) When labels mask oppression: implications for teaching psychiatric taxonomy to mental health counselors. *Journal of Mental Health Counseling,* **27**(4): 283–296.

Coyle, Adrian, and Kitzinger, Celia (eds.) (2002) *Lesbian and gay psychology: new perspectives*. Oxford: BPS Blackwell.

Crawford, Mary (2004) Mars and Venus collide: a discursive analysis of marital self-help psychology. *Feminism & Psychology*, 14(1): 63–79.

Crawford, Mary, and Chaffin, Roger (1997) The meanings of difference: cognition in social and cultural context. In Paula Caplan, Mary Crawford, Janet Hyde, and John T. Richardson (eds.) *Gender differences in human cognition*. New York: Oxford University Press, pp. 81–130.

Crawford, Mary, and Marecek, Jeanne (1989) Psychology reconstructs the female: 1968–1988. *Psychology of Women Quarterly*, 13(2): 147–165.

Crenshaw, Kimberlee (1991) Mapping the margins: intersectionality, identity politics, and violence against women of color. *Stanford Law Review*, 43(6): 1241–1279.

Crits-Christoph, Paul, Barber, Jacques P., Baranackie, Kathryn, and Cooper, Andrew (1993) Assessing the therapist's interpretations. In Nancy E. Miller (ed.) *Psychodynamic treatment research: a handbook for clinical practice*. New York: Basic Books, pp. 361–386.

Crossley, Michelle (2000) *Introducing narrative psychology: self, trauma and the construction of meaning*. Buckingham, UK: Open University Press.

Currie, Dawn, Kelly, Deirdre, and Pomerantz, Shauna (2006) 'The geeks shall inherit the earth': girls' agency, subjectivity and empowerment. *Journal of Youth Studies*, 9(4): 419–436.

(2007) Listening to girls: discursive positioning and the construction of self. *International Journal of Qualitative Studies in Education*, 20(4): 377–400.

Cushman, Philip (2002) How psychology erodes personhood. *Journal of Theoretical and Philosophical Psychology*, 22(2): 103–113.

Danziger, Kurt (1985) The methodological imperative in psychology. *Philosophy of the Social Sciences*, 15(1): 1–13.

(1990) *Constructing the subject: historical origins of psychological research*. Cambridge University Press.

Darley, John, and Latané, Bibb (1968) Bystander intervention in emergencies: diffusion of responsibility. *Journal of Personality and Social Psychology*, 8(4): 377–383.

D'Augelli, Anthony, and Patterson, Charlotte (eds.) (2001) *Lesbian, gay, and bisexual identities and youth: psychological perspectives*. Oxford University Press.

Davies, Bronwyn, and Harré, Rom (1990) Positioning: the discursive production of selves. *Journal of the Theory of Social Behavior*, 20(1): 43–65.

Day, Katy, and Keys, Tammy (2009) Anorexia/bulimia as resistance and conformity in pro-Ana and pro-Mia virtual conversations. In Helen Malson and Maree Burns (eds.) *Critical feminist approaches to eating dis/orders*. London: Routledge, pp. 87–96.

Deaux, Kay, and Major, Brenda (1987) Putting gender into context: an interactive model of gender-related behavior. *Psychological Review*, 94: 369–389.

DeLoache, Judy, and Gottlieb, Alma (2000) *A world of babies: imagined childcare guides for seven societies*. Cambridge University Press.

de los Reyes, Paulina, Molina, Irene, and Mulinari, Diana (eds.) (2005a) *Maktens (o)lika förklädnader: kön, klass and etnicitet i det postkoloniala Sverige: en festskrift till Wuokko Knocke* [*The different disguises of power: gender, class, and ethnicity in post-colonial Sweden*]. Stockholm: Atlas.

(2005b) *Intersektionalitet: kritiska reflektioner över (o)jämlikhetens landskap* [*Intersectionality: critical reflections on the landscapes of inequality*]. Malmö, Sweden: Liber.

Denzin, Norman K. (1998) The art and politics of interpretation. In N. K. Denzin and Y. S. Lincoln (eds.) *Collecting and interpreting qualitative materials*. London: Sage, pp. 313–344.

Deutsch, Francine M. (1999) *Halving it all: how equally shared parenting works*. Cambridge, MA: Harvard University Press.

DeVault, Marjorie (1990) Talking and listening from women's standpoint: feminist strategies for interviewing and analysis. *Social Problems*, 37(1): 96–116.

Diamond, Lisa (2006) Careful what you ask for: reconsidering feminist epistemology and autobiographical narrative in research on sexual identity development. *Signs: Journal of Women in Culture and Society*, 31(2): 471–491.

Diamond, Lisa M., and Butterworth, Molly (2008) Questioning gender and sexual identity: dynamic links over time. *Sex Roles*, 59: 365–376.

Dias, Karen (2003) The Ana sanctuary: women's pro-anorexia narratives in cyberspace. *Journal of International Women's Studies*, 4(2): 31–45.

Dimen, Muriel, and Goldner, Virginia (eds.) (2002) *Gender in psychoanalytic space: between clinic and culture*. New York: Other Press.

Dixon, John, and Wetherell, Margaret (2004) On discourse and dirty nappies: gender, the division of household labour and the social psychology of distributive justice. *Theory & Psychology*, 14(2): 167–189.

Dohrenwend, Bruce P., Levav, Itzhak, Shrout, Patrick E., Schwartz, Sharon, Naveh, Guedalia, Link, Bruce G., Skodol, Andrew E., and Stueve, Ann (1998) Ethnicity, socioeconomic status, and psychiatric disorders: a test of the social causation–social selection issue. In Bruce P. Dohrenwend (ed.) *Adversity, stress, and psychopathology*. New York: Oxford University Press, pp. 285–318.

Dollard, John (1937) *Caste and class in a southern town*. Garden City, NY: Doubleday.

Drinka, George F. (1984) *The birth of neurosis: myth, malady and the Victorians*. New York: Simon and Schuster.

Dryden, Caroline (1999) *Being married, doing gender: a critical analysis of gender relationships in marriage*. London: Routledge.

Duncan, Norman, Stevens, Garth, and Bowman, Brett (2004) South African psychology and racism: historical determinants and future prospects. In Derek Hook (ed.) *Critical psychology*. Lansdowne, South Africa: UCT Press, pp. 360–388.

Eagly, Alice H. (1987) *Sex differences in social behavior: a social-role interpretation*. Hillsdale, NJ: Erlbaum.

Edelman, Murray (1982) The political language of the mental health professions. In Hiram Rubenstein and M. H. Bloch (eds.) *Things that matter: influences on helping relationships*. New York: Macmillan, pp. 63–76.

Edley, Nigel (2001) Analysing masculinity: interpretative repertoires, ideological dilemmas, and subject positions. In Margaret Wetherell, Stephanie Taylor, and Simeon Yates (eds.) *Discourse as data: a guide for analysis.* London: Sage, pp. 189–228.

(2006) Never the twain shall meet: a critical appraisal of the combination of discourse and psychoanalytic theory in studies of men and masculinity. *Sex Roles*, **55**: 601–608.

Edley, Nigel, and Wetherell, Margaret (1997) Jockeying for position: the construction of masculine identities. *Discourse & Society*, **8**(2): 203–217.

(2001) Jekyll and Hyde: men's constructions of feminism and feminists. *Feminism & Psychology*, **11**(4): 439–457.

(2008) Discursive psychology and the study of gender: a contested space. In Kate Harrington, Lia Litosselito, Helen Sauntson, and Jane Sunderland (eds.) *Gender and language research methodologies.* Basingstoke, UK: Palgrave Macmillan, pp. 161–173.

Edwards, Derek (1997) *Discourse and cognition.* London: Sage.

Edwards, Derek, and Potter, Jonathan (1992) *Discursive psychology.* London: Sage.

Eichenbaum, Luise, and Orbach, Susie (1985) *Understanding women.* New York: Viking Penguin.

Else-Quest, Nicole, Hyde, Janet S., and Linn, Marcia (2010) Cross-national patterns of gender differences in mathematics: a meta-analysis. *Psychological Bulletin*, **136**(1): 103–127.

Engel, Susan (2005) *Real kids: creating meaning in everyday life.* Cambridge, MA: Harvard University Press.

Enns, Carolyn Z. (1993) Twenty years of feminist counseling and therapy: from naming biases to implementing multifaceted practice. *The Counseling Psychologist*, **21**(1): 3–87.

(2004) *Feminist theories and feminist psychotherapies: origins, themes and diversity* (2nd edn.). New York: Haworth Press.

(2010) Locational feminisms and feminist social identity analysis. *Professional Psychology: Research and Practice*, **41**(4): 333–339.

Erikson, Erik Homburger (1968) *Identity: youth and crisis.* New York: Norton.

Eriksson, Kristina (2003) *Manligt läkarskap, kvinnliga läkare och normala kvinnor* [*Masculine physicianhood, female doctors, and normal women*]. Stehag, Sweden: Förlags AB Gondolin.

Eskner Skoger, Ulrika, Lindberg, Lene, and Magnusson, Eva (2011) Neutrality, gender stereotypes, and analytical voids: the ideals and practices of Swedish child psychologists. *Feminism & Psychology*, **21**: 372–392.

Fausto-Sterling, Anne (2000a) *Sexing the body: gender politics and the construction of sexuality.* New York: Basic Books.

(2000b) Beyond difference: feminism and evolutionary psychology. In Hilary Rose and Steven Rose (eds.) *Alas, poor Darwin: arguments against evolutionary psychology.* London: Jonathan Cape, pp. 209–227.

Feingold, Alan (1994) Gender differences in personality: a meta-analysis. *Psychological Bulletin*, **116**: 429–456.

Feminist Therapy Institute (1999) Feminist therapy code of ethics. www. chrysaliscounseling.org/Feminist_Therapy.html (retrieved September 1, 2011).

Fenstermaker, Sarah, and West, Candace (eds.) (2002) *Doing gender, doing difference: inequality, power and institutional change*. New York: Routledge.

Fernando, Suman (2003) *Cultural diversity, mental health, and psychiatry: the struggle against racism*. New York: Brunner-Routledge.

Ferree, Myra Marx (2009) Inequality, intersectionality and the politics of discourse: framing feminist alliances. In Emanuela Lombardo, Petra Meier, and Mieke Verloo (eds.) *The discursive politics of gender equality: stretching, bending and policy-making*. London: Routledge, pp. 84–101.

Fine, Cordelia (2010) *Delusions of gender: how our minds, society, and neurosexism create difference*. New York: W. W. Norton.

Fine, Michelle (1989) Coping with rape: critical perspectives on consciousness. In Rhoda K. Unger (ed.) *Representations: social constructions of gender*. Amityville, NY: Baywood, pp. 186–200.

Fine, Michelle, Weis, Lois, Powell, Linda, and Wong, Mun (eds.) (1997) *Off-white: readings on race, power and society*. New York: Routledge.

Finlay, Linda, and Gough, Brendan (eds.) (2003) *Reflexivity: a practical guide for researchers in health and social sciences*. Oxford: Blackwell Science.

Flaherty, Eugenie W., Marecek, Jeanne, Olson, Kristin, and Wilcove, Gail (1983) Preventing adolescent pregnancy: an interpersonal problem-solving approach. *Prevention in Human Services*, 2(3): 49–64.

Fleck, Ludwik (1935/1979) *Genesis and development of a scientific fact* (trans. Fred Bradley and Thaddeus J. Renn) (ed. Thaddeus J. Renn and Robert K. Merton). University of Chicago Press.

Fontes, Lisa A. (2004) Ethics in violence against women research: the sensitive, the dangerous, and the overlooked. *Ethics & Behavior*, 14(2): 141–174.

Fors, Malin (2007) *Post-Oidipus* [*Post-Oedipus*]. Göteborg University, Department of Psychology.

Foucault, Michel (1965/1988) *Madness and civilization: a history of insanity in the age of reason*. New York: Random House Vintage Books.

(1969/1994) *The archaeology of knowledge*. London: Routledge.

(1975/1991) *Discipline and punish: the birth of the prison*. London: Penguin.

(1979) *The history of sexuality. Volume 1: An introduction*. London: Allen Lane.

(1980) Truth and power. In Colin Gordon (ed.) *Power/knowledge: selected interviews and other writings 1972–1977*. New York: Pantheon, pp. 109–133.

(1983) Afterword: the subject and power. In Hubert Dreyfus and Paul Rabinow (eds.) *Michel Foucault: beyond structuralism and hermeneutics*. University of Chicago Press, pp. 208–226.

(1986) *The history of sexuality. Volume 2: The use of pleasure*. London: Viking.

Fox, Dennis, and Prilleltensky, Isaac (eds.) (1997) *Critical psychology: an introduction*. London: Sage.

Fox, Dennis, Prilleltensky, Isaac, and Austin, Stephanie (eds.) (2009) *Critical psychology: an introduction* (2nd edn.). London: Sage.

Fox, Nathan, and Rutter, Michael (2010) Introduction to the Special Section on the effects of early experience on development. *Child Development*, 81(1): 23–27.

Frankenberg, Ruth (1993) *White women, race matters: the social construction of whiteness*. New York: Routledge.

Freedman, David H. (2010) Lies, damned lies, and medical science. *Atlantic Monthly*, **306**(4): 76–78, 80–82, 84–86.

Freeman, Mark (2010) The space of selfhood. In Suzanne Kirschner and Jack Martin (eds.) *The sociocultural turn in psychology: the contextual emergence of mind and self*. New York: Columbia University Press, pp. 137–159.

Freud, Sigmund (1905/1991) Differentiation of male and female. In *On sexuality: three essays on the theory of sexuality and other works*. Harmondsworth: Penguin Books.

(1952) The development of libido and the sexual organization. Part XXI in *A general introduction to psycho-analysis*. New York: Liveright Publishing Corporation.

(1963) Some psychic consequences of the anatomical difference between the sexes. In *The collected papers of Sigmund Freud. Part 8, Sexuality and the psychology of love*. New York: Collier.

Friedan, Betty (1963) *The feminine mystique*. New York: Dell.

Friend, Penelope, Kalin, Rudolf, and Giles, Howard (1979) Sex bias in the evaluation of journal articles: sexism in England. *British Journal of Social and Clinical Psychology*, **18**(1): 77–78.

Frithiof, Patricia (1984) *Kvinnor och psykoterapi* [*Women and psychotherapy*]. *Psykisk Hälsa* [*Mental Health*], **1**: 12–22.

Frodi, Ann, Macaulay, Jacqueline, and Thome, Pauline R. (1977) Are women always less aggressive than men? A review of the experimental literature. *Psychological Bulletin*, **84**(4): 634–660.

Frome, Pamela, and Eccles, Jacquelynne (1998) Parents' influence on children's achievement-related perceptions. *Journal of Personality and Social Psychology*, **74**: 435–452.

Frosh, Stephen, Phoenix, Ann, and Pattman, Rob (2002) *Young masculinities: understanding boys in contemporary society*. Basingstoke: Palgrave.

Gallagher, Ann, and DeLisi, Richard (1994) Gender differences in Scholastic Aptitude Test mathematics problem solving among high-ability students. *Journal of Educational Psychology*, **86**: 204–211.

Gallagher, Ann, Levin, Jutta, and Cahalan, Cara (2002) GRE research: cognitive patterns of gender differences in mathematics admissions test. *ETS Report 02–19*. Princeton, NJ: Educational Testing Service.

Garfinkel, Harold (1967) *Studies in ethnomethodology*. Englewood Cliffs, NJ: Prentice-Hall.

Gavey, Nicola (1992) Technologies and effects of heterosexual coercion. *Feminism & Psychology*, **2**(3): 325–351.

(1999) "I wasn't raped, but . . .": revisiting definitional problems in sexual victimization. In Sharon Lamb (ed.) *New versions of victims: feminists struggle with the concept*. New York University Press, pp. 57–81.

(2005) *Just sex? The cultural scaffolding of rape*. London: Routledge.

(2008) Rape, trauma and meaning. In Carolyn M. Elliott (ed.) *Global empowerment of women: responses to globalization and politicized religions*. London: Routledge, pp. 233–246.

(2009) Fighting rape: theory and practice. In Renee J. Heberle and Victoria Grace (eds.) *Theorizing sexual violence*. New York: Routledge, pp. 96–124.

Gavey, Nicola, and Schmidt, Johanna (2011) 'Trauma of rape' discourse: a double-edged template for everyday understandings of the impact of rape? *Violence Against Women*, 17: 433–456.

Geertz, Clifford (1973) *The interpretation of cultures*. New York: Basic Books.

(1983) *Local knowledge: further essays in interpretive anthropology*. New York: Basic Books.

Gergen, Kenneth (1985) The social constructionist movement in modern psychology. *American Psychologist*, 40: 266–275.

Gervasio, Amy H., and Crawford, Mary (1989) Social evaluations of assertiveness: a critique and speech act reformulation. *Psychology of Women Quarterly*, 13(1): 1–25.

Gigerenzer, Gerd, Swijtink, Zeno, Porter, Theodore, Daston, Lorraine, Beatty, John, and Krüger, Lorenz (1989) *The empire of chance: how probability changed science and everyday life*. Cambridge University Press.

Gilbert, Nigel, and Mulkay, Michael (1984) *Opening Pandora's box: a sociological analysis of scientists' discourse*. Cambridge University Press.

Gill, Rosalind, Henwood, Karen, and McLean, Carl (2005) Body projects and the regulation of normative masculinity. *Body and Society*, 11(1): 37–62.

Gilligan, Carol (1982) *In a different voice: psychological theory and women's development*. Cambridge, MA: Harvard University Press.

Gilman, Charlotte Perkins (1892/1980) The yellow wallpaper. In Ann Lane (ed.) *The Charlotte Perkins Gilman reader*. New York: Pantheon Books, pp. 3–20.

Glaser, Barney, and Strauss, Anselm (1967) *The discovery of grounded theory*. Chicago: Aldine.

Gluck, Sherna, and Patai, Daphne (eds.) (1991) *Women's words: the feminist practice of oral history*. New York: Routledge.

Goldberg, Philip A. (1968) Are women prejudiced against women? *Transaction*, 5: 28–30.

Goldner, Virginia (1985) Feminism and family therapy. *Family Process*, 24(1): 31–47.

(1999) Morality and multiplicity: perspectives on the treatment of violence in intimate life. *Journal of Marital and Family Therapy*, 25(3): 325–336.

Goodwin, Stephanie A., and Fiske, Susan (2001) Power and gender: the double-edged sword of ambivalence. In Rhoda Unger (ed.) *The handbook of the psychology of women and gender*. New York: Wiley, pp. 358–366.

Gough, Brendan (2004) Psychoanalysis as a resource for understanding emotional ruptures in the text: the case of defensive masculinities. *British Journal of Social Psychology*, 43: 245–267.

Gould, Stephen Jay (1981) *The mismeasure of man*. New York: Norton.

(2000) More things in heaven and earth. In Hilary Rose and Steven Rose (eds.) *Alas, poor Darwin: arguments against evolutionary psychology*. London: Jonathan Cape, pp. 85–105.

Gowaty, Patricia Adair (2001) Women, psychology, and evolution. In Rhoda K. Unger (ed.) *Handbook of the psychology of women and gender*. New York: Wiley, pp. 53–76.

Granek, Leeat (2007) "You're a whole lot of person": understanding the journey through anorexia to recovery: a qualitative study. *The Humanistic Psychologist*, **35**(4): 363–385.

Gray, John (1992) *Men are from Mars, women are from Venus: a practical guide for improving communication and getting what you want in your relationships.* New York: HarperCollins.

Greene, Sheila (2003) *The psychological development of girls and women: rethinking change in time.* London: Routledge.

Greenspan, Miriam (1983) *A new approach to women and therapy.* New York: McGraw-Hill.

Gremillion, Helen (2001) In fitness and in health: crafting bodies in the treatment of anorexia nervosa. *Signs: Journal of Women in Culture and Society*, **27**(2): 381–414.

(2003) *Feeding anorexia: gender and power at a treatment center.* Durham, NC: Duke University Press.

(2005) The cultural politics of body size. *Annual Review of Anthropology*, **34**(1): 13–32.

Grills, Scott, and Prus, Robert (2008) The myth of the independent variable: reconceptualizing class, gender, race, and age as subcultural processes. *American Sociologist*, **39**: 19–37.

Grinker, Roy Richard (2007) *Unstrange minds: remapping the world of autism.* New York: Basic Books.

Groneman, Carol (1994) Nymphomania: the historical construction of female sexuality. *Signs: Journal of Women in Culture and Society*, **19**(2): 337–367.

Guilfoyle, Michael (2008) CBT's integration into societal networks of power. *European Journal of Psychotherapy and Counselling*, **10**(3): 197–205.

Guiso, Luigi, Monte, Ferdinando, Sapienza, Paola, and Zingales, Luigi (2008) Diversity: culture, gender, and math. *Science*, **320**: 1164–1165.

Gulbrandsen, Liv Mette (1998) *I barns dagligliv. En kulturpsykologisk studie av jenters og gutters utvikling* [*Children's daily lives. A cultural psychological study of the development of girls and boys*]. Oslo: Scandinavian University Press.

(2002) Storybjenter [Girls in big cities]. In K. Thorsen and R. Toverud (eds.) *Kulturpsykologi. Bevegelser i livsløp* [*Cultural psychology. Narratives through the life span*]. Oslo: Scandinavian University Press, pp. 103–127.

(2003) Peer relations as arenas for gender constructions among young teenagers. *Pedagogy, Culture and Society*, **11**(1): 113–131.

(2006a) Fra småjenter till ungjenter: heteroseksualitet som normativ utviklingsretning [From little girls to young women: heterosexuality as a normative developmental trajectory]. *Tidsskrift for kjønnsforskning* [*Norwegian Journal of Gender Studies*], **4**: 5–20.

(2006b) *Opvekst og psykologisk utvikling: innføring i psykologiske perspektiver* [*Childhood and psychological development: an introduction to psychological perspectives*]. Oslo: Scandinavian University Press.

Guthrie, Robert V. (2004) *Even the rat was white: a historical view of psychology* (2nd edn.). Upper Saddle River, NJ: Pearson Education.

Haaken, Janice (1988) Field dependence research: a historical analysis of a psychological construct. *Signs: Journal of Women in Culture and Society*, **13**: 311–330.

(1998) *Pillar of salt: gender, memory, and the perils of looking back.* New Brunswick, NJ: Rutgers University Press.

Haaken, Janice, and Reavey, Paula (eds.) (2010) *Memory matters: contexts for understanding sexual abuse recollections.* New York: Routledge/Taylor and Francis Group.

Haavind, Hanne (1987) *Liten og stor. Mødres omsorg og barns utviklingsmuligheter* [*Small and big. Mother-care and children's possibilities for development*]. Oslo: Scandinavian University Press.

(1998) Understanding women in the psychological mode. In Drude von der Fehr, Anna Jonasdóttir, and Bente Rosenbeck (eds.) *Is there a Nordic feminism?* London: UCL Press, pp. 243–271.

(2000) *Kön och tolkning. Metodiska möjligheter i kvalitativ forskning* [*Gender and interpretations. Methodological possibilities in qualitative research*]. Stockholm: Natur & Kultur.

(2002) Forord [Preface]. In Kirsten Thoresen and Ruth Toverud (eds.) *Kulturpsykologi. Bevegelser i livsløp* [*Cultural psychology. Narratives through the life span*]. Oslo: Scandinavian University Press, pp. 7–12.

(2003) Masculinity by rule-breaking: cultural contestations in the transitional move from being a child to being a young male. *NORA: Nordic Journal of Women's Studies*, **11**(1): 89–100.

Hacking, Ian (1994) The looping effects of human kinds. In D. Sperber, D. Premack, and A. J. Premack (eds.) *Causal cognition: a multidisciplinary approach.* Oxford: Clarendon Press, pp. 351–394.

(1995) *Rewriting the soul: multiple personality and the sciences of memory.* Princeton, NJ: Princeton University Press.

(1998) *Mad travellers.* Charlottesville, VA: University of Virginia Press.

(1999) *The social construction of what?* Cambridge, MA: Harvard University Press.

Haldar, Marit (2006) Kjærlighetskunnskap: tolvåringers fortellinger om romantik og familieliv [Love knowledge: 12-year-olds' narratives about romantic relationships and family life]. University of Oslo, Department of Sociology and Cultural Geography, doctoral dissertation.

Hall, G. Stanley (1907) *Youth: its education, regimen and hygiene.* New York: D. Appleton.

Hallerstedt, Gunilla (2006) Introduktion: lidandets uttryck och namn [Introduction: the expression and naming of suffering]. In Gunilla Hallerstedt (ed.) *Diagnosens makt: om kunskap, pengar och lidande* [*The power of diagnosis: about knowledge, money, and suffering*]. Göteborg: Daidalos, pp. 11–28.

Halpern, Diane, Benbow, Camilla, Geary, David, Gur, Ruben, Hyde, Janet S., and Gernsbacher, Morton Ann (2007) The science of sex differences in science and mathematics. *Psychological Science in the Public Interest*, **8**: 1–51.

Hamberg, Katarina (2005) Biology, gender, and behaviour. A critical discussion of the biological models used for explaining cognitive and behavioural gender differences. In Janice Lee (ed.) *The psychology of gender identity*. New York: Nova Science Publishers, pp. 127–143.

Hamreby, Kerstin (2004) Flickor och pojkar i den sociala barnavården: föreställningar om kön och sociala problem under 1900-talet [Girls and boys in social work with children: ideas of gender and social problems throughout the 20th century]. Umeå, Sweden: Umeå University, Department of Social Work, doctoral dissertation.

Haraway, Donna (1988) Situated knowledges: the science question in feminism and the privilege of partial perspective. *Feminist Studies*, 14(3): 575–599.

Harding, Sandra (1986) *The science question in feminism*. Milton Keynes: Open University Press.

 (1987) *Feminism and methodology: social science issues*. Bloomington, IN: Indiana University Press.

Hare-Mustin, Rachel T. (1978) A feminist approach to family therapy. *Family Process*, 17(2): 181–194.

 (1980) Family therapy may be dangerous for your health. *Professional Psychology*, 11(6): 935–938.

 (1983) An appraisal of the relationship between women and psychotherapy: 80 years after the case of Dora. *American Psychologist*, 38: 594–601.

 (1987) The problem of gender in family therapy theory. *Family Process*, 26: 15–27.

 (1994) Discourses in the mirrored room: a postmodern analysis of therapy. *Family Process*, 33(1): 19–35.

Hare-Mustin, Rachel T., and Marecek, Jeanne (1986) Autonomy and gender: some questions for therapists. *Psychotherapy: Theory, Practice and Research*, 23(2): 205–212.

 (1988) The meaning of difference: gender theory, postmodernism, and psychology. *American Psychologist*, 43(6): 455–464.

 (1990) *Making a difference: psychology and the construction of gender*. New Haven, CT: Yale University Press.

 (1994) Asking the right questions: feminist psychology and sex differences. *Feminism & Psychology*, 4(4): 531–537.

 (1997) Clinical and abnormal psychology: the politics of madness. In Dennis Fox and Isaac Prilleltensky (eds.) *Critical psychology: an introduction*. London: Sage, pp. 104–120.

Hare-Mustin, Rachel, Marecek, Jeanne, Kaplan, Alexandra G., and Liss-Levinson, Nechama (1979) Rights of clients, responsibilities of therapists. *American Psychologist*, 34: 3–16.

Hauge, Mona-Iren (2009a) Bodily practices and discourses of hetero-femininity: girls' constitution of subjectivities in their social transitions between childhood and adolescence. *Gender and Education*, 21(3): 293–307.

 (2009b) Doing, being and becoming. Young people's processes of subjectivation between categories of age. University of Oslo, Department of Psychology, doctoral dissertation.

Hedges, L. V., and Nowell, A. (1995) Sex differences in mental test scores, variability, and numbers of high-scoring individuals. *Science*, 269: 41–45.

Hegarty, Peter (2007) Getting dirty: psychology's history of power. *History of Psychology*, **10**(2): 75–91.

Helliwell, Christine (2000) 'It's only a penis': rape, feminism and difference. *Signs: Journal of Women in Culture and Society*, **25**(3): 789–816.

Henrich, Joseph, Heine, Steven, and Norenzayan, Ara (2010) The weirdest people in the world? *Behavioral and Brain Sciences*, **33**: 61–83.

Henry, P. J. (2009) College sophomores in the laboratory redux: influences of a narrow database on social psychology's view of the nature of prejudice. *Psychological Inquiry*, **19**: 49–71.

Herdt, Gilbert (1997) *Same sex, different cultures*. Boulder, CO: Westview Press.

Herman, Judith (1992) *Trauma and recovery*. New York: Basic Books.

Hjern, Anders, Wicks, Susanne, and Dalman, Christina (2004) Social adversity contributes to high morbidity in psychoses in immigrants: a national cohort study in two generations of Swedish residents. *Psychological Medicine*, **34**(6): 1025–1033.

Holland, Janet, Ramazanoglu, Caroline, Sharpe, Sue, and Thomson, Rachel (2004) *The male in the head: young people, heterosexuality and power*. London: Tufnell Press.

Hollway, Wendy (1984/1998) Gender difference and the production of subjectivity. In Julian Henriques, Wendy Hollway, Cathy Urwin, Couze Venn, and Valerie Walkerdine (eds.) *Changing the subject: psychology, social regulation and subjectivity*. London: Methuen, pp. 227–263.

(1989) *Subjectivity and method in psychology: gender, meaning and science*. London: Sage.

Holmberg, Carin (1993) *Det kallas kärlek: en socialpsykologisk studie om kvinnors underordning och mäns överordning bland unga jämställda par* [*They call it love: a social psychological study of women's subordination and men's domination among young egalitarian couples*]. Göteborg: Anamma Publishers.

Holmberg, Carin, Stjernqvist, Ulrica, and Sörensen, Eva (2005) *Väldsamt lika och olika: om våld i samkönade parrelationer* [*Violently similar and different: about violence in same-sex couple relations*]. Stockholm: Stockholm University, Center for Gender Studies.

Holter, Harriet (1992) Berättelser om kvinnor, män och samhälle: kvinnoforskning under trettio år [*Narratives about women, men, and society: women's studies during thirty years*]. In Joan Acker et al. (eds.) *Kvinnors och mäns liv och arbete* [*Women's and men's lives and work*]. Stockholm: Studieförbundet Näringsliv och Samhälle, pp. 55–104.

Hook, Derek (2004a) Foucault, disciplinary power and the critical pre-history of psychology. In Derek Hook (ed.) *Critical psychology*, pp. 210–238.

(ed.) (2004b) *Critical psychology*. Lansdowne, South Africa: UCT Press.

Hopper, Kim, Harrison, Glynn, Janca, Aleksandar, and Sartorius, Norman (2007) *Recovery from schizophrenia: an international perspective – results from the WHO-coordinated International Study of Schizophrenia*. Oxford University Press.

Horney, Karen (1967) *Feminine psychology*. London: Routledge & Kegan Paul.

Hornstein, Gail (1988) Quantifying psychological phenomena: debates, dilemmas, and implications. In Jill Morawski (ed.) *The rise of experimentation in American psychology.* New Haven, CT: Yale University Press, pp. 1–34.

Horton-Salway, Mary (2001) The construction of M.E.: the discursive action model. In Margaret Wetherell, Stephanie Taylor, and Simeon Yates (eds.) *Discourse as data: a guide for analysis.* London: Sage, pp. 147–199.

Horwitz, Allan V. (2002) *Creating mental illness.* University of Chicago Press.

Hyde, Janet (2005) The gender similarities hypothesis. *American Psychologist,* **60**: 581–592.

Hyde, Janet, Lindberg, Sara, Linn, Marcia, Ellis, Amy, and Williams, Caroline (2008) Gender similarities characterize math performance. *Science,* **321**: 494–495.

Hyde, Janet, and McKinley, Nita (1997) Gender differences in cognition: results from meta-analyses. In Paula Caplan, Mary Crawford, Janet Hyde, and John T. Richardson (eds.) *Gender differences in human cognition.* New York: Oxford University Press, pp. 30–51.

Hyndman, Jennifer (2008) Feminism, conflict and disasters in post-tsunami Sri Lanka. *Gender, Technology and Development,* **12**(1): 101–121.

Ikunga, Ai, Nath, Sanjay, and Skinner, Kenneth (2009) Internet suicide bulletin boards in Japan: A qualitative content analysis. Paper presented at the meetings of the American Psychological Association, Toronto, Canada, August 2009.

Jadhav, Susrut (1996) The cultural origins of western depression. In Vieda Skultans and John Cox (eds.) *Anthropological approaches to psychological medicine.* London: Jessica Kingsley Publishers, pp. 41–65.

Jaffee, Sara, and Hyde, Janet S. (2000) Gender differences in moral orientation: a meta-analysis. *Psychological Bulletin,* **126**: 703–726.

James, Kerrie, and McKinnon, Laurie (1990) The "incestuous family" revisited: a critical analysis of family therapy myths. *Journal of Marital and Family Therapy,* **16**(1): 71–88.

Jenkins, Janis H., and Barrett, Robert J. (eds.) (2004) *Schizophrenia, culture, and subjectivity: the edge of experience.* Cambridge University Press.

Johannisson, Karin (2006) Hur skapas en diagnos? Ett historiskt perspektiv [How is a diagnosis created? A historical perspective]. In Gunilla Hallerstedt (ed.) *Diagnosens makt: om kunskap, pengar och lidande [The power of diagnosis: about knowledge, money, and suffering].* Göteborg: Daidalos, pp. 29–42.

Johnson, Marilyn (1976) An approach to feminist therapy. *Psychotherapy: Theory, Research and Practice,* **13**(1): 72–76.

Jordan, Judith V., Kaplan, Alexandra, Miller, Jean B., Stiver, Irene, and Surrey, Janet (1991) *Women's growth in connection.* New York: Guilford.

Jordan-Young, Rebecca (2010) *Brain storm: the flaws in the science of sex differences.* Cambridge, MA: Harvard University Press.

Kagan, Jerome (1998) *Three seductive ideas.* Cambridge, MA: Harvard University Press.

Kakar, Sudhir (1991) *Shamans, mystics, and doctors.* University of Chicago Press.

Kalat, James W. (2009) *Biological psychology* (10th edn.). Belmont, CA: Wadsworth.

Kärfve, Eva (2006) Den mänskliga mångfalden – diagnosen som urvalsinstrument [Human diversity: diagnoses as selection instruments]. In Gunilla Hallerstedt (ed.) *Diagnosens makt: om kunskap, pengar och lidande* [*The power of diagnosis: about knowledge, money, and suffering*]. Göteborg: Daidalos, pp. 59–71.

Kaschak, Ellen (1992) *Engendered lives: a new view of women's experience*. New York: Basic Books.

Kirk, Stuart A., and Kutchins, Herb (1992) *The selling of DSM: the rhetoric of science in psychiatry*. New York: Aldine de Gruyter.

Kirschner, Suzanne, and Martin, Jack (eds.) (2010) *The sociocultural turn in psychology: the contextual emergence of mind and self*. New York: Columbia University Press.

Kitzinger, Celia (ed.) (1994) Should psychologists study sex differences? (Special Feature). *Feminism & Psychology*, 4(4): 501–546.

(2001) Sexualities. In Rhoda Unger (ed.) *Handbook of the psychology of women and gender*. New York: Wiley, pp. 272–285.

Kitzinger, Celia, and Peel, Elizabeth (2005) The de-gaying and re-gaying of AIDS: contested homophobias in lesbian and gay awareness training. *Discourse & Society*, 16(2): 173–197.

Kitzinger, Celia, and Perkins, Rachel (1993) *Changing our minds: lesbian feminism and psychology*. London: Onlywomen Press.

Kleinman, Arthur (1988) *The illness narratives: suffering, healing, and the human condition*. New York: Basic Books.

Kleinman, Arthur, and Good, Byron (eds.) (1984) *Culture and depression*. Berkeley, CA: University of California Press.

Kling, Kristen C., Hyde, Janet S., Showers, Carolin J., and Buswell, Brenda N. (1999) Gender differences in self-esteem: a meta-analysis. *Psychological Bulletin*, 125: 470–500.

Knight, George P., Guthrie, I. K., Page, M. C., and Fabes, R. A. (2002) Emotional arousal and gender differences in aggression: a meta-analysis. *Aggressive Behavior*, 28: 366–393.

Koch, Sigmund (1981) The nature and limits of psychological knowledge: lessons of a quarter century qua science. *American Psychologist*, 36: 257–269.

Korobov, Neill (2004) Inoculating against prejudice: a discursive approach to homophobia and sexism in adolescent male talk. *Psychology of Men and Masculinity*, 5(2): 178–189.

(2005) Ironizing masculinity: how adolescent boys negotiate hetero-normative dilemmas in conversational interaction. *Journal of Men's Studies*, 13(2): 225–246.

Korobov, Neill, and Bamberg, Michael (2004) Positioning a 'mature' self in interactive practices: how adolescent males negotiate 'physical attraction' in group talk. *British Journal of Developmental Psychology*, 22: 471–492.

Koss, Mary (1985) The hidden rape victim: personality, attitudinal, and situational characteristics. *Psychology of Women Quarterly*, 9(2): 193–212.

Kulick, Don (ed.) (2005) *Queersverige* [*Queering Sweden*]. Stockholm: Natur & Kultur.

Lacey, Hugh (2005) *Is science value-free? Values and scientific understanding.*
New York: Routledge.
LaFrance, Marianne, Hecht, Marvin A., and Paluck, Elizabeth Levy (2003)
The contingent smile: a meta-analysis of sex differences in smiling.
Psychological Bulletin, **129**(2): 305–334.
Lamb, Sharon (1991) Acts without agents: an analysis of linguistic avoidance
in journal articles on men who batter women. *American Journal of
Orthopsychiatry,* **61**(2): 250–257.
(ed.) (1999) *New versions of victims: feminists struggle with the concept.* New York
University Press.
Lamb, Sharon, and Brown, Lyn M. (2006) *Packaging girlhood: rescuing our
daughters from marketers' schemes.* New York: St. Martin's Press.
Lareau, Annette (2003) *Unequal childhoods: class, race and family life.* Berkeley,
CA: University of California Press.
Lehrer, Jonah (2010) The truth wears off. Is there something wrong with the
scientific method? *New Yorker,* **86**(40): 52–57.
Lerman, Hannah (1986) *A mote in Freud's eye.* New York: Springer.
Lerman, Hannah, and Porter, Natalie (eds.) (1990) *Feminist ethics in
psychotherapy.* New York: Springer.
Lorber, Judith (1994) *Paradoxes of gender.* New Haven, CT: Yale University
Press.
Lukes, Steven (1974) *Power: a radical view.* London: Macmillan.
Lyness, Anne M. P. (ed.) (2006) *Lesbian families' challenges and means of resiliency:
implications for feminist family therapy.* New York: Haworth Press.
Maccoby, Eleanor, and Jacklin, Carol Nagy (1974) *The psychology of sex
differences.* Stanford, CA: Stanford University Press.
MacLean, Christopher, Carey, Maggie, and White, Cheryl (1996) *Men's ways
of being.* Boulder, CO: Westview Press.
Magnusson, Eva (1996) Jag har faktiskt aldrig lidit av att vara kvinna [I have
never really suffered by being a woman]. *Kvinnovetenskaplig tidskrift
[Swedish Journal of Women's Studies],* **17**(1): 30–46.
(1998) *Vardagslivets könsinnebörder under förhandling: om arbete, familj och
produktion av kvinnlighet [Everyday negotiations of gender: work, family and the
production of femininity].* Umeå, Sweden: Umeå University, Department of
Clinical Psychology.
(2000a) Studier av konsistens och föränderlighet i könsinnebörder – att arbeta
med dubbla analytiska ansatser [Studies of consistency and change in the
meanings of gender: working with dual analytical approaches]. In
H. Haavind (ed.) *Kön och tolkning: metodiska möjligheter i kvalitativ forskning
[Gender and interpretations: methodological possibilities in qualitative research].*
Stockholm: Natur & Kultur, pp. 220–259.
(2000b) Party-political rhetoric on gender equality in Sweden: the uses of
uniformity and heterogeneity. *NORA: Nordic Journal of Women's Studies,*
8(2): 78–92.
(2000c) Positions, powers and hierarchies in feminist research: the vicissitudes
of egalitarian interviews. Paper presented at the 25th Annual Association for
Women in Psychology Conference, Salt Lake City, Utah, March 2000.

(2003) *Psykologi och kön: från könsskillnader till genusperspektiv* [*Psychology and gender: from sex differences to gender issues*]. Stockholm: Natur & Kultur.

(2006) *Hon, han och hemmet: genuspsykologiska perspektiv på vardagslivet i nordiska barnfamiljer* [*She, he, and their home: gender, psychology, and everyday life in Nordic families with children*]. Stockholm: Natur & Kultur.

(2008a) The rhetoric of inequality: Nordic women and men argue against sharing housework. *NORA: Nordic Journal of Feminist and Gender Research,* 16(2): 79–95.

(2008b) Conflict, danger and difference: Nordic heterosexual couples converse about gender equality and fairness. In Eva Magnusson, Malin Rönnblom, and Harriet Silius (eds.) *Critical studies of gender equalities: Nordic dislocations, dilemmas and contradictions.* Göteborg: Makadambok förlag, pp. 161–179.

(2011) Women, men, and all the other categories: psychologies for theorizing human diversity. *Nordic Psychology,* 63(2): 88–114.

Magnusson, Eva, and Marecek, Jeanne (2010) Sociocultural means to feminist ends: discursive and constructionist psychologies of gender. In Suzanne Kirschner and Jack Martin (eds.) *The sociocultural turn in psychology: the contextual emergence of mind and self.* New York: Columbia University Press, pp. 88–110.

Magnusson, Eva, Sjöquist Andersson, Lena, and Wännman, Lena (1998) *Forskarens projekt – och deltagarens. En reflexiv studie av relationerna mellan forskare och deltagare i ett forskningsprojekt om kvinnors arbetsliv* [*The researcher's project – and that of the participants. A reflexive study of the relations between researcher and participants in a research project on women's work life*]. Umeå, Sweden: Umeå University, Center for Women's Studies, Report no. 7.

Malson, Helen (1997) *The thin woman: feminism, post-structuralism and the social psychology of anorexia nervosa.* London: Routledge.

Mander, Anica V., and Rush, Anne K. (1974) *Feminism as therapy.* New York: Random House.

Marecek, Jeanne (1993) Disappearances, silences, and anxious rhetoric: gender in abnormal psychology textbooks. *Journal of Theoretical and Philosophical Psychology,* 13: 114–123.

(1995a) Gender, politics, and psychology's ways of knowing. *American Psychologist,* 50: 162–163.

(1995b) Feminism and psychology: can this relationship be saved? In Domna C. Stanton and Abigail J. Stewart (eds.) *Feminisms in the academy.* Ann Arbor, MI: University of Michigan Press, pp. 101–132.

(2001) Disorderly constructs: feminist frameworks for mental health. In Rhoda K. Unger (ed.) *Handbook of the psychology of women and gender.* New York: Wiley, pp. 303–316.

(2003) Dancing through minefields: toward a qualitative stance in psychology. In Paul Camic, Jean Rhodes, and Lucy Yardley (eds.) *Qualitative research in psychology: expanding perspectives in methodology and design.* Washington, DC: American Psychological Association, pp. 49–69.

Marecek, Jeanne, and Appuhamilage, Udeni (2011) Present but unnamed: feminisms and psychologies in Sri Lanka. In Alexandra Rutherford, Rose Capdevila, Vindya Undurti, and Ingrid Palmary (eds.) *Handbook of international feminisms: perspectives on psychology, women, culture, and rights.* New York: Springer.

Marecek, Jeanne, Caron, Cynthia, and Lynch, Caitrin (2009) "Ethical bras" and "guilt-free garments": the politics of sexual harassment in the Sri Lankan garment industry. Paper presented at the 38th Annual South Asia Conference, Madison, Wisconsin, USA.

Marecek, Jeanne, Crawford, Mary, and Popp, Danielle (2004) On the construction of gender, sex, and sexualities. In Alice Eagly, Robert Sternberg, and Anne Beall (eds.) *The psychology of gender.* New York: Guilford Press, pp. 192–216.

Marecek, Jeanne, and Hare-Mustin, Rachel T. (1991) A short history of the future: feminism and clinical psychology. *Psychology of Women Quarterly,* **15**: 521–536.

Marecek, Jeanne, and Hare-Mustin, Rachel (2009) Clinical psychology: the politics of madness. In Dennis Fox, Isaac Prilleltensky, and Stephanie Austin (eds.) *Critical psychology: an introduction* (2nd edn.). London: Sage, pp. 75–92.

Markus, Hazel R. (2008) Pride, prejudice and ambivalence: toward a unified theory of race and ethnicity. *American Psychologist,* **63**(8): 651–670.

Marsella, Anthony J. (1978) Thoughts on cross-cultural studies on the epidemiology of depression. *Culture, Medicine and Psychiatry,* 2: 343–357.

Martin, Carol L., Ruble, Diane N., and Szkrybalo, Joel (2002) Cognitive theories of early gender development. *Psychological Bulletin,* **128**: 903–933.

Masters, William, and Johnson, Virginia (1966) *Human sexual response.* Boston: Little, Brown.

Matlin, Margaret (2004) *The psychology of women* (5th edn.). New York: Thompson.

Mattingly, Cheryl (2008) Reading minds and telling tales in a cultural borderland. *ETHOS,* **36**(1): 136–154.

Mattingly, Cheryl, Lutkehaus, Nancy, and Throop, C. Jason (2008) Bruner's search for meaning: a conversation between psychology and anthropology. *ETHOS,* **36**(1): 1–28.

Mays, Vickie M. (1988) Even the rat was White and male: teaching the psychology of Black women. In Phyllis A. Bronstein and Kathryn Quina (eds.) *Teaching a psychology of people: resources for gender and sociocultural awareness.* Washington, DC: American Psychological Association, pp. 142–146.

McCall, Leslie (2005) The complexity of intersectionality. *SIGNS: Journal of Women in Culture and Society,* **30**(3): 1771–1800.

McKenzie-Mohr, Suzanne, and Lafrance, Michelle N. (2011) Telling stories without the words: 'tightrope talk' in women's accounts of coming to live well after rape or depression. *Feminism & Psychology,* **21**(1): 49–73.

McMullen, Linda (2002) Learning the languages of research: transcending illiteracy and indifference. *Canadian Psychology,* **43**(3): 195–204.

McMullin, Darcy, and White, Jacquelyn (2006) Long-term effects of labelling a rape experience. *Psychology of Women Quarterly,* **30**(1): 96–105.

208   References

Mednick, Martha (1989) On the politics of psychological constructs: stop the bandwagon, I want to get off. *American Psychologist*, 44: 1118–1123.

Mehan, Hugh (1993) Beneath the skin and between the ears: a case study in the politics of representation. In Seth Chaiklin and Jean Lave (eds.) *Understanding practice: perspectives on activity and context*. New York: Cambridge University Press, pp. 241–268.

Metcalfe, William, and Caplan, Paula (2004) Seeking "normal" sexuality on a complex matrix. In Paula Caplan and Lisa Cosgrove (eds.) *Bias in psychiatric diagnosis*. Lanham, MD: Jason Aronson, pp. 121–126.

Miles, Robert (1993) *Racism after "race relations."* London: Routledge.

Miller, Jean Baker (1976) *Toward a new psychology of women*. Boston: Beacon Press.

Miller, Jean Baker, and Stiver, Irene (1997) *The healing connection*. Boston: Beacon Press.

Miller, Jody (2008) *Getting played: African American girls, urban inequality and gendered violence*. New York University Press.

Miller, Peggy J., Wang, Su-hua, Sandel, Todd, and Cho, Grace E. (2002) Self-esteem as folk theory: a comparison of European American and Taiwanese mothers' beliefs. *Parenting: Science and Practice*, 2(3): 209–239.

Mishler, Elliot G. (1979) Meaning in context: is there any other kind? *Harvard Educational Review*, 49(1): 1–19.

Morawski, Jill (ed.) (1988) *The rise of experimentation in American psychology*. New Haven, CT: Yale University Press.

(1994) *Practicing feminisms, reconstructing psychology: notes on a liminal science*. Ann Arbor, MI: University of Michigan Press.

(1997) White blood and other white conditions: locating the psychologist's race. In Michelle Fine, Lois Weis, Linda C. Powell, and L. Mun Wong (eds.) *Off-white: readings on race, power, and society*. New York: Routledge, pp. 13–28.

Mouffe, Chantal (ed.) (1992) *Dimensions of a radical democracy: pluralism, citizenship, community*. London: Verso.

Moynihan, Roy, Heath, Iona, and Henry, David (2002) Selling sickness: the pharmaceutical industry and disease mongering. *British Medical Journal*, 324(7342): 886–891.

Nanda, Serena (1998) The hijras of India: cultural and individual dimensions of an institutionalized third gender role. In Peter Aggleton and Richard Parker (eds.) *Culture, society, and sexuality*. London: UCL Press, pp. 226–238.

National Council for Crime Prevention (2008) *Våldtäkt mot personer 15 år eller äldre. Utvecklingen under åren 1995–2006 [Rape of persons 15 years of age and older. Development during the years 1995–2006]*. Report 2008:13. Stockholm: BRÅ, National Council for Crime Prevention.

Nichter, Mimi (2000) *Fat talk*. Cambridge, MA: Harvard University Press.

Nordenmark, Mikael, and Nyman, Charlott (2003) Fair or unfair? Perceived fairness of household division of labour and gender equality among women and men: the Swedish case. *European Journal of Women's Studies*, 10(2): 181–209.

Oakley, Ann (1981) Interviewing women: a contradiction in terms. In Helen Roberts (ed.) *Doing feminist research*. London: Routledge and Kegan Paul, pp. 30–61.

Obeyesekere, Gananath (1984) Depression, Buddhism and the work of culture in Sri Lanka. In Arthur Kleinman and Byron Good (eds.) *Culture and depression*. Berkeley, CA: University of California Press, pp. 134–152.

Oliver, Mary Beth, and Hyde, Janet S. (1993) Gender differences in sexuality: a meta-analysis. *Psychological Bulletin*, **114**: 29–51.

Oransky, Matthew, and Marecek, Jeanne (2009) "I'm not going to be a girl": masculinity and emotions in boys' friendships and peer groups. *Journal of Adolescent Research*, **24**(2): 218–241.

Ortner, Tuulia M., and Sieverding, Monika (2008) Where are the gender differences? Male priming boosts spatial skills in women. *Sex Roles*, **59**: 274–281.

Paludi, Michele A., and Bauer, William D. (1983) Goldberg revisited: what's in an author's name? *Sex Roles*, **9**(3): 387–390.

Parlee, Mary Brown (1992) On PMS and psychiatric abnormality. *Feminism & Psychology*, **2**(1): 105–108.

(1994a) Comment/Reply. Commentary on the literature review. In Judith H. Gold and Sally K. Severino (eds.) *Premenstrual dysphorias: myths and realities*. Washington, DC: American Psychiatric Association, pp. 149–167.

(1994b) The social construction of premenstrual syndrome: a case study of scientific discourse as cultural contestation. In Mary G. Winkler and Letha B. Cole (eds.) *The good body: asceticism in contemporary culture*. New Haven, CT: Yale University Press, pp. 91–107.

Perry, Pamela (2003) White means never having to say you're ethnic: white youth and the construction of "cultureless" identities. In James Holstein and Jaber Gubrium (eds.) *Inner lives and social worlds: readings in social psychology*. New York: Oxford University Press, pp. 362–380.

Peterson, Abby, and Ålund, Aleksandra (2007) Etniciteter: ras, kön, klass, identitet och kultur [Ethnicities: race, gender, class, identity, and culture]. In Abby Peterson and Mikael Hjerm (eds.) *Etnicitet: perspektiv på samhället* [*Ethnicity: perspectives on society*]. Malmö: Gleerups, pp. 11–26.

Phillips, Lynn M. (2000) *Flirting with danger: young women's reflections on sexuality and domination*. New York University Press.

Piran, Niva (2001) Re-inhabiting the body from the inside out: girls transform their school environment. In Deborah L. Tolman and Mary Brydon-Miller (eds.) *From subjects to subjectivities: a handbook of interpretive and participatory methods*. New York University Press, pp. 218–238.

Plato (1972) *Phaedrus*. Cambridge University Press.

Polkinghorne, Donald P. (1990) *Narrative knowing and the human sciences*. Albany, NY: SUNY Press.

Potter, Jonathan (1996) *Representing reality: discourse, rhetoric and social construction*. London: Sage.

(2005) Making psychology relevant. *Discourse & Society*, **16**(5): 739–747.

Potter, Jonathan, and Wetherell, Margaret (1987) *Discourse and social psychology.* London: Sage.

Prins, Baukje (2006) Narrative accounts of origins: a blind spot in the intersectional approach? *European Journal of Women's Studies,* 13(3): 277–290.

Quinn, Naomi (ed.) (2005) *Finding culture in talk: a collection of methods.* New York: Palgrave Macmillan.

Rabinowitz, Vita C., and Weseen, Susan (2001) Power, politics, and the qualitative/quantitative debates in psychology. In Deborah L. Tolman and Mary Brydon-Miller (eds.) *From subjects to subjectivities: a handbook of interpretive and participatory methods.* New York University Press, pp. 12–28.

Radtke, H. Lorraine (2009) Theorizing mothering in the context of intimate partner violence. In Thomas Teo, Paul Stenner, Alexandra Rutherford, *et al.* (eds.) *Varieties of theoretical psychology: ISTP 2007.* Concord, Ontario: Captus Press.

Råstam, Maria, Gillberg, Christoffer, and Wentz, Elisabet (2003) Outcome of teenage-onset anorexia nervosa in a Swedish community-based sample. *European Child and Adolescent Psychiatry,* 12(Suppl. 1): 78–90.

Reddy, Gayatri (2005) *With respect to sex: negotiating hijra identity in South India.* University of Chicago Press.

Rennie, David L. (2006) The grounded theory method: application of a variant of its procedure of constant comparative analysis to psychotherapy research. In Constance T. Fischer (eds.) *Qualitative research methods for psychologists: introduction through empirical studies.* San Diego, CA: Elsevier Academic Press, pp. 59–78.

Reynolds, Jill, Wetherell, Margaret, and Taylor, Stephanie (2007) Choice and chance: negotiating agency in narratives of singleness. *Sociological Review,* 55(2): 331–351.

Rhodes, Lorna Amarasingham (1995) *Emptying beds: the work of an emergency psychiatric unit.* Berkeley, CA: University of California Press.

Richards, Graham (1997) *'Race', racism and psychology: towards a reflexive history.* London: Routledge.

　(2010) *Putting psychology in its place: a critical historical perspective* (3rd edn.). London: Routledge.

Richardson, John T. E. (ed.) (1996) *Handbook of qualitative research methods for psychology and the social sciences.* Leicester: BPS Books (British Psychological Society).

Richardson, Robert C. (2010) *Evolutionary psychology as maladapted psychology.* Cambridge, MA: MIT Press.

Rigné, Eva Marie (2002) Profession, science and state: psychology in Sweden 1968–1990. Göteborg University, Department of Sociology, doctoral dissertation.

Ristock, Janice L. (2003) Exploring dynamics of abusive lesbian relationships: preliminary analysis of a multisite, qualitative study. *American Journal of Community Psychology,* 31(3–4): 329–341.

Robinson, Daniel N. (1995) The logic of reductionistic models. *New Ideas in Psychology,* 13(1): 1–8.

(2000) Paradigms and 'the myth of framework': how science progresses. *Theory & Psychology*, **10**: 39–47.

Rodin, Judith, Silberstein, Lisa, and Striegel-Moore, Ruth (1984) Women and weight: a normative discontent. *Nebraska Symposium on Motivation*, **32**: 267–307.

Rogler, Lloyd (1997) Making sense of historical changes in the *Diagnostic and Statistical Manual of Mental Disorders*: five propositions. *Journal of Health and Social Behavior*, **38**: 9–20.

Rogoff, Barbara (1995) Observing sociocultural activity on three planes: participatory appropriation, guided participation, and apprenticeship. In James Wertsch, Pablo del Río, and Amelia Alvarez (eds.) *Sociocultural studies of mind*. Cambridge University Press, pp. 139–164.

(2003) *The cultural nature of human development*. New York: Oxford University Press.

Roman, Christine (2004) *Familjen i det moderna. Sociologiska sanningar och feministisk kritik* [*The family in modernity. Sociological truths and feminist critique*]. Malmö: Liber.

Root, Maria P., and Brown, Laura (1990) *Diversity and complexity in feminist therapy*. New York: Routledge.

Rose, Hilary, and Rose, Steven (eds.) (2000) *Alas, poor Darwin: arguments against evolutionary psychology*. London: Jonathan Cape.

Rose, Nikolas (1989) *Governing the soul: the shaping of the private self*. London: Free Association Books.

(1996) *Inventing ourselves: psychology, power and personhood*. Cambridge University Press.

Rosenberg, Rosalind (1982) *Beyond separate spheres: intellectual roots of modern feminism*. New Haven, CT: Yale University Press.

Rosenwald, George, and Ochberg, Richard (eds.) (1992) *Storied lives: the cultural politics of self-understanding*. New Haven, CT: Yale University Press.

Rossiter, Amy, deBoer, Catherine, Narayan, Jasma, Razack, Narda, Scollay, Virginia, and Willette, Chris (1998) Toward an alternative account of feminist practice ethics in mental health. *Affilia*, **13**(1): 9–30.

Rowold, Katharina (1996) *Gender and science: late nineteenth century debates on the female mind and body*. Bristol, UK: Thoemmes Press.

Rubin, Lisa, Fitts, Mako, and Becker, Anne E. (2003) 'Whatever feels good in my soul': body ethics and aesthetics among African American and Latina women. *Culture, Medicine, and Psychiatry*, **27**(1): 49–75.

Rush, Florence (1980) *The best kept secret: sexual abuse of children*. New York: McGraw-Hill.

Russell, Glenda, and Bohan, Janis (2006) The case of internalized homophobia: theory and/as practice. *Theory & Psychology*, **16**(3): 343–366.

Russell, Shona, and Carey, Maggie (2003) Feminism, therapy, and narrative ideas: exploring some not so commonly asked questions. *International Journal of Narrative Therapy and Community Work*, **2**: 67–91.

Russett, Cynthia E. (1989) *Sexual science: the Victorian construction of womanhood*. Cambridge, MA: Harvard University Press.

Rutherford, Alexandra, Marecek, Jeanne, and Sheese, Kate (in press) The psychology of women and gender. In Donald Freedheim (ed.) *The history of psychology* (2nd edn.). New York: Wiley.

Sadker, David, Sadker, Myra, and Zittleman, Karen (1994) *Still failing at fairness*. New York: Simon & Schuster.

Sameroff, Arnold (2010) A unified theory of development: a dialectic integration of nature and nurture. *Child Development*, **81**(1): 6–22.

Scarborough, Elizabeth, and Furomoto, Laurel (1987) *Untold lives: the first generation of American women psychologists*. New York: Columbia University Press.

Scott, Joan W. (1986) Gender: a useful category of historical analysis. *American Historical Review*, **91**(5): 1053–1075.

Sears, David O. (1986) College sophomores in the laboratory: influences of a narrow data base on social psychology's view of human nature. *Journal of Personality and Social Psychology*, **51**(3): 515–530.

Seavey, Carol, Katz, Phyllis, and Zalk, Sue (1975) Baby X: the effect of gender labels on adult responses to infants. *Sex Roles*, **1**(2): 103–109.

Sex Roles (2008) Gender: an intersectionality perspective. *Sex Roles*, **59**, whole issue 8.

Seymour-Smith, Sarah, and Wetherell, Margaret (2006) 'What he hasn't told you ...': investigating the micro-politics of gendered support in heterosexual couples' co-constructed accounts of illness. *Feminism & Psychology*, **16**(1): 105–127.

Sharps, Matthew J., Price, Jana, and Williams, John K. (1994) Spatial cognition and gender: instructional and stimulus influences on mental image rotation performance. *Psychology of Women Quarterly*, **18**: 413–426.

Sherif, Carolyn Wood (1979) Bias in psychology. In Julia Sherman and Evelyn Beck (eds.) *The prism of sex: essays in the sociology of knowledge*. Madison, WI: University of Wisconsin Press, pp. 93–133.

Sherman, Julia A. (1978) *Sex-related cognitive differences: an essay on theory and evidence*. Springfield, IL: Thomas.

Shields, Stephanie (1975) Functionalism, Darwinism, and the psychology of women: a study in social myth. *American Psychologist*, **30**: 739–754.

(2008) Gender: an intersectionality perspective. *Sex Roles*, **59**: 301–311.

Showalter, Elaine (1987) *The female malady: women, madness and English culture, 1830–1980*. London: Virago Press.

Shweder, Richard A. (1991) *Thinking through cultures: expeditions in cultural psychology*. Cambridge, MA: Harvard University Press.

Shweder, Richard A., Goodnow, Jacqueline, Hatano, Giyoo, LeVine, Robert A., Markus, Hazel, and Miller, Peggy (1998) The cultural psychology of development: one mind, many mentalities. In William Damon and Richard Lerner (eds.) *Handbook of child psychology*, vol. I (5th edn.). New York: Wiley, pp. 865–937.

Sidorowicz, Laura S., and Lunney, G. Sparks (1980) Baby X revisited. *Sex Roles*, **6**(1): 67–73.

Siegler, Miriam, and Osmond, Humphrey (1974) *Models of madness, models of medicine*. New York: Macmillan.

Silberschatz, George (2005) *Transformative relationships: the control mastery theory of psychotherapy*. New York: Routledge.

Silverstein, Louise B. (2001) Fathers and families. In James P. McHale and Wendy S. Grolnick (eds.) *Retrospect and prospect in the psychological study of families*. Mahwah, NJ: Lawrence Erlbaum, pp. 35–64.

Slife, Brent D., Reber, Jeffrey S., and Richardson, Frank C. (eds.) (2005) *Critical thinking about psychology: hidden assumptions and plausible alternatives*. Washington, DC: American Psychological Association.

Slife, Brent, and Williams, Richard (1995) *What's behind the research? Discovering hidden assumptions in the behavioral sciences*. Thousand Oaks, CA: Sage.

Smedley, Audrey, and Smedley, Brian (2005) Race as biology is fiction, racism as a social problem is real. *American Psychologist*, 60(1): 16–26.

Smith, Jonathan A., Flowers, Paul, and Larkin, Michael (2009) *Interpretative phenomenological analysis: theory, method and research*. London: Sage.

Smith, Roger (2007) *Being human: historical knowledge and the creation of human nature*. New York: Columbia University Press.

Spackman, Matthew, and Williams, Richard (2001) The affiliation of methodology with ontology in a scientific psychology. *Journal of Mind and Behavior*, 22(4): 389–406.

Speer, Susan A. (2005) *Gender talk: feminism, discourse and conversation analysis*. London: Routledge.

Spelke, Elizabeth (2005) Sex differences in intrinsic aptitude for mathematics and science? A critical review. *American Psychologist*, 60: 950–958.

Spence, Donald P. (1982) *Narrative truth and historical truth: meaning and interpretation in psychoanalysis*. New York: W. W. Norton.

Stacey, Judith (1988) Can there be a feminist ethnography? *Women's Studies International Forum*, 11(1): 21–27.

(1995) Disloyal to the disciplines: a feminist trajectory in the borderlands. In Domna Stanton and Abigail Stewart (eds.) *Feminisms in the academy*. Ann Arbor, MI: University of Michigan Press, pp. 311–329.

Stam, Henderkus J. (2006) Pythagoreanism, meaning and the appeal to number. *New Ideas in Psychology*, 24: 240–251.

Stanko, Elizabeth A. (1995) *Intimate intrusions: women's experience of male violence*. London: Routledge and Kegan Paul.

Statistics Sweden (2010) *Women and men in Sweden – facts and figures*. Örebro, Sweden: Statistical Prognosis Unit.

Staunæs, Dorthe (2005) From culturally *avant garde* to sexually promiscuous: troubling subjectivities and intersections in the social transition from childhood into youth. *Feminism & Psychology*, 15(2): 151–169.

Staunæs, Dorthe, and Søndergaard, Dorte Marie (2008) Management and gender diversity: intertwining categories and paradoxes. In Eva Magnusson, Malin Rönnblom, and Harriet Silius (eds.) *Critical studies of gender equalities: Nordic dislocations, dilemmas and contradictions*. Göteborg: Makadambok, pp. 135–160.

Steele, Jennifer, James, Jacquelyn B., and Barnett, Rosalind C. (2002) Learning in a man's world: examining the perceptions of undergraduate women in male-dominated academic areas. *Psychology of Women Quarterly*, 26: 46–50.

Stewart, Abigail, and McDermott, Christa (2004) Gender in psychology. *Annual Review of Psychology*, **55**: 519–544.

Stiles, William B., and Angus, Lynne (2001) Qualitative research on clients' assimilation of problematic experiences in psychotherapy. In Jörg Frommer and David Rennie (eds.) *Qualitative psychotherapy research: methods and methodology*. Lengerich, Germany: Pabst Science Publishers, pp. 111–126.

Stokoe, Elizabeth H. (2004) Gender and discourse, gender and categorization: current developments in language and gender research. *Qualitative Research in Psychology*, **1**(2): 107–129.

Stoppard, Janet (2002) Navigating the hazards of orthodoxy: introducing a graduate course on qualitative methods into the psychology curriculum. *Canadian Psychology*, **43**(3): 143–153.

Stratton, Terry D., McLaughlin, Margaret A., Witte, Florence M., Foxxon, Sue E., and Nora, Margaret (2005) Does students' exposure to gender discrimination and sexual harassment in medical school affect specialty choice and residency program selection? *Academic Medicine*, **80**(5): 400–408.

Striegel-Moore, Ruth H., and Bulik, Cynthia (2007) Risk factors for eating disorders. *American Psychologist*, **62**(3): 181–198.

Summerfield, Derek (2001) The invention of post-traumatic stress disorder and the social usefulness of a psychiatric category. *British Medical Journal*, **322**(7278): 95–98.

    (2006) Depression: epidemic or pseudo-epidemic? *Journal of the Royal Society of Medicine*, **99**: 161–162.

Swedish Department of Justice (1976) *Sexuella övergrepp: förslag till ny lydelse av brottsbalkens bestämmelser om sedlighetsbrott. Betänkande av Sexualbrottsutredningen* [*Sexual abuse: proposition of new legislation on vice crimes*] (SOU 1976: 9). Stockholm: Government Department of Justice.

Swedish National Agency for Education (2006) *Könsskillnader i måluppfyllelse och utbildningsval* [*Sex differences in goal achievement and educational choice*]. Stockholm: Skolverket, Report 287.

    (2007) *PISA 2006. 15-åringars förmåga att förstå, tolka och reflektera – naturvetenskap, matematik och läsförståelse* [*PISA 2006. 15-year-olds' abilities to understand, interpret, and reflect – science, mathematics, and reading comprehension*]. Stockholm: Skolverket, Report 306.

Swedish National Board of Health and Welfare (2008) *Folkhälsa och sociala förhållanden* [*Public health and social conditions*]. Stockholm: National Board. www.socialstyrelsen.se (retrieved April 2, 2010).

    (2009) *Folkhälsorapport 2009* [*Public health reports 2009*]. Stockholm: National Board.

Swedish National Council for Crime Prevention (2002) *Att förebygga våld mot kvinnor i nära relationer. Lokalt brottsförebyggande arbete* [*Prevention of violence against women in close relations. Local preventive work*]. Stockholm: Report 2002: 8.

Swedish National Institute of Public Health (2004) *Prevention av ätstörningar – Kunskapsläget idag* [*Preventing eating disorders: state of the art*].

Report 2004: 40 (n.d.). www.fhi.se/upload/PDF/2004/rapporter/
r200440preventionavatstorningar.pdf (retrieved February 1, 2010).

Swedish Social Security Agency (2010) *Statistik och analys: försäkringsanalys*
[*Statistics and analysis: analyses of insurance costs*]. www.forsakringskassan.se/
nav/294730460e8405ed12f0a1c9b2be7cc2 (retrieved March 4, 2010).

Szymanski, Dawn M., Kashubeck-West, Susan, and Meyer, Jill (2008)
Internalized heterosexism: a historical and theoretical overview.
The Counseling Psychologist, **36**(4): 510–524.

Tannenbaum, Cara, and Rochon Ford, Anne (2006) Women and psychotropic
drugs. *Women, mental health, mental illness, and addiction in Canada: an
overview.* www.cwhn.ca (retrieved February 1, 2010).

Taylor, Jenny Bourne, and Shuttleworth, Sally (eds.) (1998) *Embodied selves:
an anthology of psychological texts, 1830–1890*. Oxford: Clarendon Press.

Thompson, Becky W. (1994) *A hunger so wide and deep: American women speak
out on eating disorders*. Minneapolis, MN: University of Minnesota Press.
(1996) Multiracial feminist theorizing about eating problems: refusing to
rank oppressions. *Eating Disorders: The Journal of Treatment and Prevention*,
4(2): 104–114.

Thompson, Clara M. (1964/1971) *On women*. New York: New American
Library.

Thorne, Barrie (1993) *Gender play: girls and boys in school*. New Brunswick, NJ:
Rutgers University Press.

Thorsen, Kirsten, and Toverud, Ruth (eds.) (2002) *Kulturpsykologi. Bevegelser i
livsløp* [*Cultural psychology. Narratives through the life span*]. Oslo:
Scandinavian University Press.

Tiefer, Leonore (1991) Historical, scientific, clinical, and feminist criticism of
"the human sexual response cycle." *Annual Review of Sex Research*,
2(1): 1–23.
(2004) *Sex is not a natural act and other essays*. Boulder, CO: Westview Press.
(2006) Female sexual dysfunction: a case study of disease mongering and
activist resistance. *PLoS Med*, **3**(4): 178. www.plosmedicine.org/article/info:
doi/10.1371/journal.pmed.0030178 (retrieved June 1, 2010).

Tolman, Deborah L. (2002) *Dilemmas of desire: teenage girls talk about sexuality*.
Cambridge, MA: Harvard University Press.

Tolman, Deborah L., and Brydon-Miller, Mary (eds.) (2000) *From subjects to
subjectivities: a handbook of interpretive and participatory methods*. New York
University Press.

UK Mental Health (2011) *The poverty site*. www.poverty.org.uk/62/index.shtml
(retrieved February 1, 2011).

Unger, Rhoda (1979) Toward a redefinition of sex and gender. *American
Psychologist*, **34**: 1085–1094.
(1989) *Representations: social constructions of gender*. New York: Baywood.

Ussher, Jane (2010) Are we medicalizing women's misery? A critical review
of women's higher rates of reported depression. *Feminism & Psychology*,
20(1): 9–35.

Viestad, Astrid (1977) *Opprør eller sykdom? Om kvinner og psykiske problemer*
[*Revolt or disease? About women and mental disorder*]. Oslo: Pax Press.

Voyer, Daniel, Voyer, Susan, and Bryden, M. Philip (1995) Magnitude of sex differences in spatial abilities: a meta-analysis and consideration of critical variables. *Psychological Bulletin*, **117**: 250–270.

Walby, Sylvia (2007) Complexity theory, systems theory, and multiple intersecting social inequalities. *Philosophy of the Social Sciences*, **37**(4): 449–470.

Wang, Caroline, and Burris, Mary Ann (1997) Photovoice: concept, methodology, and use for participatory needs assessment. *Health Education & Behavior*, **24**: 369–387.

Wang, Vivian Ota, and Sue, Stanley (2005) In the eye of the storm: race and genomics in research and practice. *American Psychologist*, **60**(1): 37–45.

Watters, Ethan (2010) *Crazy like us: the globalization of the American psyche.* New York: Free Press.

Weatherall, Ann (2002a) *Gender, language and discourse.* London: Routledge.
    (2002b) Towards understanding gender and talk-in-interaction. *Discourse & Society*, **13**(6): 767–781.

Weinehall, Katarina, Jonsson, Marie-Louise, and Eliasson, Mona (2007) *G(l)ömda: en studie om kvinnor och barn med skyddade personuppgifter* [*Forgotten and hidden: a study of women and children with protected identities*]. Umeå: Umeå University, Department of Law.

Weisstein, Naomi (1971/1993) Psychology constructs the female. In Vivian Gornick and Barbara Moran (eds.) *Woman in sexist society: studies in power and powerlessness.* New York: Basic Books, pp. 207–224. Reprinted in *Feminism & Psychology*, 1993, **3**(2): 195–210.

Weller, Ann C. (2001) *Editorial peer review: its strengths and weaknesses.* Medford, NJ: Information Today.

Wennerås, Christine, and Wold, Agnes (1997) Nepotism and sexism in peer-review. *Nature*, **387**: 341–343.

Wertsch, James (1997) Narrative tools of history and identity. *Culture & Psychology*, **3**(1): 5–20.

Wertsch, James, del Río, Pablo, and Alvarez, Amelia (eds.) (1995) *Sociocultural studies of mind.* Cambridge University Press.

West, Candace, and Zimmerman, Don (1987) Doing gender. *Gender & Society*, **1**(2): 125–151.
    (2009) Accounting for doing gender. *Gender & Society*, **23**: 112–122.

Wetherell, Margaret (1998) Positioning and interpretative repertoires: conversation analysis and poststructuralism in dialogue. *Discourse & Society*, **9**(3): 387–412.
    (2001) Debates in discourse research. In Margaret Wetherell, Stephanie Taylor, and Simeon Yates (eds.) *Discourse theory and practice: a reader.* London: Sage, pp. 380–399.
    (2003) Paranoia, ambivalence, and discursive practices: concepts of position and positioning in psychoanalysis and discursive psychology. In Rom Harré and Fathali Moghaddam (eds.) *The self and others: positioning individuals and groups in personal, political, and cultural contexts.* London: Praeger, pp. 99–120.
    (2005) Commentary: unconscious conflict or everyday accountability? *British Journal of Social Psychology*, **44**: 169–173.

(2007) A step too far: discursive psychology, linguistic ethnography and questions of identity. *Journal of Sociolinguistics*, **11**(5): 661–681.

(2008) Subjectivity or psycho-discursive practices? Investigating complex intersectional identities. *Subjectivity*, **22**(1): 73–81.

Wetherell, Margaret, and Edley, Nigel (1998) Gender practices: steps in the analysis of men and masculinities. In Karen Henwood, Christine Griffin, and Ann Phoenix (eds.) *Standpoints and differences: essays in the practice of feminist psychology*. Thousand Oaks, CA: Sage, pp. 156–173.

(1999) Negotiating hegemonic masculinity. *Feminism & Psychology*, **9**(3): 335–356.

Wetherell, Margaret, and Potter, Jonathan (1992) *Mapping the language of racism: discourse and the legitimation of exploitation*. Hemel Hempstead: Harvester Wheatsheaf.

Wetherell, Margaret, Taylor, Stephanie, and Yates, Simeon (eds.) (2001) *Discourse theory and practice: a reader*. London: Sage.

White, Merry I., and LeVine, Robert A. (1986) What is an *ii ko* (good child)? In Harold Stevenson, Hiroshi Azumi, and Kenji Hakuta (eds.) *Child development and education in Japan*. New York: Freeman, pp. 55–62.

White, Michael (2007) *Maps of narrative practice*. New York: W. W. Norton.

Wicks, Susanne, Hjern, Anders, Gunnell, David, Lewis, Glyn, and Dalman, Christina (2005) Social adversity in childhood and the risk of developing psychosis: a national cohort study. *American Journal of Psychiatry*, **162**(9): 1652–1657.

Widiger, Thomas A., and Trull, Timothy J. (2007) Plate tectonics in the classification of personality disorder: shifting to a dimensional model. *American Psychologist*, **62**: 71–83.

Wilkinson, Sue (1988) The role of reflexivity in feminist psychology. *Women's Studies International Forum*, **11**(5): 493–502.

Willig, Carla (2008) *Introducing qualitative research in psychology* (2nd edn.). Buckingham: Open University Press.

Wilson, Mitchell (1993) DSM-III and the transformation of American psychiatry: a history. *American Journal of Psychiatry*, **150**(3): 399–410.

Wilson, Terence G., Grilo, Carlos, and Vitousek, Kelly M. (2007) Psychological treatment of eating disorders. *American Psychologist*, **62**(3): 199–216.

Windh, Anna Indra (2005) *Skärningsytor mellan terapeutisk yrkesutövning och feministiska utgångspunkter – tretton svenska behandlares berättelser och brottningar* [*Intersections between therapeutic work and feminist thought: thirteen Swedish psychotherapists' narratives and struggles*]. Lund University, Department of Psychology.

Woolgar, Steven (1996) Psychology, qualitative methods and the ideas of science. In John T. E. Richardson (ed.) *Handbook of qualitative research methods for psychology and the social sciences*. Leicester, UK: BPS Books (British Psychological Society), pp. 11–24.

Woolley, Helen Thompson (1910) A review of the recent literature on the psychology of sex. *Psychological Bulletin*, **7**: 335–342.

(1914) The psychology of sex. *Psychological Bulletin*, **11**: 353–379.

Worell, Judith, and Remer, Pamela (1992/2002) *Feminist perspectives in therapy: an empowerment model for women* (2nd edn.). New York: Wiley.

World Health Organization (1979) *Schizophrenia: an international follow-up study.* New York: Wiley.

Wylie, Mary Sykes (May/June 1995) Diagnosing for dollars. *Networker*, 23–34, 65–69.

Yanchar, Stephen (2011) Using numerical data in explicitly-interpretive, contextual inquiry: a "practical discourse" framework and examples from Engeström's research on activity systems. *Theory & Psychology*, **21**(2): 179–199.

Yanchar, Stephen, and Hill, Jack (2003) What is psychology about? Towards an explicit ontology. *Journal of Humanistic Psychology*, **43**(1): 11–32.

Young, Allan (1995) *The harmony of illusions: inventing post-traumatic stress disorder.* Princeton, NJ: Princeton University Press.

Zuckerman, Marvin (1990) Some dubious premises in research and theory on racial differences: scientific, social, and ethical issues. *American Psychologist*, **45**(12): 1297–1303.

Index